D1491655

THE LADIES OF ALDERLEY

HENRIETTA MARIA STANLEY

From The Book of Beauty

THE
LADIES OF ALDERLEY

being the Letters between
MARIA JOSEPHA, LADY STANLEY
OF ALDERLEY

and Her Daughter-in-Law
HENRIETTA MARIA STANLEY

during the Years
1841—1850

Edited by
NANCY MITFORD

With a Foreword by
LORD STANLEY OF ALDERLEY

London
CHAPMAN & HALL LTD
Eleven Henrietta Street, W.C.2

First published
1938

Printed in Great Britain by
The Whitefriars Press Ltd.
London and Tonbridge
Bound by G. & J. Kitcat Ltd.
London
Flexiback Binding Patent
No. 441294

"Gibbon used to lament that Maria Josepha was not a boy, saying she would maintain a contest well with Charles James Fox."

LORD SHEFFIELD.

"The outstanding Victorian woman is a blend of the great lady and the intellectual woman, not yet professional, and we can graduate the proportions until, at the opposite ends of the scale, we encounter the limiting instances of the Queen herself and Harriet Martineau."

G. M. YOUNG.

FOREWORD

By LORD STANLEY OF ALDERLEY

THE craving to read letters not intended for oneself and to meddle in other people's private business is one which is more widely spread than many of us would care to admit. It is, further, a craving which may be the means of causing infinite trouble in our domestic lives.

Here, then, is a book designed to give a legitimate outlet to these dangerous practices. I hope that the reader may find within its covers a substitute for the letters which your sisters, your cousins or your aunts are always leaving lying about so carelessly. Or again, if Little Joshua's behaviour at the family breakfast table leaves something to be desired, I hope that this book will teach you to bear with him and not to be too severe in your condemnation. Remember he, too, may become, like my great-uncle Algernon, a high dignitary of the Romish Church.

So let these letters (which were certainly never meant to be read by you, dear reader) take the place of more dangerous correspondence, and let my forbears become the patron saints of all who have written secrets to keep. Let them, further, become the universal subject for gossip and criticism. They would welcome it, knowing, as they did, the keen pleasures of criticising others.

My cousin, Nancy Mitford, has deserved well indeed of her public in placing a book of such high moral purpose at the disposal of the world, and for my part I am only too glad to have been able to supply her with the material from the papers at Alderley. I can only hope that those to whom she is already known as the creator of Eugenia Malmains and other curious characters will not be disappointed in her latest introduction to them of characters who, because they were real, may seem somewhat less curious.

STANLEY OF ALDERLEY.

5th April, 1938.

CONTENTS

ILLUSTRATIONS

PREFACE

HERE is the picture of a dead world, past and gone. It is, within its limits, an extraordinarily clear and detailed picture, and the portraits in it are those of real people, carefully drawn. They are all ghosts now, their bodies lie, according to their various beliefs, in the north transept of Alderley Church, in ground hallowed by the rites of Mahommed close by, and in a far off Roman grave; the house which is the background of the picture has also vanished and is a ghost house. We who are being herded in this terrible twentieth century towards, we suppose, a brave new world, may care to examine that other world, to peer into the picture and to see how human beings behave when they neither drive nor are driven, but live in peace. The people within the frame of this picture, that is to say the minor nobility of England a hundred years ago, were people situated so that they could live their lives, develop their personalities and cultivate their talents in perfect security. Secure in their financial situation, they could indulge the natural wish for a large family without thought for the future. Secure in their domestic relations, husband and wife could build up the fabric of marriage without considering the possibility of a divorce. Secure in their religious beliefs and in the knowledge of immortality, they were able to regard this life as an incident rather than as the whole experience of man. Above all, secure in their Whig outlook, they never questioned the fact that each individual has his allotted place in the realm and that their own allotted place was among the ruling, the leisured and the moneyed classes. This peace and this security, which are to-day outside the experience of any but the rich and heedless dolt, had been enjoyed by their ancestors for hundreds of years, were to them the natural order of things, and, like the music of the spheres, went unheard because too familiar. Now that the music has stopped its echo must have a nostalgic charm, even for those who believe that effort and warfare are essential factors in human development.

The following letters consist chiefly of the correspondence between a mother-in-law, Lady Stanley of Alderley, and her son's wife, Mrs. Edward Stanley. There are also some between Mrs. Edward Stanley and her husband. They deal with family life in a setting of public affairs and were written during a decade (1841–51) which is one of the most important in the whole length of English history from a political, a social and a religious point of view. During those years the English people began to feel their own power and the weight of public opinion. Curious changes were seen upon the political horizon. In 1842 Income Tax was levied, an expedient never before resorted to in times of peace and which has never since been abolished. In 1846 Sir Robert Peel sacrificed his own career and the immediate future of the Tory party to the country's demand for total repeal of the Corn Laws. This was a blow to the upper classes, most of whom were against a measure so directly opposed to their own interest. From that time Free Trade prevailed and the country flourished. Progressive and hopeful spirits meanwhile agitated for the Charter, which was looked upon by politicians, Whig and Tory alike, as a piece of crazy anarchy, but five of whose six points have now become part of our constitution. (The six points of the

Charter were : A vote for every Englishman. Voting
to be by secret ballot. Every Englishman should be
eligible to stand for Parliament. A salary of £400 a year
for M.P.'s. All constituencies to be of equal size. A
new election every year.)

During these years, unknown certainly to the writers
of the Letters, Karl Marx lived, worked and starved in
London. Meanwhile the condition of poor people in
industrial areas before Lord Shaftesbury's reforms is too
well known to require description.

In Ireland the Nationalist movement began to make
itself felt under the leadership of Daniel O'Connell, the
Roman Catholic, whose election to Parliament in 1828
and his disability to sit, owing to his religion, led to the
Emancipation of the Catholics. In 1848 the potato crop
failed and the terrible famine which ensued more than
decimated the population of Ireland.

European politics were not less momentous. The
blessings which had been bestowed upon the peoples of
Europe by the French Revolution were being finally
rejected by Germany and Austria, who, alone among
nations, turned their back upon democracy and by doing
so laid the foundations of all the misery to come. In
1848, it is true, the German people made a last half-
hearted attempt to shake off their chains, but the forces
of reaction proved too strong for them. In the same year
the French, helped by the fact that his matrimonial
meanderings in Spain had lost him all his friends abroad,
got rid of Louis Philippe in a bloodless revolution and
elected as President Louis Napoléon.

From a social point of view (to use the word in its
narrowest sense) England was still undented by the
Industrial Revolution, and the aristocrats and old landed
families were supreme. The death of Lady Holland in

1845 put an end to the glories of Holland House (many of whose habitués curiously enough died at much the same time), and Whig society was no longer a constellation of stupendous wits, but was still absolutely exclusive of the newly enriched middle classes.

The snobbishness of those days seems to us, in view of modern ideas, extremely funny. A railroad director, calling to see Lord Stanley, is shown into the drawing-room but obviously made to feel, by the ladies of the household, that he narrowly escaped another place. The cotton magnates from Manchester, no doubt very rich and important people, are known at Alderley as the Cottontots, and Lady Stanley complains that they are more annoying as trespassers at Alderley Edge than the " operatives," because it is not so easy to handcuff or great dog them. A cadet of the family, Lord Stanley's nephew, marries a banker's daughter—an eventuality which nowadays would probably be hailed with delight. Lady Stanley, however, assuming that the banker would be vastly flattered by the connexion and greatly exalted that she should have called upon him, bewails the fact that his family is so common, and his livelihood, she supposes, so precarious. These ridiculous ideas persisted among the more sheltered members of the aristocracy even into the twentieth century. A small boy was taken to see my great-grandmother (the Blanche of the Letters) as an old woman of ninety ; asked what he was going to be when grown up, he said that he was going into business. " Oh, no, dear child," with great firmness, " no gentleman ever goes into business." It is only fair to say that this attitude came partly from the tradition that it was for a gentleman to serve his country in some capacity or other, and not to indulge in the purely selfish pursuit of money making. There is also a family legend to the

effect that Rosalind Countess of Carlisle, when addressing
a public meeting, said that she would prove once and for
all that she was a true democrat. " Stand up, my
middle-class sons-in-law," whereupon two learned and
distinguished men meekly exhibited themselves as a
living testimony to their mother-in-law's democratic
feelings.

The age of reason was dying, the age of science was
hardly born, and among educated people a sort of
muddled mysticism began to prevail. Inspiration was
sought by artists, poets and priests in the Middle Ages,
classicism was rejected and the muggy Gothic past
revived. An unwholesome movement in the Church,
headed by Pusey, began to show leanings towards the
Romish ritual of the Early Fathers. Ruskin and his
friends made a ludicrous road which led to nothing.
The pre-Raphaelites, with their dying knights, dead
virgins and wild roses, were founding the rottenest and
most decadent school of art ever seen in England, Gilbert
Scott was soon to fascinate his contemporaries with the
Albert Memorial.

All this is the frame of the picture, within the frame is
portrayed the Stanley family, which we will now consider.

The Stanleys are said to have been descended from
Charlemagne. They crossed the Channel in 1066 and
proceeded according to plan by marrying into the Anglo-
Saxon landed gentry, and, except for a certain younger
son of the family, they sat back on the lands thus acquired
and were never heard of for some eight hundred years.
The aforesaid younger son was ennobled after the battle
of Bosworth and his descendants have always been
actively concerned with public affairs ; it would probably
be true to say that Lord Derby is to-day the most impor-

tant unofficial man in the country. It is, however, of the idle elder branch that we treat.

John Thomas Stanley, descendant, after Charlemagne, of a succession of bucolic knights and baronets, was born in 1766. A man of more enterprise than his immediate forbears, he fitted out and led, in his youth, an expedition to Iceland ; was a member of the Royal Society and the first Lord Stanley of Alderley. In 1796 he married Gibbon's little friend, Maria Josepha Holroyd, the elder of our two Ladies of Alderley. She already has a small niche in English literature as co-editor with her father, Lord Sheffield, of Gibbon's posthumous documents. Two volumes of her own early letters were published in 1897 under the titles of " Childhood and Girlhood of Maria Josepha Holroyd " and " Early Married Life of Maria Josepha Stanley " ; there is nothing very impressive about their style : they could have been written by any young woman of intelligence and reveal neither the enormous vocabulary nor the fearful outspokenness of her later years. They are, however, interesting enough from the matter they contain.

Lord Sheffield was a horrified but fascinated observer of the French Revolution, and in 1792 he gave his wife and daughter the treat of witnessing it at close quarters. They arrived in Paris on the very day that Louis XVI and Marie Antoinette were brought back from their attempt to escape. Maria Josepha was told that " four determined men could have carried them out of France even after they had been taken a great way back towards Paris." She found everywhere the greatest contempt for the king. A week later the tourists attended the Apotheosis of Voltaire, Maria Josepha and Lady Sheffield dressed, like all the women present, in a white dress with a blue sash and a wreath of red roses. " Mama wore her wreath on her cap which was not correct." The Apotheosis seems to have been a very gimcrack affair, rather like the Lord Mayor's Show. When they had had their fill of Revolution the Sheffields and Maria Josepha went on to visit Gibbon at Lausanne, where they met with many French refugees and heard many tales of horror. The death of Gibbon in 1794 is minutely described in these early letters, and indeed it is mainly from Maria Josepha that its circumstances are known. The terms of his will, too, curious in that he left nothing to his good stepmother and nothing to Lord Sheffield, his greatest friend, are fully discussed. In 1795 Maria Josepha was helping her father to collect, sort and edit the historian's papers. Although she was only thirty when the eighteenth century drew to its close, and although she was destined to live another sixty-three years in the nineteenth, she remained, as will be seen, a purely eighteenth century character to the end.

Maria Josepha married John Stanley for love and she loved him devotedly all her life. As portrayed in the following letters, he is a shadowy figure, old, dirty, curmudgeonly and crippled with gout. He does emerge for one glorious moment in a great diatribe against *Letter 186* Roman Catholics, the Irish, Guizot and the annexation of Cracow. That and a copy of his farewell letter to Girdlestone, the offending parson, were all of his that I could find. Lord and Lady Stanley had nine children, Edward and William, who were twins, and seven daughters. In 1841, when the following correspondence begins, there were three unmarried daughters living at home, Maria Margaret (Rianette), the eldest child, Louisa and the hysterical Emmy.

Edward Stanley, eldest twin son of Lord and Lady Stanley of Alderley, was, like his father, a man of some ability and also married a remarkable woman. He held various posts in various Whig Governments, was made a peer before the death of his father, and ended in a burst of glory as Postmaster-General with a seat in the Cabinet. He was known in London as Benjamin Backbite and was, as will appear in the Letters, a very disagreeable character indeed. I have heard it said, and hope it is true, that on his death bed he apologised to his wife and children for his great nastiness to them at all times. His wife was Henrietta Maria Dillon, member of an expatriated Irish Jacobite family, whom he met and married in Florence. She loved him so much in spite of everything that during his lifetime her personality was completely suppressed, and she appears in her letters to him a gentle, complaining creature. When he died, however, she became the terror of all who were in contact with her. She threw herself with unbounded energy into the championship of women's rights and higher education, and was among the founders of Girton, Queen's College, London, and High Schools for girls.

The fusion of what Maria Josepha calls "the sluggish blood of the Stanleys" with that of these two intelligent and masterful women was destined to produce eccentric results. Henrietta, like her mother-in-law, had nine surviving children, amongst whom there was not one quite ordinary human being. Their common characteristics were a sort of downright rudeness, a passion for quarrelling, great indifference to public opinion, an unrivalled skill in finding and pointing out the weak points in other people's armour, thick legs and eyebrows, lively minds and a great literary sense. Their religious opinions, generally adopted to annoy some other member of the family, were various and peculiar, and included Mahommedanism, Roman Catholicism, Agnosticism, and

Anglicanism both high and low. During the years covered by this book they are all children or only just grown up, but their individual characters are so plainly delineated that it may be of interest to summarise their careers.

Henry, who started life as such a dear little boy, became, as we shall see, a complete misogynist at a sadly early age, perhaps owing to the fact that he was deaf. The passion for Africa, which always obsessed his mind, led to his becoming a Mahommedan, in the rites of which faith he was buried at Alderley. He was the third Lord Stanley of Alderley. He bigamously married a Spanish lady who, like Proserpine, seems to have spent half the year with him and half with her husband in Spain ; they had no children.

Johnny went into the army. He served with the American Red Cross all through the Siege of Paris and the Commune, and remarked in his letters home (which are very interesting) that no doubt the poor fellows whose wounds he dressed were glad to be attended to by a gentleman. He married a charming Miss Mackenzie, whom he bullied unmercifully, and died a colonel. His widow then married Sir Francis Jeune, afterwards Lord St. Helier, and became a very well known hostess.

Lyulph survived his two elder brothers and inherited the baronies of Stanley of Alderley, Eddisbury and, through Maria Josepha, that of Sheffield, by which title he was always known. His wife was a beautiful Miss Bell, and the present Lord Stanley is their grandson.

Algernon went into the Church. He became a Roman Catholic in order to annoy his brother Henry, who refused to give him the family living. He rose in his profession to the rank of bishop in partibus, and was for many years a figure in Roman society. When asked, however, by his brother Lyulph to give an exposition of the Roman Catholic religion he is reported to have said, " Dear boy, it is all great nonsense." He died rich.

Alice married a Colonel Fox Pitt or Pitt Rivers. She had a great many children whom she is alleged to have starved, for Alice was a miser.

Blanche was the beauty of the family. She married the Earl of Airlie and became a great autocrat to his dependants. She embroidered many hundreds of yards of rough white linen in a curious Tudor design and had six children.

Maud did not marry. She invented girls' clubs and had a literary salon in her house in Smith Square. She was very ugly.

Kate married Lord Amberley, the son of Earl Russell (better known as Lord John). Her short life and arresting character have been recorded by her son, Bertrand Russell, in " The Amberley Papers."

Rosalind married the Earl of Carlisle. She was another family autocrat and an unreasoning enthusiast for the cause of temperance. She gained so much ascendancy over her delightful, artistic husband that she induced him to make a most unjust will to the advantage of her favourite child.

Alderley Park is in Cheshire, about four miles from that strange phenomenon of nature, Alderley Edge, whose fate is much discussed in the Letters. Until 1779, when it was gutted by fire, the Stanleys lived at Alderley Hall, which a contemporary picture shows to have been a beautiful Jacobean red brick house. It is said that Sir John and Lady Stanley were at their town house in Chester at the time and that the news was broken to them by a tearful housekeeper in the following terms : " Yes, Sir John, all the furniture—yes, My Lady, all the silver—yes, Sir John, all the pictures, but (brightening considerably) your Ladyship will be very glad to hear that we managed to rescue all your Ladyship's jams and preserves."

Sir John and Lady Stanley, after the fire, went to live temporarily at the bailiff's house, called the Park House, where the bailiff's wife and daughter cooked for them, intending to rebuild the Hall. By degrees, however, they found themselves so comfortably installed that they gave up the project and built on to the Park House instead. Their son, John, and grandson, John Thomas (Maria Josepha's husband), continued enlarging it to suit the size of their families and requirements, and in the end the little Park House had become a north facing mansion of some sixty bedrooms and of very small architectural merit. The present Lord Stanley pulled it down five years ago, leaving two large sitting-rooms and a few little bedrooms, the result being a residence very well suited to modern requirements. The Ladies of Alderley were evidently not women of much taste, the furniture for the house was sent down from London in suites as it was required, and in all that waste of rooms it was quite difficult to find enough good pieces to furnish the house in its present reduced size. Henrietta Maria admits in one letter that she has no ideas on the subject of house decoration ; we find her ordering a red and yellow carpet for her Adam drawing-room, and worst of all she speaks in a most deprecating way of beautiful Winnington, her home for several years, which she refers to more than once as a " dirt hole."

The great and undoubted charm of Alderley, however, a charm which has been felt by many generations of Stanleys, their children and grandchildren, lies in its exterior surroundings. The park, with its mere flanked

by beech woods, its undulating ground, lovely trees
and old deer house, is extraordinarily fascinating. The
estate abounds in farm houses in the black and white
architecture that looks so well in its appointed place, so
frightful when copied. Soss Moss Hall and Chorley
Hall are famous examples of this style and quite unspoilt
to this day—the farm kitchens are still farm kitchens and
not drawing-rooms with chintzey furniture and bridge
tables. Over the flat, domestic countryside frowns
Alderley Edge, rising like a great cliff and affording a
really spectacular view from its summit.

There are, in a loft at Alderley, some ten thousand
letters, mostly written after the year 1840. Although
they were evidently no more fond of each other than is
usual in a mother and daughter-in-law, Maria Josepha
and Henrietta Stanley wrote to each other every day,
partly, no doubt, in order to receive and dispatch news
and family business, and partly to preserve that family
solidarity which both considered valuable. Maria
Josepha is a born writer and her own pleasure in the
details of life communicates itself to the reader. Henrietta
by comparison writes a poor letter, but, living as she did
in the political and social world at a time of great interest,
she has much to relate. Like all women she is perfectly
self-revealing when she writes to the man she is in love
with. Each letter is very long and in order to make a
readable book I have had to cut a good deal. There is
always much about illness, generally minor disorders such
as colds (of which everybody seems to have had a per-
manent one) or chilblains, resulting no doubt from the
cold atmosphere of the large unheated rooms, with stone-
flagged floors, in which they lived. The weather also
occupies many lines, as does the health and condition of
carriage horses, a matter of some importance. There is

usually at least a page devoted to plans and arrangements, and when Henrietta is in London her mother-in-law, who sends a regular supply of provisions from Alderley, has a good deal to say about the non-return of hampers, tins, egg boxes, etc. Family news of all sorts was faithfully copied out and sent on, and I have omitted many a dreary anecdote of the Adeane family, of the sporting activities of Colonel Scott and of the religious propensities of Lucy Hare's children. Unfortunately, by no means all the letters they must have written have been kept, and often there are most tantalising gaps in the correspondence. The writing, except for the numberless abbreviations, is fairly legible unless one or other correspondent is abroad, when, for economy, they write on such thin paper that everything shows through. Punctuation seems to have been unknown and spelling, even of the names of relations, most erratic : thus Catherine Stanley is spelt with a K or a C indiscriminately and by the same person, and Maud and Adeane sometimes have e's, sometimes not. Most of these things I have regulated for the sake of the reader. I have also, very occasionally, taken sentences out of one letter and put them, in their context, into another written the same or the next day, simply in order to keep the continuity. Capital letters to nouns I have suppressed.

It is quite hard to believe that a world so different from our own can have existed less than a hundred years ago. The very relationships between human beings seem to be changed. What wife, nowadays, would support year after year the neglectful gallivantings of an Edward, what husband would support the continual reproaches and complaints of a Henrietta ? To write as she wrote about Lady Emily de Burgh would be to ensure that, King's Proctor permitting, a modern husband would be married to the odious creature within a year. What mother-in-law of our time would dare to behave as Maria Josepha did, advising, hectoring and insulting ? She would soon find that her son as well as her son's wife would be off her visiting list, for but little respect is now paid to the agéd as such. Naughty boys, like mothers-in-law, had a wonderful field for their activities : surely hunting the housemaids with spears is a sport beyond the dreams of modern children ? Or is it that naughty boys are becoming as rare a species as housemaids ? Young ladies, we learn, might not travel with their maid only and without male escort, although they were quite grown-up young ladies, for fear of being squeezed in an omnibus. Delicious freedom of the twentieth century—young ladies are continually being squeezed in omnibuses and nobody cares. On the other hand, there are certain aspects of family life which do not alter. Complaints of the dreariness of sisters-in-law and the ill manners and ignorance of their children ; comparisons between the behaviour of mama-in-law and that of mama, greatly to the benefit of the latter ; denigration of any rather spectacular friend whom another member of the family may happen to acquire ; and underlying all an immense solidarity displayed in times of crisis—these are typical of any family in any age. Instantly recognisable, too, are the Boothbys, those old friends to whom we cling and of whose doings we like to hear, heaven knows why. " B. Boothby is a tedious bore," says Edward, but that does not prevent a minute chronicling of B. Boothby's plans and prospects.

It has been suggested to me that the interest I have felt in the Letters is due to the fact that Maria Josepha and Henrietta are my ancestresses. Surely, however, a great-great-great-grandmother is too remote a figure for anybody to take an interest in her as such. Lady

Dillon, who also wrote to Henrietta every day and all of whose letters are in preservation, stands in the same relationship to me, but her letters are unreadable from their extreme dullness, and not if she were my own sister would I think otherwise.

I can only remember, among the shadows of my childhood, two of the characters who appear in the book, my great-grandmother, Blanche Airlie, an image so awful that I must confess to a certain satisfaction in finding her spoken of as " live lumber " ; and Algernon the Bishop of Emmäus, whom, as children, we firmly believed to be the Pope. Neither have I ever heard much about those past Stanleys, for my Grandmother, the daughter of Blanche, disliked the Stanley connexion and rarely mentioned any of them.

Therefore I do feel that my critical faculties in this respect are as unbiased as those of the general reader, who will, I hope, find the lives of The Ladies of Alderley as fascinating and their jokes as good as I do.

NANCY MITFORD.

14th March, 1938.

ACKNOWLEDGMENT

LORD STANLEY allowed me to forage about at Alderley and to find, and use, these letters. Mr. Williams and Mr. Newall helped me to forage, and Mr. Williams has taken an infinity of trouble ever since. Mrs. Rowbotham made me happy and comfortable while I was there.

My mother lent me a peaceful roof to work under. Lord Clarendon gave me the facts concerning his grandfather's association with Borrow. The Dowager Lady Stanley of Alderley, Mrs. Allhusen and Mr. Alfred Sotheby lent me various pictures in their possession. Miss Sigrid Enersen simplified my life in a thousand ways. My brother, Tom Mitford, provided me with an 1850 copy of Burke's Peerage. My husband read the manuscript and encouraged me. Mr. Igor Vinogradoff found out about " The Discipline of Life " for me. Mrs. Butcher typed my manuscript for me most beautifully.

To all these I wish to tender my very grateful thanks.

NANCY MITFORD.

FAMILY TREE

The Family of Sir John Stanley (1735–1807) and Margaret Owen, Heiress of Penrhos

John Thomas (1766–1850), *m.* Maria Josepha Holroyd (1771–1863) and had issue.

Edward (1779–1849), Bishop of Norwich, *m.* Kitty Leycester and had issue.

Mrs. Gibson.

Lady Leighton.

Mrs. Carpenter.

The Family of John Thomas 1st Lord Stanley of Alderley and Maria Josepha, Daughter of the 1st Earl of Sheffield

Rianette (1797–1882).

Lucy (1798–1869), *m.* Marcus Hare and had issue.

Louisa (1799–1877).

Isabella (1801–1839), *m.* Sir Edward Parry and had issue.

Edward (1802–1869), *m.* Henrietta Maria Dillon (1808–1896) and had issue.

William, twin with Edward (1802–1884), *m.* Ellin Williams.

Alethea (1805–1888), *m.* General Scott and had issue.

Maude (1806–1850), *m.* H. Adeane of Babraham and had issue.

Emmeline (1809–1906), *m.* Albert Way and had issue.

xxxi

THE FAMILY OF EDWARD 2ND LORD STANLEY OF ALDER-
LEY AND HENRIETTA MARIA, DAUGHTER OF THE 13TH
VISCOUNT DILLON

Henry (1827–1903), 3rd Lord Stanley of Alderley.
Alice (1828–1910), *m.* Colonel Fox Pitt and had issue.
Blanche (1829–1921), *m.* Earl of Airlie and had issue.
Maud (1832–1915).
John (1837–1878), *m.* Miss Mackenzie and had issue.
Lyulph (1839–1929), 4th Lord Stanley of Alderley and
4th Lord Sheffield, *m.* Miss Bell and had issue.
Kate (1842–1874), *m.* Lord Amberley and had issue.
Algernon (1843–1928), Bishop of Emmäus (in partibus).
Rosalind (1844–1921), *m.* Earl of Carlisle and had issue.

———————

THE FAMILY OF EDWARD BISHOP OF NORWICH AND
MISS LEYCESTER OF TOFTS

Owen (1811–1850), Captain R.N.
Arthur Penrhyn (1815–1881), Dean of Westminster, *m.*
Lady Augusta Bruce.
Charles Edward (1819–1849), *m.* Miss Clayton, who
d. 1901.
Mary (*d.* 1879).
Catherine (*d.* 1899), *m.* Dr. Vaughan.

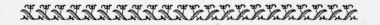

1841

LADY STANLEY OF ALDERLEY TO
MRS. EDWARD STANLEY

(1)   ALDERLEY 10*th* *Jan*/41.

DEAR HEN:

It is indeed woeful weather & I think the country &
ones *own home* in it much the best place to be in. There
was a heavy fall of snow again last night & I wish Henry [1]
was here to build up a snow man in the centre of the
sweep before the hall door, by which operation a good
drive might be made round it for a carriage. My Lord
keeps well & does not complain more than usual, of
course he does not put his nose out of doors. Emmy [2]
suffers the most, she cannot get any warmth into her &
has bad headaches in consequence.

I have been carrying Swinnerton's bill about the house
to get some of the items owned which I disclaim & I am
told that Elegant Extracts £1—1—0 calls you mistress.

There was another letter from Maude [3] this week—
she & baby very well—*quite out of conceit* with Naples &
the high station they are in & the *naughty people* that

---

[1] Henry Stanley, Mrs. Stanley's eldest son.
[2] Emmeline Stanley, one of Lady Stanley's unmarried daughters.
[3] Mrs. Adeane, Lady Stanley's daughter.

L.A.   I   B

Mr. Adeane is obliged to meet in society. She is a funny person & *rayther* absurd at times. It is gone to Ally[1] so perhaps she could show it to you before it proceeds.

Do you care about *The Times* ? That is sending it the same day—if you do I will order it for ourselves. Goodbye.

Yours affecly   M. J. S.

(2)   ALDERLEY. *Jan.* 27.

I do wish you did not always write in such a deuce of a hurry—for you never have time to make any observations beyond the absolutely needful—how *can* you read Humphrey's[2] last numbers & not *indulge* me with an ejaculation or two about it—are you satisfied with the disposal of Quilp ? My Lord is not, says it is too easy a death & that he should have had more time to *feel* his punishment. Will Nelly die ? I think she ought.

The Bishop of N[3] dines with the Queen on the 10th. I suppose he will be at Lord Cardigan's[4] trial if Bishops ever attend on such occasions. I am afraid he will be pronounced *not* guilty on the *honour* of a *Peer*. A poacher has as good a right to be tried by *his* peers in equity & justice & it is my opinion both lord & poacher have an equal chance of being acquitted in such case.

A note from Maude [Adeane]—she declares her two girls grow more gigantic & their mouths larger than

---

[1] Mrs. Scott, daughter of Lady Stanley, married to Colonel, afterwards General, Scott.

[2] Master Humphrey's Clock, the periodical in which were serialised The Old Curiosity Shop & Barnaby Rudge.

[3] Edward Stanley, Bishop of Norwich, was Lord Stanley's brother.

[4] Lord Cardigan was tried for wounding a Captain Tucket in a duel. He was acquitted amid great popular disgust.

ever & that they must set the Thames on fire by their
wit for they never will by their beauty. I think Alethea
will be a handsome or what is called a *fine woman* if she
does not stop short in growth. Baby flourishes with her
Italian cow.

(3)   ALDERLEY. *March* 3/41.

I do not like the manner & tone in which the Globe
has noticed Peel & Catholicus. Peel's speech was fault-
less & if it bore the marks of a *new* light having broke
in upon him it should not have been received with such
rude & I think vulgar irony. Is it known who wrote
Catholicus ? I see the Globe says he is an Oxford
dignitary. We have noticed all his letters, in my opinion
they are not clever, & certainly the only conclusion a
candid mind can come to after reading them is that
ignorance is the safest ground work of the Xian religion.

Emmy was seized with one of her hysterical attacks
last night, so violent that her screams were terrible &
she declared she was dying. We sent for [Dr.] Nightingale who immediately decided upon taking some blood
from her, & tho' only a tea cup full it relieved her
instantly.

The Mainwarings are coming today to have a talk
about their affairs which seem to be worse & worse. Sir
Harry ought to throw up the management of the estate
& go abroad.

(4)   ALDERLEY. 18*th March*.

Invalids going on well except Rianette[1] gains very
little in strength. My Lord much better & can bear

[1] Lady Stanley's eldest child, living at home, unmarried.

3   B 2

Emmy's eloquence without fatigue but has not elicited much that is new or satisfactory from her. I should not like to die under any doctor if I could help it but I think more than I ever did that the singing bird is as likely to keep one alive as Chambers, Holland & Co., if it is not one's Kismet to die.

I am obliged to be very *clever* indeed in reading your letters as sundry small winged words are sometimes omitted—" the newspapers meant Sewell [1] for the dignitary but he is not at all known." Query, Is *he* an *obscure* man or is it only not known whether he is the author [of Catholicus]—I conclude the latter as he is a very well known individual in the Pusey-ite arena.

I hope you are all well as I hear Louisa Parker [2] is to howl at your house soon.

[Lady Stanley, having sent My Lord and Rianette to Leamington to recover from the severities of an Alderley winter, now took the other two unmarried daughters Louisa and Emmy on a visit to the Stanleys at Norwich. These two families were very intimate as Edward Stanley was rector of Alderley for 32 years before, in 1837, he accepted the Bishopric of Norwich.

" Oh," says Augustus Hare (in " Memorials of a Quiet Life "), " the charm of a rectory inhabited by a Reginald Heber or an Edward Stanley," and he goes on to paint an idyllic picture of the Alderley rectory, its wide verandah covered with roses and hung with bird cages, the beautiful scenery around and the delightful family within.

As Bishop, Edward Stanley was much beloved in his diocese, although his liberal principles and strangely

---

[1] William Sewell, 1804-1874, Tractarian, early friend of Keble and founder of Radley.
[2] A Cheshire neighbour.

modern point of view got him into trouble with the more reactionary members of his flock, who seem to have been particularly outraged by his great friendship for Jenny Lind.

Kitty Stanley, born a Miss Leycester, of Tofts in Cheshire, was chaperoned in London for the two years previous to her marriage by Lady Stanley and there was a great devotion between the sisters-in-law. She was a favourite, as a girl, with the Holland House circle and Sydney Smith spoke of her as having a " porcelain understanding."

The Stanleys had five children, Catherine who married Dr. Vaughan, Headmaster of Harrow, Mary, who went to the Crimea in charge of fifty nurses under Miss Nightingale, Charley, Owen, a sailor, and Arthur, who became Queen Victoria's beloved Dean of Westminster.]

(5)   L Y N N .   *April* 2.
DEAR HEN,

We have had two as unpleasant days journey as needs be—rain & wind all through the Derbyshire Hills & to Nottingham on Wednesday. Fog & cold damp across the very ugliest country that was ever left bare by the sea, for that is the character of almost all the scenery we came through yesterday. We remain here today & hope to reach Norwich in good time tomorrow, & I shall not be very sorry that Uncle dines with the judges so that I shall have Kitty all to myself for the evening.

Emmy was much overcome on her arrival here—the Cresswells are so much mixed up with all her Norfolk recollections, being the best friends the Parrys [1] had, &

1 Sir Edward Parry, " explorer of the Icy Seas," was the widower of Lady Stanley's daughter Isabella.

indeed his oldest of whom Emmy saw a great deal when at Congham. She had a slight hysteric, but had a good night and is pretty well today. Her visit to Castle Rising [1] will try her however but nothing will induce her to forego it. I am not at all tired now I am out of the barouche which is my abhorrence in cold rainy weather, whether open or shut.

Rianette will have told you how & why I forgot the *hair*—she promised to send some she had by her, but I have just cut off a fresh lock as you & he may prefer the present date to any former state of existence, though the present may bear more marks of time.

Yrs. affecly   M. J. S.

I cannot admire Macaulay's speech or arguments. There seems to me a wider difference between Jews & Christians than between different shades of opinion & belief—& I do not see how a Jew can conscientiously judge in a Christian court, besides it would be a grievous cause of offence to so many & might as well have been left alone.

(6)   P A L A C E ,   N O R W I C H . *April 6th/41.*

I am *so* glad I have come. It is very satisfactory & I am very happy here & indeed it is something to have come away from nothing but sick people & to be able to laugh & hear laugh, & I hope the sick couple left behind will soon be all the better for their move [to Leamington] also. Emmy is very tolerable & not more tired than one must expect—for the journey was fatiguing & the visit to Castle Rising trying for her, as well as

---

[1] A ruin.

being with Mrs. Cresswell of whom she saw a good deal when in that melancholy scene with poor Mitty.[1]

I was really rather ashamed of Maude's letter with the numerous bores she complains of & the *small* interest she seems to take in anything she sees. I wonder if a different husband would have made her a different woman, perhaps not if she had had as many children for she seems almost worn out, poor thing.

Is the little Princess [2] *blind ?* I wish for a positive assurance from you that she is not for poor dear Miss Lander's satisfaction who is *quite grieved* about it. I forget if you have seen her yourself.

Adieu   Affecly yours   M. J. S.

Was there ever such a complete Girdlestonian epistle as that of Newman ? I could fancy it written by our enemy, who by the way, is in London, probably advising with his lawyers, professedly taking his eldest boy to school & looking for a curate.

[Mr. Girdlestone was at that time rector of Alderley. He had quarrelled with Lord Stanley over some question of tithes, after which the whole family refused to have anything to do with him and indeed seem to have derived a particularly subtle pleasure from their hatred for him.]

(7)   NORWICH   *April* 9/41.

DEAREST HEN,

I have had so much writing since I came here that I *could* not do more for you, & Louisa has had a bad face

---

[1] There is much in Emmy's life that I cannot clarify. The melancholy scene may have been the death bed of her sister Isabella some two years previously, or it may have had something to do with an affair of the heart, hinted at in letter 104.—N.M.

[2] The Princess Royal.

ache & been fully occupied besides, for somebody or other worth listening to has been constantly coming in. It really is a treat after the dullness of Alderley since you left.

I am disappointed to find from Ally's letter this morning that she had not a few days ago told you about Sir Edward [1]—as I thought he had requested her to do so & I rather wished you to hear it from her than have to write a long story—& I could not have touched upon it without being led on to say much more than I had time or inclination for—& it was desirable to keep it quite secret until it was all but certain, as I think it is now. I hope & trust that it will be as happy in its completion as it appears to me it must be in prospect. There are so many circumstances in her favour which could not be the same in any other person & *some change* I am sure was necessary for the advantage of his children as well as for his own comfort & happiness.

Adieu   Yrs. affecly   M. J. S.

(8)   D O V E R   S T R E E T.[2]   *May 3rd.*

Edward looks rayonnant so I suppose he is enjoying the tangled skein they are preparing for the Conservatives to unravel for I cannot suppose he expects to *hold on* much longer—& so his colleague deserts govt.[3]   I hear there was a pitched Battle between them at Brooks's yesterday —rather warm words—but I suppose the Treasury is accustomed to them.   I suppose you are too discreet to repeat what I say.

[1] Sir Edward Parry remarried in 1841 a Mrs. Hoare.
[2] The Stanleys' London house, now the Arts Club.
[3] Edward Stanley was Patronage Secretary to the Treasury until June 1841 when he was made Paymaster General of the Forces.

Probably E will not have had time to tell you he had a letter from Girdy [1] on Friday—I suppose intended to be conciliatory but it was only in words of regret that so & so should have been unavoidable—no proposal of *coming to*, yet it could mean nothing if it did not mean he had a hope that the matter might be brought to some conclusion thro' E. He has answered it extremely well suggesting that if Mr. G really means well by this communication a reference to the Com: must be the only method of settling the business to the satisfaction of both parties.

What *are* they doing in the Green Park ? I know I shall never be able to take poor Cherry there with their abominable *improvements*—will nobody say a word for kite flyers, little dogs & the pleasure of rambling over green turf in whichever direction you please, without hurdles to save the grass for the sheep.

The Father says he is better, but nothing of coming up.

Yrs. affecly   M. J. S.

(9)   *Undated.* ALDERLEY.

DEAR HEN,

I should think your coach could be of very little use to you here, as if E. or you wanted to visit anywhere there are here choice of carriages at your service, & you could not indeed use your coach if you had it, I suppose, without 4 horses. I hope the rail-road will not have a *spasmodic* [2] effect upon you.

Our party is doing very well, no trouble at all & it is not very numerous. I am really very glad to see some

---

[1] Girdlestone, the hated parson.
[2] Mrs. Stanley was very much afflicted by spasms.

9

people & care nothing for their politicks as there are plenty of other subjects to converse upon—My Lord seems quite *happy* with Sir Philip geologising & mineralogising. Ralph [1] is a goose & his manners not what one should like in a person one cared about—Mrs. L. is easy & not *short* in her manner & seems to wish to be agreeable, but I do not fancy her much—lackadaisical I think she is in her manner—but you will be too busy to want any more descriptions of our visitors.

I shall like the satin pelisse much & the price also & will do without the boa. If I had one I should prefer the fox—can get it bye & bye if I find I really want it.

Very glad to hear of Johnny's [2] *improvement*, hope it will bear *minute criticism* & that he will not feel instigated to make grimaces at his Grandpapa—of course it will not do to say anything about it or it wd put it into his head.

Would it not be the best way to send half a dozen wine to Henry at Eton either for his own keeping or some servant to be trusted at Pickerings. Have you ever inquired of him if any boys have wine ?

Yrs affecly   M. J. S.

Written on the envelope.

So Lou [3] is gone to Norwich, I am sorry for Mary who seems to have acted an heroic part & expressed a *wish* she should come—Lou's total want of tact to know when her company & *attentions* are welcome & when not must always make her an unpleasing companion to all but her prejudiced adorers purchased by her well applied flattery.

Is there any truth in the change of religion of Ld &

---

[1] Ralph Leycester, a neighbour.
[2] Mrs. Stanley's second son, a naughty boy.
[3] Louisa Clinton, a niece of Lady Stanley.

Ly Holland? I think Henry's recluseness may have more reasons than mere love of study & anxiety for success. Childish or boyish sports are not in his way not naturally his choice—you know that the society of his *elders* has always been preferred by him & I feel almost sure that Etonian ways have no charm for him, & I do not think you ought to mind this, but leave him to follow the bent of his inclinations in this way. It will be better for him now, at his age to educate himself, much passes in his mind, I feel certain, that does him more good then general intercourse with his fellows who think him an *odd boy* & throw him back upon himself only the more—but I am at the end of my paper & cannot pursue the subject. Perhaps you are not Aunt Kitty (how can you) to understand me without doing more than sketch my subject.

MRS. STANLEY TO EDWARD STANLEY

(10)   GROV: CRES. *June 23rd.*

MY DEAREST LOVE

I made the most prosperous journey without a single incident. I found Henry very uncomfortable from pain & fever & I believe his throat is very bad. I was very glad I came for he wants to be kept up, he is very low & was very much frightened last Sunday. It seems he had a bad thumb which inflamed up his arm & he was *staying out* for that. Woodhouse had the scarlet fever slightly & as a lower boy they sent Henry into his room with drink so he caught it & on Sunday mg fainted twice. When Pickering found he was ill he sent him home—that was right but he sent him alone & he nearly fainted on the R.R. & some one at the station seeing how ill he was charitably put him in a cab & when he was with Mama he was pinched & blue with the cold fit. I believe Pickering felt he had been careless for he came up to enquire for him.

I met Lady Georgina Wortley at the door enquiring, your mother came here this evg & said some very unfeeling things to me about (Henry) having already suffered for want of care & altogether I thought of the plaisir secondaire tho' I lose the first of pleasures being with you.

Johnny was so *obstreperous* that they have been obliged to send a maid to take care of him—if he goes on like this he will require a keeper. Williams [1] can hardly speak having slept, or rather waked in Henry's little den of which door & window are kept open all night, wind or rain. Henry cannot swallow a strawberry, that will give you an idea of his throat.

I hope you will keep up your spirits for your canvass. God bless you my darling. Your affec wife   H. M. S.

(11)   GROSVENOR CRESCENT.
MY DEAREST LOVE

I went to Dover Street according to Lady Stanley's wish but she was gone out & I only saw Ld Stanley. He seemed very fearful of the expense of the election & wishes you were in the H of Lds not in his place tho'— he asked me if I was to return to Alderley but I told him Lady Stanley was afraid of me. She has never seen Henry. It is fortunate for him all his relations were not equally afraid.

Williams is really the best creature in the world so quiet & so indefatigable.

---

[1] The children's nurse, generally called Wee.

I wrote to Lady Holland to say I was in town as I thought she wd be good natured & she sent me a book & I dare say will send Henry food.   Goodbye my dearest love pray write or desire Simpson [1] if too busy

Yr affec wife   H. M. S.

(12)   GROSVENOR CRESCENT *June 25.* 1841.
MY DEAREST LOVE

Henry is going on perfectly well—I am with him from morning till towards 8 o clock when I go to Mama.

I am very much vexed at the suddenness of your election, it is very unfair.   I feel uneasy about it & it is a great disappointment to be away—but it cannot be helped, it is yr last I hope.

Lady Stanley keeps asking me what are my plans.   I don't know what she means, I can make no plans which can interest her as she is decided upon neither myself nor Henry going to Alderley—tell me what she says if anything occurs on this subject ; besides it is useless speculating until the election is over.

Dr Seymour [2] says the having had a quack doctor, a friend of Sir F. West to dine at the Palace has confirmed the suspicion of Prince Albert being ill—it is a sad thing he shld be in such bad hands.   Henry wants me to read to him so goodbye dear

(13)   GROV: CRES: *June 26th.*
MY DEAREST LOVE

I hardly like to write half I have to say to you for I feel yr mind must be so engrossed with yr present

---

[1] The estate agent at Alderley.
[2] Edward Seymour (1796–1866) was doctor to the Stanley family.

anxious work—but you will be glad to hear Henry is going on very well. Dr Seymour does not wish him to be out of his care till the 3 weeks are finished as in as severe cases of fever as his Dropsy sometimes occurs at the end of the fortnight. It suits me also to be here to hear the news of yr dreadful day. The difficulty was what to do with the children but Mama as usual will do impossibilities. Margaret[1] will keep Lyulph, & Johnny come home as most people do not fear the scarlet fever twice as Lady Stanley seems to do for the Parry children who have *had* it.

I have got the newspapers today, thanks to you. Lady Holland wanted me to go to her last night but Ly Clanricarde was there & she might be afraid—I am going there this afternoon. I saw Ld Fitzgerald[2] yesterday he said he heard yr election wd not be 100 either way & so very close run tho the Tories said they were sure. I say nothing of you dearest for I know nothing, but am so anxious I cannot sleep for thinking of it

Yr affec wife   H. M. S.

LADY STANLEY TO MRS. STANLEY

(14)   ALDERLEY *June* 30/41.

DEAR HEN:

Edward was very well received at Macclesfield. There were hustings prepared for him down by the waters & he spoke for an hour to about 4000 people—was frequently questioned, had no doubt ready answers to give. There was no riot or confusion & all *appeared* unanimous

---

[1] Mrs. Stanley's sister, Mrs. Hamilton.

[2] Lord Fitzgerald and Vesci, President of the Board of Trade under Lord Melbourne.

in his favour, but he saw several enemies who came to listen, but they did not interrupt or say anything & he met with great applause. The Tory breakfast at the Macd Arms kept quite snug & he neither saw nor heard of them or their proceedings. He had heard they gave out he would not dare face the people of Maccles:— which determined him to go there & if they hear the *truth* I think they will be satisfied they were under a mistake, both as to his courage & the feeling of many towards him.

The Bishop seems to have been very much pleased with his dinner & reception—I hope Victoria will rival Adelaide & recover his good graces.

Mrs. Leycester had gone 6 weeks beyond her time. Emma L came here yesterday to sleep having nearly given up all expectation of a real Baby. Charlotte came to fetch her this morning Mrs. L having been taken ill in the night & delivered of a fine girl which just breathed only having come the wrong way & the foolish (I think) Dr said being *a month older* than she should be the skull was too hard to give way. Mrs. L doing well but suffered severely.

Yrs affecly   M. J. S.

[Lord Melbourne's government having fallen there was now a general election in which Edward Stanley lost his seat and the Whig party their majority.]

(15)   PENRHOS[1] *Aug.* 27/41.
DEAR HEN

I was very glad to hear of your expedition to Norwich I am sure you will enjoy it much & K be delighted to

---

[1] A property in Anglesea belonging to the Stanley family and inhabited by Lady Stanley's second son William and his wife Ellin.

have you, but it will be a poor compensation for Henry, only the exchange of one town for another. I suppose you go to Yarmouth as you speak of a night at sea, I hope you will be as lucky by sea as you usually are on land in your journeys.

I expect E. will pick up a seat in Scotland perhaps. If I were him I should long to let them fight it out without me & lay by for the right moment.

(16)   PENRHOS *Sept.* 10.
DEAR HEN

I have not written to *you* as I have done so to K & I knew the contents of my letters would be in common. I just wanted to know all you told me. I was not sure where you had sent the children, wanted to know also what sort of a lodging they had got (*don't* understand why you should wish it *not* to be *very* romantic) I hope none of them will be *very* ill—very *odd* you will say of course you would hope so—but did you read in the Globe of the barbarous conduct of the Broadstairs people towards a young woman who was ill & it was thought *might* die, how she was bundled out in the cruellest manner for *fear* she should bring *discredit* on the lodging, & then a little boy was blown over the cliff, I don't suppose it was Johnny or mention would have been made of a fat woman jumping after him.

My leg—Walthen complained it was a very *indolent* wound so he *enlivened* it with caustic which has made it *actively* painful since but he says it is all right & he wishes to cause healthy granulations to appear & then it would heal. I daresay you will understand all about it tho I am not sure whether you consider yourself as clever a surgeon as physician.

MARIA JOSEPHA
LADY STANLEY OF ALDERLEY

We do grumble so much at another Honble Miss
E Stanley [1] or any Stanley at all at Court that is not us.

MRS. STANLEY TO LADY STANLEY

(17)   PALACE NORWICH *Sept* 12.
MY DEAR LADY STANLEY

Catherine [2] had a doz leeches on again last night &
18 just now The pain seems obstinate, but still as her
countenance is good & the skin moist I hope the Doctors
are right in saying danger is over—I quite feel it is.
Still, in her weak state it is vexatious to be obliged to
bleed so much.

I heard from Broadstairs they say two days sunshine
have revived them—when I said romantic I meant damp
which what with creepers and thatched roofs always
seems to me synonymous.

My head aches so you must excuse more

                    Your affec daughter   H. M. S.

(18)   PALACE *Sept* 15.
MY DEAR LADY STANLEY

I have indeed a most melancholy account to give you
today for we are all in the deepest anxiety—All day
Catherine was comfortable tho' she still had the pain—
I saw her at two & perceived that the disease had shifted,
it was evident that the pain was in the region of the
bladder. Dr Lubbock did not come till 7 & then she
had the first very acute paroxysm of pain, her pulse had

---

[1] Emma-Caroline, granddaughter of Lord Derby.
[2] Catherine Stanley, daughter of the Bishop.

mounted up to what it had been in the previous attack—
it was a fresh inflammation—24 leeches were applied
immediately & at 12, 12 more leeches but still no relief.
She saw Lubbock alone & asked him candidly her state—
that of danger but he did not at all despair. She is quite
calm. Poor Uncle quite gives up all hope—Aunt is
beautifully calm & composed. I cannot leave them
indeed I feel they wish me to stay. This week is ever
to be one of grief to me—last year I was in agony about
Alice,[1] the year before ——[2]
$\frac{1}{2}$ *past* 2 We are more at ease. From 9 till 2 she has
been in fainting fits, Mary, Arthur & I have sat in the
extreme of anxiety. She is still cold but the collapse is
going off. I trust she will be spared to us I cld not bear
to think of her poor mother.

LADY STANLEY TO MRS. STANLEY

(19)   PENRHOS *Sept* 18/41.
DEAREST HEN

What a comfort it is to have you *there* & *they* do feel
it is a great one to them. I *hope* much from the latter
part of your letter but one hardly knows what to express
in the fearful doubt of what may have occurred in the
long space of time between writing your letter & receiving
this. I have not heard any mention of warm baths, which
seem as if they ought to have been the first thing thought
of—I have been just speaking to Walthen about it & it
was a satisfaction to hear that inflammation in the bladder
was much less dangerous than the bowels. May it

---

[1] Mrs. Stanley's eldest daughter.
[2] Mrs. Stanley lost a little girl, Cecilia, in 1839.

prove so.   I can well imagine dear Aunt's calmness &
external composure ; as long as she knows & feels how
necessary it is she should exert herself the power will be
there during the progress of the disorder, but *either way*
I fear for her when *anxiety* is over.   Poor Uncle, I know
his nature is to despond at once in severe illness & no one
will feel more deeply than he under this severe & *first*
affliction.

Pray write me a few lines straight to Alderley, in case
you have not done so already

MRS. STANLEY TO LADY STANLEY

(20)   PALACE.

MY DEAR LADY STANLEY

We are all prepared to part with dear Catherine but it
is hard to bear the fluctuations of hope & fear—*she* is
better for having us all.   I read to her this mg from the
Xian year & she made Blanche sing a hymn for her.
She is so happy & so cheerful that while one is with her
one is elevated above all earthly cares.   She is so tender
& has often said she was so glad I was here ; when all
together she said, " pray talk of me always when I am
gone & never say poor Catherine."   She desired to be
buried in the North Transept,[1] gave all directions.   I
cannot feel she is for this world she is too heavenly
minded & Dr Lubbock says tho' her symptoms are not
so bad he never saw a patient recover who had such a
strong feeling of death.   Uncle went through the whole
Communion service with great firmness.   I can never be
sufficiently thankful to have been here at this time.   I
have always loved Catherine dearly & her mother has
ever been to me the kindest & best of friends.   This

[1] At Alderley.

19   c 2

sorrow in which I am allowed to share will ever be a bond of union between us—& dear Mary so forgetful of self, yet so bowed down, I feel I am a comfort to her

Yr affec daughter   H. M. S.

MARY STANLEY TO LADY STANLEY

(21)   PALACE 10 o'clock

DEAREST AUNT STANLEY

All hope is gone & the last 10 hours we have all been in her room & we have been raised above this earth. The Soul seems already winged for flight—she is lying in the most heavenly state, speaking a word of comfort to each, quite alive to everything that passes.   Mamma is *quite* calm.   Papa is very much overcome.

11 *O'clock.*   The Drs have just been & say there is certainly a change for the better, she has taken a quantity of milk with comfort & tho' we dare not encourage the idea, still the hour of her departure seems delayed.   I hardly can rejoice, *recovery* seems impossible & the suffering she has gone through is so severe that I dread any more.

In Mrs. Stanley's handwriting :

I think she is sinking—we are all round her bed—she cannot speak even for a moment.   Uncle & Aunt quite calm.

LADY STANLEY TO MRS. STANLEY

(22)   PENRHOS *Sept* 21.

DEAREST HEN

I have longed for a letter from you for some days—I want to hear more of the dear Child's bodily state & less

of her mental or spiritual, because I consider the instances
given of that as bordering on fever, & certainly proving
great excitement, & it is incomprehensible to us all that
she should have been allowed to be so surrounded, & to
talk so much, & above all, the extreme excitement of
constant Cathedral musick—keeping her hearing &
feeling on the constant strain.   I really think you have
all lost your wits—have got into the seventh heaven of
enthusiasm & forgot every thing sublunary.   You gave
her over & then seemed to think she must be indulged
in all her fancies without considering whether they might
be hurtful—& have fancied her under inspiration almost,
forgetting that the greatest criminals & villains frequently
go out of the world exulting at the gallows in their
assurances of eternal happiness & really, I have no doubt,
feel what they say. . . . I could not say all this or ask
for these *medical* particulars if I was not very sanguine
of her recovery.   In Mary's last letter she talks of
brandy every hour, this looks like weakness—K the day
before mentions pulse at 120, that was strength—nothing
can be more tantalizing than the accounts of the last
3 days—but as Life still remained & Youth was on her
side we cannot help hoping on   It is very pleasing to
hear what a *blessing*, I may say, you are to them—more
than a comfort.

We leave this on Friday, I hope I have told you so we
shall not lose a letter.   Emmy is better than I expected—
she was so much overset by the Friday's acct that I was
afraid of one of her fits of hysterics, but she recovered
herself.   It is a very uncomfortable time for getting
letters of great interest—8 in the evening but we
cannot wait for the next morning when they are to
be got.

How are you dearest Hen: affec yrs   M. J. S.

MRS. STANLEY TO LADY STANLEY

(23)   PALACE Sept 20th.

MY DEAR LADY STANLEY

We are so happy a favourable change took place yesterday at 6 & since that time our darling Kate[1] has been going on as well as anyone could wish. She sleeps & takes nourishment. She is weaker than a baby & only speaks in a whisper. The Doctor : " the exhaustion is great, the prostration extreme, the countenance bad "—many many times have we seen death on it but it has receded. Aunt is *very* well—the dear Bishop behaves so very well, he does restrain his natural irritation so perfectly & even does not ask questions when we tell him not. Arthur has been a great comfort to Mary.

I hear from Edward,[2] he is very low.

Yr affec daughter   H. M. S.

(24)   PALACE NORWICH Sept 21.

MY DEAR LADY STANLEY

I must answer your letter. From the time of the recovery from the collapse Wed 15th till Sunday evg no change took place, there was no pain, no disease, yet the prostration was complete during that period—3 times the change of death came over her face & humanly speaking it was Kate's *perfect* & *entire* subjugation to live or die that brought her thro'—there was no excitement but there was extreme depression from the fatigue, the *dead* weight of the body, & nothing but the hope of speedy change could have supported a patient in such a distressing state. *Our* being with her (for I may say she

[1] Catherine lived to marry the Headmaster of Harrow.
[2] In Scotland.

loves me most dearly) was to her an inexpressible comfort
& sanctioned by the Doctors, who said they *dared* not
refuse to one so near the grave the consolation of expressing her last wishes to her friends & partaking of the
consolation of religion. She *said she felt* she would
recover as soon as the physicians did & there has been
no change in manner since, the same even cheerfulness
thro' out

Yr affec daughter   H. M. S.

LADY STANLEY TO MRS. STANLEY

(25)   PENRHOS *Sept 23rd.*

DEAREST HEN

How your letter has revived us all so far beyond
expectation but I have always *felt* she would recover &
have been much the most hopeful of the party even from
the slender information we have had. I am afraid my
last letter would make you very angry with me but I
could not help it I was so vexed at getting no particulars
of the bodily symptoms or the suffering, & thought so
silly to rest your fears upon the highly wrought expression
of feeling in a person who supposed herself dying. You
are a very dear creature & we shall all love you a hundred
times better than we did for all the comfort you have
been to that family.

Louisa & Emmy are enjoying their last day here
hunting out the poor people & relieving their wants just
before our departure, & there is plenty of this work to do.
Poor Edward I suppose does not see a seat in prospect
for him—& does not fancy the shelf & *idleness*, indolent
though he is. Adieu—are you quite well? Affecly

M. J. S.

MRS. STANLEY TO LADY STANLEY

(26)   GROS: CRES: *Oct.* 4/41

MY DEAR LADY STANLEY

I find this house dreadfully dull & quiet, but at 3 I meet Mama & stay with her, when I do not dine out, the rest of the day. I am going to meet the new French ambassador today at Mrs Damer—I dine with Miss Berry[1] on Wednesday—I will give " Oh Buller yr me page " tomorrow. A letter from Edward with great complaints of the weather & bad sport. I suppose you will hear when he will be at Alderley. There is as you say *much* to consider as to our future plans & were I alone I could settle them easily but such is not the case, the uncertainty about Parliament is a perplexity. Haywood wd be very convenient in many respects & in none more to me than that I should get rid of *your* having the annoyance of the children ; & have a greater chance of having Edward with me than in another place, but if we let our house in the Spring would Edward like to be so out of reach of London, should I like to be confined there, would it be the best place for the children all the year ? My confinement is most inconvenient as it will necessitate my being housed by the beginning of March. I am quite willing to do what is most agreeable to all parties, always preferring that which will separate me least from Edward—that was a great reason for wishing to go abroad he would not have got away there.

[Haywood, or Heawood Hall is a small manor house on the Alderley estate and was at that time occupied by a family called Bell. Lady Stanley was always offering it to the Edward Stanleys—who probably did not wish to take up their abode quite so near to his parents. The

---

[1] Walpole's friend, now over 80.

WINNINGTON

(*Photo: Courtesy of Imperial Chemical Industries Ltd.*)

alternative suggestion, which they finally accepted, was an estate called Winnington belonging to the Stanley family some eighteen miles from Alderley, which consisted of a small but beautiful Adam house standing near salt mines. Mrs. Stanley, for some reason, always detested the place. Winnington now belongs to Imperial Chemical Industries and the house has been made into a country club for their employees. One of the rooms boasts an unique Chinese wall paper, and the whole is as graceful a building as could be wished for, but no Stanley in any letter makes a reference to its beauties.]

LADY STANLEY TO MRS. STANLEY

(27)   ALDERLEY *Oct 5/41*.

DEAR HEN:

As I have never seen Edward's handwriting since he left London I am not likely to know when he wishes, intends, or expects to come to Alderley—but as I said the end of October for the whole family I supposed he had arranged accordingly. The Philip Egertons have offered themselves for the 25th & I hope he would be able to make up his mind to treat them & any others we might be obliged to ask to meet them, civilly & not be annoyed with their being here.

I do not see Heawood quite in the light you do— certainly you ought to be confined in London but you might be glad of the Children being longer in the country than you would like yourself sometimes—but the truth is, & an unpleasant truth it is, that Edward has no taste for the company of Wife & Children by themselves & that you are afraid of being set down at Heawood & left there when he is amusing himself in Town. . . . I am certain there is scarce another son, of E's age, & daughter in law with a family so large in Great Britain who would not eagerly seize on such an opening—I know what E would like, to quarter his family upon us for the greater part of the year & be elsewhere himself.   I do not wish to conceal that my opinion is decidedly in favour of your going abroad—you might live handsomely & without restraint in expence for 2000, Maude Adeane has not spent 3000 tho' moving about so much & with 9 children & in expensive places.   Education, society, every thing could be attained much easier than on the same income in England.   I am not sure you would have a bit *more* of E's company abroad but you could hardly have much *less* & you might find pleasant society yourself—& if not in Parliament of what possible advantage can it be to him, politically, to remain in England for the next year or two—he can hardly expect a change in that time & I am very much afraid, as regards selfish interests, that the Country will go on a very great deal better under the present[1] than the former Govt & it will take much longer than one or two years to make the people, the rational weighty people of England, dissatisfied with them, & Heaven defend us from the *extreme* party which I *dread* seeing Edward attach himself to, I would much sooner see him turn Tory, the *amended* Tory of the present day, & you will find My Lord very much of this opinion.

Nightingale is in disgrace, Moomie[2] had a very decayed tooth which gave her a great deal of pain—he pulled out the next door neighbour which was perfectly sound, & his coolness about it was more provoking than the mistake itself.

---

[1] Sir Robert Peel's.
[2] Lady Stanley's old nurse, who lived in a cottage at Alderley.

(28)   *Oct* 14.

We shall be ready to receive you next week & I think you will not be sorry to stop house keeping in such a melancholy state of your finances—I can only say we *sympathize* with you & the last 200 run us so dry that I was obliged to desire Goslings to sell out in order to carry us on till the next rent day.

1 8 4 2

ALDERLEY *Jan* 25.

If a High Churchman was to be appointed[1] is not Gilbert as good or better than some ? Better than Hook for instance & of course a very *liberal* man was not likely to be named, & it is a good thing he should have arrayed himself against Puseyism at all events, & his bigotry if he is a bigot is turned to good account in this. How delighted Miss Lander will be—quite a well pleased fly upon the coach wheel enjoying her *important* situation.

I am very glad you turn your thoughts towards Winnington : you must give me a positive decision before I send Worthington the notice, not to give him unnecessary trouble. I think Edward might find a very sufficient interest in the concern[2] there & *practise* the management of an estate which he may do without interference, or he may *take the whole*, securing 7000 a year to My Lord, but I would not advise him to do that, being a fluctuating & insecure concern with great drawbacks. My Lord is never likely to go near the place again, certainly not in the way of doing business & all is done through Simpson, it may as well be done through him under Edward as not. But *perhaps* this view of mine may not be the best inducement I could hold out to a man

[1] To the Bishopric of Chichester. A. T. Gilbert (1786–1870) was appointed.
[2] Salt mines.

who likes idleness, so you need not press it. It is certainly more desirable than Heawood, & my reason for proposing the latter was only that you had always been so vehement against the other.

Such a storm last night & it has done us tree haters a service—blown down the elm in front of the house & given us so much more light & space it is quite delightful. William has had a grand wreck near Holyhead, it must have been a fine sight but he did not see it at the grand moment. The crew escaped in their boat with difficulty.

(30)   *Jan* 30/42.

I will write to Mr. Worthington immediately—& if any wonderful revolution takes place to put an end to your wishing for it there is no great harm done—the loss is not great—he is a fidgetty tenant.

(31)   NORTON PRIORY[1] *Feb* 2.

What a stupid woman Mlle Alyse is—I wrote today I liked my caps very much but I wanted one for evening rather more dressy—with a few white flowers—but did not I suppose say anything of mourning as I thought she had been fully apprised of that from your order. Yesterday arrived as pretty a cap as I ever saw, but any one I had would do just as well—blonde & flowers with coloured leaves. It will be no loss, only I could have saved the present expence & done without it for a long time to come, as I have a good stock of smart caps out of mourning.

[1] Seat of Sir Richard Brook.

We have found here only the Kayes & Townley
Parkers. Do not direct here if you should write tomorrow for Sir Richd does not care for news or letters &
the post arrives late in the day after we should be gone.

Yrs affecly   M. J. S.

(32)   ALDERLEY *Feb* 4.

Just come home after luncheon, since which had to
read letters & endure a visit from Col. Dixon very mal à
propos at such a moment so I have only just time to say,
another woodcock has been caught & is just going off
with a goose a hare & your wools. A very dull visit,
the Kayes & Townley Parkers were all, nobody else came
except a vile Tory, Hill, who quizzed the K. of P.[1] &
Prince Albert, & made me lose a game at chess by
exciting my attention & indignation so that I could not
mind my business.

Very sorry for Marcus'[2] affliction—the brothers all
loved one another with a love surpassing common fra-
ternal affection—I cannot help hoping Mr. F. is wrong
about the connexion of his leg & bowels especially as we
had been told that the disease of the former had *not*
affected the bowels.

(33)   ALDERLEY *Feb* 6/42.

It must have been an extraordinary delusion that, Mr.
Mill[3] doubting whether *you* & Louisa liked him—I
remember the dinner well—it is before my eyes now—

---

[1] The King of Prussia, having begun his reign with a few negligible reforms,
was supposed to have very Liberal ideas.
[2] Marcus Hare, husband of Lady Stanley's daughter Lucy.
[3] John Stuart Mill (1806–1873) was afterwards a great friend of the family.

more probable that he should have feared you would pull caps for him, if he could have fathomed the motives of actions. Was not Louisa in a very interesting conversation with him at dinner & did not you set your bull dog on to divert it, & did not you in the drawing room draw him off to a corner & keep him in a tete a tete conversation all the time we remained. Very stupid man, or your conversation must have been very problematical if he thought you did not like him then. I am glad you have convinced him now.

I have always forgot to ask what the paragraph in the paper meant, about the *ball* at Windsor being put off on acct of the Queen's sudden indisposition in the evening —had she ate too much, was there to be any ball & is it true that the Archb of C[1] prefaced " all mankind being born in Original Sin " with " may it please your Majesties " but I must ask Uncle this question as he was there.

(34)   ALDERLEY *Feb* 13.
DEAR HEN

Indeed this attack has been most unconscionably long & unusually so, you have not kept up your Mother Hubbard's dog's credit at all. My Lord was forming a theory & coming to a conclusion yesterday that all these neuralgias & *new* illnesses are caused by the adoption of so many poisons in the pharmecopia—certainly we never heard of such ailments in our young days. He is quite well, spins such long yarns with or rather to Mr. Boothby, who is an excellent listener, just putting in a proper word, at the proper places & occasional pauses. He is very well informed & very sensible certainly more-

---

[1] At the christening of the Prince of Wales.

over he brought Mathilda with him in which he has been thoroughly engrossed in a morning & sometimes in the evening also & we have been tantalized with it as he did not produce her at first & now we shall be obliged to leave off in the most interesting part as he goes to-morrow. I do like a French novel so much better than an English one *when* it is readable but I suppose I am to be *shocked* before I come to the end.

The Bells [1] have accepted our offer of remaining in part of Heawood, thankfully at last—I believe Sarah Anne was the only objector at first.

Marcus & Julius [Hare] feel deeply the disappointment of being excluded from the guardianship of F's children—but I cannot wonder that Ann should have used her utmost influence to have them left entirely to her she has probably as great a dislike to them & their ideas as they can have to her & hers.

(35)   ALDERLEY *March* 1.

I shall rejoice in the sight of Edward's writing, hoping that the letter contains good news of you, & I shall begin to look out for it very soon.

The rail road will be open for the publick on the 14th April—the Directors propose coming down to inspect it by the middle of this month, but the various stations will not be completed so soon.

I propose sending your hog immediately—Mrs. Thomson objected on account of the hams not being sufficiently ripe, but I suggested that as you may possibly leave Town early in Spring you may as well have the present advantage. There is also a litter of pigs—per-

---

[1] The Bell family lived in the neighbourhood for many years to come and eventually had a school for young ladies at Winnington.

haps one may run your way if you will keep up to eat it
—& now as it is a fine afternoon I must wish you good-
bye   affecly yrs   M. J. S.

LADY STANLEY TO EDWARD STANLEY ON
THE OCCASION OF THE BIRTH OF KATE
(AFTERWARDS LADY AMBERLEY)

(36)   ALDERLEY *March 6th.*
DEAR EDWARD

Your news was most welcome on every account—a
girl is better than a boy as you have plenty of the latter
& there is less trouble & expence in setting the former
forward in the world, let alone their being often greater
comforts to parents, whereby I assure you I mean no
reflection however—& it is well you & Hen are set at
liberty for future designs.

All well with us—I do not write a separate letter to
Hen today, having nothing more to add.   Give her our
best loves & say how much I regret the pig was *wasted*,
as far as she was concerned.

                              Affec yours   M. J. S.

(37)   ALDERLEY *March 9th/42.*
DEAR HEN

Practise makes perfect it appears—& I trust you will
go on as well as you have begun—Lady Dillon's [1] report
today is as good as can be, but the better you are in these
early days the more I am afraid of imprudence.   I can
think of nothing to say, except that Fleetwood [2] wants a

---

[1] Mrs. Stanley's mother, widow of 12th Viscount Dillon.
[2] The gamekeeper for many years at Alderley.

new net & wants to give £30 for one & I think " want
will be his master " tho he talks grandly of Mr. Stanley
knowing that a new net is wanted & that a larger one
would be better—I hope E does not *uphold* him in these
hard times. You may as well ask him if he does really
know a new one is wanted. How very distressing the
news from India must be to all who have friends in such
an alarming situation as our troops are in.

I am very glad the young thing is to be Katharine

Yrs affec   M. J. S.

(38)   A L D E R L E Y *March* 11
I can hardly tell which is the most horrible tale, Zanoni
or the accounts in the papers of Caubul—I was reading
one & Rianette the other this morning after breakfast &
we were each making exclamations, not in unison certainly,
as to the subject, but as to the horror—*I* was just at the
part where poor Viola has her fears excited for her child,
knowing that the Monster with burning eyes is at her
side. But the frightful news & fear of the worst from
India which is *real*, real at all events in parts & in the
misery all must suffer who have friends in that country—
are they all massacred or not—& are the ladies grinding
corn & thanking heavens they are not put to a worse use.
My Lord fails entirely in making me understand why
we sacrifice so much blood & treasure to cram down the
throats of the people a Sovereign they do not chuse to
have. I would send them back Mr. Dost [1] at once, but
only on condition that his son should be hanged & the
town of Caubul razed to the ground. Some expiation is
necessary.

Yr affec   M. J. S.

[1] Dost Mahommed was reinstated by the British, Cabul was razed to the
ground.

(39)　　　　　　　　ASHBOURNE *March* 18.

I think the Income Tax [1] a very disagreeable thing but so I do blue pills, rhubarb or castor oil, & as it does appear clear that a strong dose of help is necessary for the finances of the country, & that it cannot go on with half measures or experiments any longer, I would like to ask those who object to this Tax to point out another that would certainly answer as well ; & if they cannot I should like them not to stir up a factious & useless opposition. Our dear Queen how nobly she has acted & like her own Whig self—are the rest of the Royal Family exempted from taxes by law as well as the Queen—if so will they follow her example ? Poor D of Sussex will not like it, Adelaide can afford it.

I am very much interested in Mme. d'Arblay's [2] 2 Vol: from remembering so much of the society she frequented when I was young & knowing some of them well, but I do not expect *modern* people will like it. Goodbye—

　　　　　　　　　　　　　　Yr affec　M. J. S.

Love to Henry—if he is in your way pack him off to Alderley.

(40)　　　　　　　ASHBOURNE [3] *March* 21/42.

DEAR HEN

I remember once before you talked of sending Henry to Alderley & his Papa grudged the cash & as he & you certainly ought to think twice before you spend any 5£ that you can avoid I send you a bit of silver paper to

---

[1] Introduced by Peel to make up for the loss in Revenue consequent upon his Free Trade policy.
[2] Fanny Burney, her reminiscences.
[3] Seat of Sir William Boothby.

settle that difficulty as I think he will enjoy the country as *fish will begin to bite*.[1] I must only bargain with him that he shall always appear at luncheon *unless* I know that he is in safe company & not alone on any distant expedition.

It has not been a very pleasant visit—no company here except two young cousins who do not bring an accession of sense & interest into the society—& the *Fellow* is in a distant humour—no allusion please in return—

I think the Morning Chronical's turn to the Queen's handsome conduct is too absurd & I do think Sir Robert knocks down any argument on the other side like so many straws so Adieu affec yrs.

M. J. S.

(41)   ALDERLEY *March* 23.
DEAR HEN

I think I never saw him [Henry] less deaf & I am sure no complaint could be made of his spirits & they are quite up this morning. I am so glad to have him, he is such a dear boy—I was almost sorry Iser did not come, though we have dogs enough certainly, she is so part & parcel of him—& there is no dog love in after life equal to that of the boy for his first dog, & Hannah had put a covering to his bed in expectation, which Henry stated as a touching circumstance. The hedges & horse chestnuts are showing green buds in spite of the weather.

Adieu   affec yrs   M. J. S.

---

[1] Henry's great love of fishing lasted all his life. Mr. Haydon, the keeper at Alderley, well remembers rowing him, as an old man, for hours together on the Mere.

(42)   ALDERLEY *March* 30.

I have not put Henry's case in my mind quite so strong as to see him actually a dumb animal—but I am rather rejoiced that he is an eldest son & will not have to carve his way in the world—his deafness is sadly against him & keeps him back. But he is so very amiable & never shows the least irritability at being lectured—great distress however with tears silently rolling down his cheeks when I found Aunt Louisa had set him to learn Lo ! the Poor Indian he said he *could* not learn it he had tried all he could it was impossible. He would be after Fleetwood all day & as F says he is obliged to hurry in a morning very much to get his work done in time I have requested he would *occasionally* say he was *busy* & could not go about all day with Henry

Good morning to you for I must go out   affec yrs

M. J. S.

(43)   ALDERLEY *April* 3

Julius Hare [1] has published a charge against attacking pews & now the *black monsters* that warm churches & he is very anxious to put to shame all brides who are not virgins, he does not absolutely mention a white sheet but some sort of penance he would have—I am afraid he will find this reformation a difficult one to effect & it is no *new* custom—for as long as I can remember hearing about such things. Sussex was very much in that way as well as Cheshire.

Goodbye   Yr affect M. J. S.

[1] Rector of Hurstmonceaux, brother-in-law of Lady Stanley's daughter Lucy.

(44)   A L D E R L E Y *April* 12.

I hope Henry told Wee that she sent him with one nightshirt only which he wore for 10 days before Louisa found out—he is a dirty boy & has a hydrophobia— very averse to washing. Very much love to him however.

How entertaining Wakeley & Milnes were the other day—about poets—W. speaking *so* disrespectfully of Wordsworth & M placing eminent poets on an equality with the Bible.

LETTER FROM HENRY STANLEY AT EMS
WHERE HE WAS WITH HIS FATHER AND
MOTHER

(45)   *July* 18

MY DEAR GRANDMAMMA

I have to thank you again for your kindness in sending me here, I have enjoyed myself so much. The passage was very smooth & pleasant. There was a very amusing person on board called Captain Kean, he had commanded the British Queen after it was sold to the Belgians, he was rather easy, I suppose from having been frequently in America.

At Antwerp we visited the Museum in it is Ruben's chair & some of his best pieces. I liked best the adoration of the Magi, the Crucifixion & a dead Christ. In this town wherever you go you see a white Spitz dog with a curly tail & black eyes & each has got a wire muzzle as it is the dog-days. [Much more in this vein.]

In Mrs. Stanley's handwriting on the envelope

The King of Hanover is here, Schlegel, an animated old professor, told us a great deal & mentioned an anecdote of him. The K of H having dismissed 5 of his professors from Gottengen for resisting some arbitrary acts of his, was exceeding enraged at the King of Prussia having employed 3 in his own universities—took the opportunity of a large dinner at which xxx, the King of Prussia & Humboldt were present to ask the King what had become of his runaway professors. The K of P answered they were honourable men & at this moment were doing great good to Prussia by their services, upon which the K of H said in a loud tone in the coarsest manner—" Comedians, Courtezans & Professors can always be had for money." Humboldt retorted " with the first two I am not acquainted but as I belong to the last class I must request your maj: to make no satirical reflections upon them."

[Several very dull letters from Mrs. Stanley at Ems and Carlsbad describing the social life there, the chief excitement at Ems was the engagement of Lady Sarah Amherst to Sir John Williams. Lady Stanley comments " she has neither youth nor beauty and this probably facilitated his courtship, but in all other respects she will be a wife he could hardly have expected to get."

Henry says : " The other day we saw a man put a handkerchief over his head & then rush against the bank with a pick axe & then he ran along the road yelping & howling. We found out from the donkey man he had attacked a wasps nest. Goodbye dear Grandmamma your affectionate son Henry Stanley."

While Mrs. Stanley was abroad her household and children moved into Winnington which was to be her home until the death of Lord Stanley in 1850.]

MRS. STANLEY TO LADY STANLEY

(46) CARLSBAD *Aug* 22.

MY DEAR LADY STANLEY, I was very glad indeed to get
your letter from Winnington tho' the first impression of
it was disagreeable. I feared Maud had been very ill
from your staying the night—but I came to the conclusion
that it was your kindness to see how she was going on &
perhaps you were not sorry to see after your business
there.

. Since I wrote I have had the Bath fever or Crisis, that
is to say the dissolvent properties of the water have put
more blood from the torpid liver in action than the
system could manage, & accordingly, as my head is my
strong point I have had no headache etc, but I had
violent palpitations which were relieved by 15 leeches on
the heart.

LADY STANLEY TO MRS. STANLEY

(47) ALDERLEY *Aug* 15

If Galignani[1] tells you we are in a state of insurrection
he will tell you the truth—therefore you will like to hear
that we are only plundered civilly—the Weavers go about
in parties of from 7 to 17 levying Black Mail—they have
been *out* since Thursday & during the intermediate time,
the whole country & towns too have been at their mercy
—a battalion of Guards & detachment of Artillery came
down last night to Chalford & troops have also come
from Dublin & other places. On the application of the
Macclesfield magistrates to General Warre[2] at Man-

[1] The library at Carlsbad where people went to read the papers.
[2] Lieut.-General Sir William Warre (1784–1853), a veteran of the Peninsular
War.

chester, on Friday for assistance, he said he could not
spare them any regular force & they must defend
themselves or employ the yeomanry—These have been
called out & responded most cheerfully to the call &
have conducted themselves with the greatest coolness &
prudence.   Their Adjutant, Hill, is, I believe a good &
intelligent officer.   Louisa & I were at Head Quarters
on Thursday & Friday—Tatton [1]—& all was very
interesting, hearing all the accounts that came in &
expresses from different quarters beseeching help—
10,000 then being on the march, stopping not only all
the mills, in every direction, but every other employment
& trade.   The Tatton troop marched to Macd—William
Egerton commands them & Ralph Leycester was obliged
to follow soon after to join his which is the Macd one,
tho' his Lady was beginning to squeak—she was brought
to bed of a little girl a very few hours after he went &
Wm E having the Colonel's orders to release him as soon
as possible he reached home a quarter of an hour after
the business was over.

Tomorrow a great meeting is announced at Manchester to celebrate Peterloo [2]—& the next day to settle
the rate of wages—but I trust the large force collected
will not look on quietly & that the Queen's Proclamation
will encourage the authorities to lay hold of some of the
ringleaders.

The 250 who have come to our door this morning in
detachments have had a small piece of bread & cheese
& one horn of diluted small beer, each, with which they
have appeared quite satisfied, & each party moved off
as soon as they had finished.   Some liked butter milk
better.   They *professed* themselves the Turned Out &

---

[1] Seat of the Egerton family.
[2] The so-called battle of Peterloo took place 16th August, 1819.

not the Turnouts & all said they did not dare work till the week was passed but I guess there were a few Chartists amongst them very willing to help in the matter.

I cannot move his Lordship to Penrhos he says he cannot bear the journey—I shall take Maude & Blanche[1] as I think it will do them a great deal of good & at all events will give them pleasure. The Winnington children quite well—I am sending a little gig, Ally's former donkey carriage to draw the boys & Williams about the grounds. . . .

I have been so engaged watching the Weavers from the windows that I have no more today. My Lord talked to one party who sent in a letter, they were very respectful, very eloquent & much apparent fairness of complaint against the manufacturers—they of course attacked the Corn Laws. Adieu I hope I shall hear soon

Yrs affec   M. J. S.

(48)   Undated.

DEAREST HEN:

We are all safe & quiet at Alderley although we did give bread cheese & beer *on compulsion* to 500 on Monday & about 100 on Tuesday—not the compulsion however of threats or even rude demand but acting under the influence of prudence when we had no means of resistance —if they had been refused, & offered to take what was not given. Since that day the whole County has been swearing in special constables—My Lord assisted Glegg in swearing in 350 of the Parish & adjacent townships & we think we could now defend ourselves against hundreds if not thousands—The main body has never

---

[1] Mrs. Stanley's girls.

come our way; the visitors have been, generally, I
believe those who were turned out tho' one man was
heard to say he was a Chartist & gloried in the name.
But these were only words in conversation with each
other, overheard, for there was not one un-civil word or
look from any ; & all expressed themselves thankful for
what they got & went away in packs as they came, never
waiting the arrival of another to join them tho' they came
pouring into the yard in quick succession. I have not
heard that the Mills at Macd are again at work—but it
was expected they would begin today. There has been
no military there except two troops of the yeomanry who,
with the help of the constables have kept everything
quiet, but a great deal of charity of the same nature as
ours has been distributed among the mob by tradespeople
& farmers, & I find the worst feature of the business is
that these people have not left a single house in the
neighbourhood unvisited, not even the poorest cottage,
& they have asked, & had, from those who could ill
afford it. There has not, as yet, been any collision
between the military & the assemblies as the latter have
always dispersed as soon as the former appeared in sight.
The fights have been in the towns & in taking prisoners ;
Fred Clinton is at Manchester with a battalion of Gren:
Guards, wrote us word yesterday that several prisoners
had been taken & it was supposed some of the Ring
leaders were amongst them agt whom there were warrants
out.   There is a large force collected at Manchester &
Sir William Arbuthnot [1] is just sent down to take command of them & General Warre, the General of the
District bears a high character for decision & firmness,
& he is a Whig also.   I am very glad the present Govt

[1] Brigadier-General Sir Thomas Arbuthnot, sent by Wellington to deal
with the Chartists.

has to battle this out for I do not suppose you could flatter yourselves all would have been different had you remained in power. It is said that the Queen is going to Scotland. If she does I shall think it the first foolish step she has taken since her accession & a *very* foolish one too. It is surely not the moment for her to run about amusing herself, & removing herself from the seat of government when everyone should be at his post.

There is a general meeting of the Magistrates today at Knutsford which My Lord is gone to—at present the great object should be to protect those people who are willing to work & once set a-going I should hope it would not be in the power of the evil ones, to disturb them again.

The Chartists have luckily betrayed their object which was to gain their ends by the instrumentality of those who cared not for the 6 Points but for the sake of wages they should receive, & many of the operatives are aware of it & will not make common cause with them.

MRS. STANLEY TO LADY STANLEY

(49) CARLSBAD *Sept* 2.

MY DEAR LADY STANLEY

We received yesterday your letter of the 22nd & we were very glad to hear that the country was all quiet again. We were quite surprised to hear you were going to take Johnny to Penrhos but very grateful you should take that trouble—I daresay it will do him great good, but I do not like him being so delicate. I send him many kisses & I hope he will be a good boy & not disturb grandmama. We start next Tuesday certainly I am sure I have had water enough, for if I stayed much

longer I should have no insides left.   Mrs. Austin has
given us the July Edinborough a great treat as you may
believe—I am sorry the Queen has gone to Scotland at
this time as the colliers may insist on seeing her.   We
were very glad to hear Lord Stanley was so well as to be
able to be so active going to Knutsford & swearing in
the constables, I dare say it did him good.   Henry who
seizes upon letters with the family avidity was much
interested in yours last night, but thinks very unkind no
one should have mentioned Iser since he has left England.

Goodbye dear Lady Stanley, my dearest love to my
children.   I hope Johnny will behave so as to win golden
opinions from all.   Mlle. R writes in such enchantment
at going to Penrhos & so penetrated with all your
kindness   Love to Louisa.

Yr very affec & grateful daughter   H. M. S.

(50)   L O N D O N, *Thursday.*
DEAR LADY STANLEY

We arrived this morning at 8—good passage 23 hours
from Rotterdam.   I am now writing at Cartwright,
Henry has a little decay on a front tooth & Parkinson is
out of town so I came here.   I shall never be sufficiently
grateful for all your love to my children—it has been a
source of constant pleasure to Edw: & myself   I am
not alarmed about Baby, with a nurse they get over so
many things, but I shall be glad to be with her.

Yr affec daughter   H. M. S.

I am sorry to say I am now with Cartwright & he has
found Henry's four front teeth decayed.   The poor boy
nearly fainted at first but is behaving very well now—I

45

hope Edw: will see how right I was but it is disagreeable
to assist & only mamas could do it.

(51)   W I N N I N G T O N *Sept* 22.
MY DEAR LADY STANLEY

Rianette will have told you of an expedition to
Alderley where I left Edward yesterday & *Spitz* who was
as much admired by his new master as was compatible
with his tenderness for Blackie's feelings.   It is very cold,
but I walked to Northwich to order a dog basket & other
trifles it is a great convenience having a town so near &
at the same time it is not a place where one could be
tempted to spend money.   I feel quite settled now & the
library only wants a little litter to look very comf:

They have mown the grass in front of the bow window
which is a great improvement, I do not find the grass or
trees at all as black as I expected & the sheep look very
respectable, altogether I am agreeably surprised.   Mr.
Bratten came himself to take the measure for the blinds—
I was to tell you he has no chests of drawers by him—
they will have to be made.   He brought 3 carpets, one
which yr ladyship *greatly admired*, red & yellow, will do
nicely—I could not help surmising a portion of the
admiration was lent by Mr. Bratten, but it is a very
estimable carpet   Yr affec daughter   H. M. S.

LADY STANLEY TO MRS. STANLEY

(52)   P E N R H O S *Sept* 21

Very glad indeed to hear the rabbits are *extinct*—I have
done all I could to bring about that desirable circumstance,
you shall be supplied from Alderley or E can turn out

Henry's rabbits from the Poultry Court I have just put in a new couple there (not rabbits), pray make acquaintance with the woman & see if she is a nice person.

Colonel Scott [1] in washing his feet in a *bidet*, & resting all the weight of one leg in it, broke through & cut himself badly about the ankle—don't expect me to explain how he could do such a strange awkward thing for I do not understand it myself tho' Ally has endeavoured to make me sensible.

I am rather amused by the usual topsy-turveyism of tastes in successive generations—the dear bow rooms, above & below, looking on that beautiful lawn, neglected by the masters & the gravel road preferred. The Library is full South, not East, as you might have guessed, otherwise the sun would not have *annoyed* you *all* the morning—you can easily imagine My Lord & I never wished to exclude the smallest ray of his light & warmth. Bratten shall put some blinds up. I also wonder a little that you should prefer the square to the 3 corner, with its London yard look out.

(53)   A L D E R L E Y *Friday.*

A seventh Miss Adeane made her appearance on Thursday last.

I forgot to tell you yesterday that the next night after the poachers shot Mr. Dixon's dog they were met by Glegg's keeper, who fancying he & a watcher had but one man to deal with, attempted to seize him but more of the gang were at hand & the keeper was severely beaten. The police have been set on the alert in consequence & this morning Fleetwood tells me that the two Hassalls & Okell have been taken up, at Hassall's house

---

[1] Husband of Lady Stanley's daughter Ally.

where they had assembled & he heard they had made resistance & knocked one of the constables about a good deal. My Lord proposes giving the keepers police hats, Fleetwood says they had been thinking to buy them themselves.

Louisa has had one of her worst headaches the last 2 days—she is better today but *creechy*. So glad you like your dinner set, tell me of anything else.

(54)   ALDERLEY *Nov* 13.

DEAR HEN

I think it is *unfair* in *you* to grudge Edward to his parents on his 40th birthday—especially as you know how much pleasure Ld S has in his being present & as it is entirely optional on your part *not being with him*. If as I think is probable *you* could not enjoy the day without your children I still think this is unreasonable. If we are so troublesome as to live some years longer you must learn to look forward, either to be seldom with us, which I should regret or *not* having all your children nor any large portion of them at once, often with you. A rassemblement at Christmas I shall always wish for & hope to enjoy as long as life & health remain. I am *sometimes* distressing myself to think how soon, in the way in which I think you will wish to push forward instead of keeping back *your* daughters (as I should for their own sake) how soon I say there will be two [Alice and Blanche] expecting to take their place at table & in society, & if you continue to keep them in the same state of reserve & distance from me they will be only so much live lumber & no pleasure at any time. Really I did not intend to say all this when I began but only to reproach

48

you *gently* for going away. Neither of us, however, need
distress ourselves much on the subject, the progress of
years must bring such things to an end before many are
passed. It has been a pouring day—the coachman must
rejoice he does not belong to an episcopal or over pious
family, for finding both Bishop & Kitty would have
walked rather than not go a second time I had the
carriage out again.

(55)   *Tuesday.*

Why did you not tell me, or did you not know that
game must be sent *cooked* to Eton—poor Henry was
obliged to refuse what I sent & ordered to return it—
which he thought would be *very* uncivil & so he forwarded
it to Aunt Scott. I suppose I never treated Edward &
William to such dainties for I do not remember knowing
of such a stern law.

(56)   ALDERLEY *Nov:* 22

Capital news from China—I suppose it may be
depended on. My Lord talks of nothing but Hong
Kong being part of Q. Victoria's dominions. I wish
Edwd would let you off Hooton—I think he might just
as well go by himself, only you may as well go & look
after him as I hear two accounts of Mrs. J. S. one, that
she is an innocent little thing etc. & another that men
can, & do, say *anything* to her—but I cannot think it a
respectable house for any woman of decent habits, let *her*
be what she may.

Why do Blanche & Maud look wretched?

Yrs affecly   M. J. S.

Fuchsias are not splet Fucias [*sic*].

(57) ALDERLEY *Wednesday.*

Spitz is a beast, dirtied both my room & my quilt, bad dirt, last night—at least I can be sure of the *room* as Puppy cannot jump on the bed if he got off so I know he was not down all night, & they plague me by playing all day & wanting each other's bone. Spitz follows me about everywhere—& there now they are got to play again & I have no peace or quiet, as bad as children only they are dumb.

Two more of Dr. Parry's daughters *have been* given over, he has buried two within a year, grown up, beautiful girls—Sir Edward [Parry] sent me a letter of his brother in which, after speaking of his own severe sufferings he says " God bless you & your children, but do not love them " I said to Rianette this was *truth* of feeling & I had not faith in the *truth* of those who say, at the *moment* of trial Thy will be done, this is all in Mercy & Love. Resignation may come, on reflection, to those who have a deep, habitual, trustful faith, but not at first.

1843

ALDERLEY 6th Feb.

DEAR HEN

Fleetwood having mentioned to one of Lord Derby's people that our Swan establishment was low, it reached Lord Derby, who has written the kindest letter possible to My Lord, saying how glad he is to be able to furnish him with whatever he wishes for in that way & assuring him it is not any favour as he shall be quite glad to diminish his number. So Fleetwood will go himself, take a little holiday with his friends & bring back a Cob & a Pen. Our Lordship wrote a pretty answer, taking the opportunity as he always does of adding a little genealogy[1] into the bargain. He has been very much interested lately with some genealogy William has picked up from the Isle of Wight, whence came the wife of Sir Peter Stanley[2]—a Miss Leigh of Northcote, & this has tacked on well with some imperfect knowledge he had before & besides is very entertaining in itself—for instance the act of an old gentleman who hoped his grandson would revenge the ill conduct of his son towards him when he (the boy) was grown up but alas ! Dio dispone & the little boy died before his grandfather who lived to be 83. The son was a wicked chap certainly

[1] The Alderley Stanleys claim to be an elder branch of the family.
[2] In the 17th century.

E 2

for he used to say he wished he could repeat the first line of the Lord's Prayer, with reference to his earthly father. But tell Edward that he took the best way possible to enable him to await with patience, for he married three wives, all with a great deal of money & very much improved the family property.

The wood stealers were sent to prison for a month or pay 20/– Fleetwood thought My Lord would not wish them to be transported & put the value of the wood at 1/–

In haste   Yrs affecly   M. J. S.

(59)   GREEN BANK   *Feb* 10/43.

Louisa has sent me your most entertaining letter. What folly will next seize the fashionable world ! Dogs in a London drawing room ! A soiree of stars, with the accompaniment of barking curs & chattering ladies overlaying all rational, instructive, scientific or political conversation. I imagine to myself My Lord in Macaulay's skin trying to put in his word on the physiology of the canine species while internally groaning over the frivolity of the female creation & I can *hear* Miss Berry screaming in a higher key than all the party put together. Well— I am very glad you get such amusing evenings, set off by an occasional lonely studious one.

MRS. STANLEY TO LADY STANLEY

(60)   GROS: CRES: *Feb* 14*th*.

MY DEAR LADY STANLEY

I dined at the Palmerstons, Ed: Mr. Oswald, Lord Auckland,[1] Miss Eden,[2] the Clanricardes & Clarendons

---

[1] Afterwards Viceroy of India.
[2] Lord Auckland's sister, author of "A Semi Attached Couple."

—an agreeable dinner & yesterday we had a very pleasant
dinner at Lady Holland's, Rogers,[1] Luttrel, Baring,
Wall, Fonblanque[2] & Lady Charlotte Lindsay—Rogers
told me as usual how he loved me I told him he had
always said so but I saw no proofs so he answered he
loved *me* but not my husband. He was in great force in
the evening & told many anecdotes.

We dine at Lansdowne House tomorrow & Miss
Berry Thursday. Thank you for the Times.

Yrs affec daughter   H. M. S.

LADY STANLEY TO MRS. STANLEY

(61)   ALDERLEY *Feb* 16

Your dinner was a constellation indeed.

The housemaid went to Town this morning & has
taken Blanche's book & the Bible in Spain Louisa read
hard at last, to get it done & I did not like to lose this
gratis opportunity. She has been extraordinarily amused
by it. My Lord will not believe it—I hope you will see
Lord Clarendon[3] & ask him about the man for he must
know all about him & whether he is to be depended on.

Lord Newburgh went this morning & Sir Gardner
Wilkinson is just arrived. We are colder than cold, My
Lord has taken to his great coat & will not stir out, he is
very well—only grieving over Blackey who cannot live
long I think, she is so weak she can hardly stand & will
scarce eat anything.   affecly yrs   M. J. S.

---

[1] Samuel Rogers (1763–1855), " banker bard of St. James's."
[2] Albany Fonblanque (1793–1872), leader writer to *The Examiner*.
[3] Lord Clarendon was Minister Plenipotentiary in Madrid when Borrow
was disseminating his Bible.

53

Lady Combermere [1] miscarried of twins at Brighton—
how droll of those old ladies. Very strange nobody
comes after your house while Margaret's & the Bishop's
always let directly & well. The Bishop however *may* be
in a scrape as Kethick did not tell them the lady is going
to lay in & she *may* not be a good reckoner & be ready
to move at Easter, moreover she has a French daughter
in law who reads in bed, & *may* set fire to the house.

(62)   ALDERLEY *Feb* 21*st*.

How poor Milnes [2] is attacked & laughed at in the
papers, why will he talk so of being young—but he has
caught it now, the Morn: Chron: says his speech savours
of the ignorance of youth with the garrulity of old age—
& both sides seem to have cheered him with peals of
laughter.

Poor Blackey died this morning & I have just seen
her deposited between Cavack & Coll in the Yew Arbour.
My Lord looks very disconsolate, but it is a release both
to him & the old dog.

MRS. STANLEY TO LADY STANLEY

(63)   GROV: CRES: *Feb* 22*nd*.
MY DEAR LADY STANLEY

I am very sorry Lord Stanley has lost his dog for I am
afraid he will not find it easy to replace one who suited
him so well—pray tell him we all spoke most tenderly
of the poor mother of the dogs.

[1] Lord Combermere was over 70.
[2] R. Monckton Milnes (1809–1885).

54

Edward has set up a nervous headache in half his head at a fixed hour every day—I am attacking his stomach.

No houses are letting—I have been to every agent in London. We dined yesterday at Lady Holland. Ld. Radnor Sir William Russell both silent Mr. Rutherford [1] agreeable & Sydney Smith [2] disgusting—he was ever the first to scoff at things of good repute, described how the whole Church was in expectancy ready to make a rush on China—a Bishop of Hong Kong in the bake-house. Then saying he was sorry the Bishops had shown even less than of their usual sagacity in finding fault with Ld. Ellenborough's want of Xianity, which is abundantly satisfying to the Rev: S. S. He was dull upon the whole, being full of an imaginary wit & having none of his own.

in another handwriting

Mama has been so interrupted by people that she has not time to write another word.

Yr affec & dutiful Grand Alice

LADY STANLEY TO MRS. STANLEY

(64)   *Feb 28th*

Did you dine with Ld. Clarendon & not ask him about Borrow ? I am very glad Edwd has consulted Seymour & hope he will follow his directions—if not— eat nothing one day & a gourmand's dinner the next. You are very good in writing so much about all your invalids.

The Bum Bailiffs were after George Bell yesterday—

[1] William Rutherford, 1798-1871, Editor of *The Mathematician*.
[2] Sydney Smith, 1771-1845, Canon of St. Paul's.

55

I wish that disgrace to his family & the parish could be sent farther off.

Lucy[1] is quite well & has been writing some very interesting letters lately, about the poor Brixham fishermen who were lost, in their sight (had they been looking out) & at least they saw the boats in the Bay seeking the dead bodies. And about the Channel Missions, have you ever heard of them? Under the direction of a Dr. Ashley who preaches to the wind bound ships in the Bristol Channel & has met with great encouragement in his missionary capacity.

(65)   ALDERLEY *March* 7.

You are indeed a jewel of a correspondent, & Lord Clarendon's testimony to Borrow's veracity is quite satisfactory, especially to Louisa who was ready to vouch for him before on internal evidence of sympathy for his enthusiasm. Is Lord Clarendon likely to have written the article in the Edinburgh on the book, it is very clever & seems worthy of him & there is a tone in it also which appears, to us, to suit him.

My Lord bestowed an anathema upon you, for being discontented with too much good company—I think it is the great advantage of early London that you *can* live in a set.

Henry is a distressing case for I fear Eton will not do for him—& between his ailment & his cough he should be carefully attended to. Is there no place where he could be advantageously situated with good teaching & good care—as home education seems out of the question both from expense & inconvenience.

[1] Lady Stanley's daughter, Mrs. Hare.

His poor Lordship is still suffering from gout in the *sole* of his foot, quite a new & strange place for it. Emmy was rather poorly yesterday so chilly & headachy, but she is much better on the whole.

Affec yrs   M. J. S.

(66)   ALDERLEY *March* 12*th*.

DEAR HEN,

Thanks for poor dear Henry's note—I wish he had been at the catching of a 10 lb Pike yesterday with the Colonel [1] who is quite as eager an Isaac Walton as Henry. All you say about him & the difficulties as to the best way of disposing of him for a few years is perfectly true & correct.   There is much to make one anxious about him, but there is so much to console one in his character —which is also much better suited to an elder than a younger son.

My Lord has been very much entertained with The Last of the Barons & has been searching old chronicles & histories to see what authority Bulwer had for some of his charges against Edward.   I think he has managed his story very well, though he has made rather too much of the *steam engine* & old Wizard.

I think Mlle. R will be just the thing for Lady W in one respect—that she will not excite her jealousy.   I have heard it said that the place is avoided by young & respectable females.   I do not think Ly. W will find her any treasure in other ways—how glad I am I shall not see her face again nor hear her thick voice.

Sneaking fellows those Bishops are, take them all in all.   Where were London, Salisbury & St. Asaph who

---

[1] Colonel Scott, Lady Stanley's son-in-law.

I believe were certainly all in Town & perhaps many more.[1]

Yrs affecly   M. J. S.

(67)   ALDERLEY PARK   *March 25th/43.*

Only *news* as it was confirmation of my more than suspicions—from many little things & words & the probability of the case.   It is really too much in these hard times & maybe harder to come to bring such an annual rent charge upon an estate.   But I am glad to find you are so well & nothing of the same kind as last time to apprehend—very hard to have such a state to meet all your troubles in—& not out of them yet——

It does seem wonderful that good or even tolerable governesses should be so scarce & that their expectations should be so exhorbitant in times when one might suppose many would wish for a governess who cannot afford to pay them high, & that very many well educated persons must be wanting bread.   I am much afraid you will not get *all* you require under £100—but certainly my own opinion is that so very few governesses are capable of *teaching every thing* that I should prefer an humbler *professor* at 80 & spend the remaining 20 in Masters.   They are sufficiently grounded in German to be able to go on with the language—Musick is the only thing a governess ought to know enough of to keep them up well in their practising, but I must say I do not think they have musical bumps.   It certainly seems to me they want most general knowledge & a sensible woman about them who will improve their minds & be able to converse with them on what they read hear or see

---

[1] No doubt this refers to a division in the House of Lords.

& above all one who will take an interest in them & not, like Mlle. R throw them off entirely except at lessons.

I quite agree with you that the *manners* of a gentle-woman are *essential* especially as they generally though not always prove the *mind* of one besides.

Poor Koelle was found dead in the ice house gardens there is something mysterious about her end—Louisa fancies she had been drinking *bullocks blood*.

(68)   A L D E R L E Y *April 2nd.*

DEAR HEN

Yesterday was such a gay day for Alderley, the hounds met on Alderley Edge & Emmeline went in the phaeton with the two [Scott] girls, the Col: & Louisa on horse-back, & a beautiful sight they had—finding in the High Lees & running the fox the whole length of the Edge, through the Clock House woods & under the Beacon, back again to the starting place where they killed. They started 2 foxes, one a lady with cubs—how Mr. White found this out I do not know, but he ordered the earth to be opened, much to the surprise of some of the sportsmen who were not in the secret. Mrs. Fox got home safe, we suppose, & Mr. Fox, having less strong parental feelings thought he should secure his safety best by flight & suffered from his imprudent choice. Louisa & Marchioness followed the hounds nearly because Mar-chioness would stand on her hind legs if Louisa wanted her to stand still—so for safety's sake she thought it better to gallop along behind the hunters, & besides John [her groom] she had Mr. Shakerley & Harry Brooke with her—& I suppose she gained great applause for her horsemanship & spirit, for about half an hour after she got home the whole field rode up to the door for Mr. White to present the brush to Miss Louisa. The Col: went to call Louisa & it was some time before she would appear, being convinced he was making an *April Fool* of her. *I* was quite sorry to be obliged to speak civilly to Mr. White, after the account we had heard of his behaviour to Lord Pomfret. Mr. Glegg was the leader in this presentation & the others who came up to the door were Mr. Shakerley, H. Brooke & Humphrey Trafford. They looked very pretty, going away over the park, it was a very large field but almost all rubbish from Macclesfield. The little girls were delighted— never saw a hound before nor so many red coats (except Uncle Scott's soldiers in the Park).

(69) A L D E R L E Y *Sunday.*

Tell Henry Miss Moomie took it very much to heart he did not turn up to take leave of her—I don't think he had seen her for three days. If she had been a *large carp* I am sure he would not have forgot her.

I expect Carlyle tomorrow or next day.

(70) A L D E R L E Y *May 3rd/43.*

You send a very poor account of yourself indeed—but you know I never do bestow much commiseration upon you trusting that you are up & laughing before this reaches you, & such ups & downs are usual in your unhappy predicament—

Carlyle ! My Lord began by fancying rather than finding some grains of corn in all the chaff they were buried in but he is ending utterly disgusted. Surely he will be shut up at last, not My Lord but the Monomaniac.

Just had the pleasure of civilly assuring a large party that neither the Hall the Garden nor the Wood were acessible—& the Edge only by permission on certain days, being also private property.

Terrible hard times these for dillettantes. My Lord & Simpson have just settled that we must allow the tenants 10 pr. ct. out of their rents, but it will be done by means of manure & so, do double good—to them & the landlord through the land, instead of leaving the tenants to misuse the allowance.

I am glad your dinner went off well, but, with daughters so near grown up, I should have been better pleased if the line, so almost universally drawn between a divorcée & a well regulated family, had not been passed. Did you expect the Bishop & Kitty would have come to you, had they been able ? I should have been a little surprised if they had—at least I think they are not acquainted so why make a beginning ?

Have you been to see a picture of the Queen painted by a German artist for Louis Philippe—Sir Edward [Parry] says it is like *you*. He says you may laugh, but I have seen the likeness in one or two of her portraits. This is a beautiful painting he says.

Yrs affec   M. J. S.

(71)   ALDERLEY *May 31st/43.*

Poor Margaret, what an account you give of her. After this is over I think you must recommend Mr. Hamilton to go on some foreign mission for a year or two & give her a respite. I daresay she will only have one after all, but she will be liable to greater discomfort every time having once got into this way.

61

I went to fetch Emmy home yesterday, she had enjoyed her visit very much—& tho' Smith Barry may not be a Solomon he is very lively, full of Irish humour & good humour, fond of his place & not ungentlemanlike—though he may not be highly polished. I believe her [Mrs. Smith-Barry's] influence keeps him quite aloof from all low company such as his father liked.

(72)   ALDERLEY *June 8th/43.*

Alas ! It has been raining all night & blowing too & thunder showering all the morning. My Alas ! is that between 2 & 3000 school boys, teachers & Ministers have been permitted to come to the Edge today. The teachers are anxious this week to provide amusement for their scholars as far from Manchester Race Course as they can & take them out each day in Whitsun week. They are to walk round the Edge in procession, in pairs, & then adjourn to sundry fields that have been hired from the farmers for them to eat buns & play about, the buns having had part of a special train allotted to them. I hardly know how many schools & of what persuasions, but I daresay there will be no polemical discussions amongst them.

Surely you do not send Henry alone to the play with Gerald [1] unless you think it high time to initiate him into the knowledge of London. I should fancy, but it may be only fancy, he is not a very good companion for Henry —however you should know your own brother best, only sometimes peoples own relations do *not* know them best. I hear the thunder rumbling, very vexatious.

Yrs affecly   M. J. S.

[1] Gerald Dillon, Mrs. Stanley's brother, only four years older than Henry.

(73)   ALDERLEY *June 9th.*

The day was very showery & very windy but never-
theless the *thousands* enjoyed themselves much, & all
went away without doing any mischief early in the evening. Many of the men, apparently Sunday school
teachers expressed themselves so thankful for the indul-
gence, & so worthy of it from the pleasure they said they
had in seeing such scenery & breathing such pure air.
The Edge, that is all about the Holy Well & Stormy
Point was covered, but I don't think they rambled far.

(74)   ALDERLEY *June* 18/43.

[A long discussion as to the respective merits of two
tutors for Henry, to neither of whose establishments he
finally went.]

And now to the subject of next importance, Lena.
I suppose you was the culprit who had the charge of her—
just walking from G.C. to Lady Dillon's thinking of
something else, was it not so ? Or I think you would
have said who she was with. I *do* think you are a
heroine of forbearing economy, & that I should have
raised my offer—but very probably you are right & she
would have disappeared again if you had shown yourself
anxious. Is it not shameful however, that the Law
should not protect such property more strictly, property,
as Louisa says, so wrapped up in our affections & doubly
shameful that people should dare so openly to confess
the possession of stolen property & bargain for its return.
I hope to hear on Tuesday that you have got her again.

I really should not have been very sorry if it had been
that abominable Spitz who does lead us such a life with
her ill temper. If she had not taken such a violent

63

affection for me & shewn me personally none but her winning ways I should have put her in the hands of a thief at once.

We took advantage of a *closed day* on the Edge yesterday to enjoy the view. The new sign is up [1] The Wizard of the Edge—very well painted, but as the man has omitted putting the name or what is meant I expect people will take the figure for My Lord in his dressing gown.

(75)   ALDERLEY *June* 21/43.

My Lord will answer for himself—I think a nightingale a nuisance because he eats raw meat but it has always been one of his desideratums therefore I am glad Edward should have the pleasure of gratifying him. He (My Lord) has also realized another of his tiresome fancies, a fountain near his mulberry tree which puts me out of all patience because he wants it to play when the watering is going on, which interrupts very much, besides thinking it a great foolery.

If your children had been sent into the country a month ago I daresay they would not have been invalids but—I am going to affront you—you half kill them with your novelty education mania. If the Course has continued along with the drawing lessons I am not surprised at any petite santé in the world. Lady Katharine Boileau spoke of the drawing class that poor, unfortunate, delicate, ailing Blanche attends. She said the room was so crowded & hot she would not on any account allow her girls to go there—she had got a drawing master to attend at home instead.

William tells me you have not got Lena back—how

---

[1] Of the public-house.

can you expect to for 1£. If you care for the dog you
must down with the 3£ & deny yourself that much in
odds & ends of dress—anyhow you will hear enough of
your *carelessness.* I was quite sure it was you because
children are in general so very watchful of dogs.

Yrs affecly   M. J. S.

I am quite *ashamed* of My Lord for assisting you
[he sent the money for Lena.]

(76)   A L D E R L E Y *June* 22/43.

We were very glad to hear of Margaret's *delivery* [1]—
in the full sense of the word on this occasion.

If the restoration of Lena depended on money I hope
yesterday's dispatch was in time to *save her life*, but My
Lord desires me to tell you that the whole transaction of
offering money for stolen goods comes under the head
of compounding for felony & is liable to the punishment
of the pillory, if it can be proved. You may say this is
an obsolete custom, but why should the Clergy alone
have the privilege of reviving excellent old practices.

I am very much pleased to hear Henry's destination
is as good as settled—it must answer well, a man who
will be able & willing, probably, to enter into his favourite
pursuits. I am sorry that his holidays must be shortened
but I am inclined to say the sooner the better considering
the situation of their place.

The little carriage will go [to Winnington] on Saturday,
& the cow (whose happy calf has gained 10 days by your
delay). I am about purchasing a second hand piano-
forte not to move ours or hire, the Adeanes have given

---

[1] Margaret Hamilton had seven children. Her eldest son was 10th Lord
Belhaven and Stenton.

the one here full work.   They play very well & have
been very well taught—Miss Meredith is a perfection of
a governess.

(77)   Y O R K *June* 2 5*th.*

What will you & still more sober Edward say on
hearing of the wonderful frisk Ellin Emmy & I have
taken ?   On Thursday evening we talked of going to
Manchester next day, partly to shop, partly to take Louisa
to show her eye to Wilson, Flora having put her foot in
it as they were gambolling together.   Some sudden
inspiration (of folly My Lord thought) suggested how
easy it would be to go on to York & see the Minster—
Rianette to return from Manchester with Louisa.   Ellin
& Emmy were quite *mad* about it, when it once got hold
of their imagination.   Well, My Lord thought we were
crazy but whether or not he believed we were in earnest
I do not know, but as he did not forbid, we set off at
2 o'clock on Friday—saw the Collegiate church for
Emmy's amusement & did all the business that evening
at Manchester—left it at 11 yesterday morning, got here
at 3, dined, saw the Minster & much more in the city,
such a contrast to Manchester—so clean so clear & so
beautiful.   We saw the sun set in an unclouded sky,
illuminating the noble building & showing it off to the
greatest advantage, from the walls, which are more
perfect than Chester, have been to Morning Service &
propose being home again tomorrow evening.   Emmy
does not appear to be at all the worse for it, I thought
the rattle & noise of the railroad would have knocked us
all up, how it did screech & worry us !   And we stopped
very often though a 1st class, because there are so many
branches from the main road.   It is a most extraordinary

sight, traversing so many miles of manufactories, tall
chimneys, smoke, & houses innumerable, every appearance of trade prospering but they say things are not going
on very well & at Leeds very badly.

(78)   ALDERLEY *June* 27/43.

Safe home again, very much pleased with our trip &
quite sorry we came back so soon as we found nobody
expected us, took for granted that we should fly further
off.   We left York at 3 yesterday afternoon & were
drinking tea here before 9. Nobody is tired & I always feel
the better for going from home & seeing something new.

Very glad you have recovered Lena—but it does
exasperate one to think how you have been obliged to
connive with villany, however *now* the dog is known &
the thieves also, I think if you should lose her again you
would have no scruple in making use of all your acquired
knowledge of their haunts.

I have been looking over all my Eton accounts to see
about the payments [1] to Keate & the tutor but can find
no entry of that sort, direct—but anyhow I suppose there
is no avoiding what is usual, which you can easily learn.
In going over the accounts however I find how much
reason Edward has to be satisfied with Henry's modera-
tion in expence [2] ; in one of Plumtrees letters is this post-
script " Query—is not 5/– an *enormous* weekly allowance ? "   Yet I fear E cannot say he left no debt at
Eton & the tradesmen's bills were also pretty big.

[Lady Stanley goes over to Winnington to see that all
is ready for the family arrival from London.]

[1] On leaving school the boys were accustomed to tip the headmaster £5.
[2] Henry throughout life was noted for his parsimony.

(79)　　　ALDERLEY PARK *June 30th.*

I thought Miss West looked very ill—so deadly pale & she complained of a very bad headache—poor thing thought I when I heard the incessant clatter of Johnny & Lyulph. I like her manners & appearance very well—but she looks quite like a governess, much above a bonne or nursery governess—all the better however as she must associate with *the* governess. I hope they will be good friends.

I think there can be no doubt but that Mr. Dean is fully competent to the accouchement part, & especially for you who manage that part so well. The recovery is everything & I should prefer London for you in that part of the business if it could be managed, but I have great confidence in Mr. Dean's skill, notwithstanding his garrulity which is a great take off from the pleasure of his company.

Tell Edward that there is a large gang of gypsies encamped near Adlington—& that young Legh [1] is very attentive & liberal to them—allows them to take rabbits & fish & whatever they like. It is said there is a very pretty girl in the camp.

(80)　　　ALDERLEY *Aug: 8th.*

Blanche is just gone from the door, with Aunt Louisa, on the two ponies to enjoy the Edge, a reserved day & a hot day, & is not likely to go fast enough to add to the *inconvenience* of yesterday's ride with both Aunts. She was rather tired in the evening but not at all desirous of shortening her ride, as she declined coming home with

[1] The Leghs of Adlington are a very old Cheshire family.

Louisa who gave up sooner than Emmy on account of the flies which plagued Marchioness.

Carried all our hay yesterday & today will finish the mowing. Every prospect of fine weather.

MRS. EDWARD STANLEY TO LADY STANLEY

(81)   WINNINGTON *Sept 6th*.

. . . Apropos of Tatton you can imagine nothing so tame as the poor fern & heath they have planted to look wild in the Pine. The flowers were looking very well but not arranged with taste, no beds all of one sort but bad mixtures like Dahlias & Holyhocks. I saw two very pretty flowers I doubt you having at Alderley—dobilia racimosa, beautiful blue & treble the size of the little ones, & viscaria occulata. If you know these well do not scoff at my humble beginnings, but it is so different looking at flowers with interest in their identity & merely thinking them pretty, I feel as if I had a new sense.

All the Rhine party, Mama, Lou, Gerald & the Hamiltons were to go up the Rhine last Monday leaving the children at Köningswinter. Margaret very well & comfortable but only able to do the necessary work of life. If she is spared having any more children she will get strong in time but Mama says she perfectly dreads another pregnancy.

LADY STANLEY TO MRS. STANLEY

(82)   NORWICH *Sept* 8/43.

Nothing can have gone off better than this rather dreaded visit, dreaded I suspect by the Bishop himself. It seemed a great relief when he found there was to be no publick reception or notice of the Father whatever & that Mathew [1] had no intention of putting himself forward. He said he never allowed any flags or crosses or popery inscriptions to be carried before him. The Bishop asking him if it was true, what he had been assured of, that the Crucifix was often carried before him, he said that in his own country the poor people, anxious to do him all the honour in their power had frequently come out to meet him, with every holy article they could get from the churches, but that he objected to such demonstrations & always sent them back. He was the advocate of Temperance only, not aiming to make proselytes to the Catholick faith & equally ready to give the Pledge to Catholick or Protestant. Emmy & Arthur went to the evening meeting (J. J. Gurney in the chair) with the Bishop. The speeches had begun before they arrived, Uncle not wishing to make himself a prominent feature by being waited for. He spoke third—Emmy says his speech was excellent & much more quiet in tone & action than she ever heard him.

Father Mathew spoke after the Bishop—he does not seem to have any of the graces of eloquence. Stafford Jerningham was on the platform, he has taken the Pledge—the Gurneys, Mrs. Opie & a few more were there, but few clergymen, who are almost universally against, not Father Mathew but the Temperance Society, probably because the Bishop has taken it up. The Father had not intended to give any Pledges last night, but there was such a rush forward at the end of the meeting of people saying they had come many miles for

[1] Theobald Mathew, 1790–1856, Irish priest and temperance reformer, received a pension from Lord J. Russell. Cf. "Queen Victoria's Letters," vol. 2.

the purpose that he consented & when the Bishop came away he left many crowding into the hall.

Our fine weather continues & certainly blue sky is bluer in Norfolk than elsewhere, there is such a clearness in the *atmosphere*, every object stands out so distinct in its edges.   Yrs affecly   M. J. S.

[Alderley Edge is a great cliff which rises very suddenly out of the flat Cheshire landscape and thus affords many dramatic view-points. Until this time it had been peaceful and secluded, particular to the Stanley family on whose estate it was. With the coming of the railways, however, it became the objective of expeditions from Manchester and other towns in the district. The Stanleys, whose Liberal principles seem to have rather deserted them over this affair, struggled to keep the public away but gradually were obliged to give in, as will presently appear. The place now has a flourishing car park, tea garden, etc., and has certainly lost all the charms which it must have had a hundred years ago.]

MRS. STANLEY TO LADY STANLEY

(83)   ALDERLEY *Sept 8th.*

MY DEAR LADY STANLEY

We received the pictures safe—I like Stormy Point view. Poor Edge I feel one loves it more for the insecurity of the tenure. If you have got my letter to Louisa you will not be surprised when I tell you today's story—as we were at luncheon yesterday we saw a man walk up whom his Lordship feared was a Parson. I feared a Rail Roadian & so the case proved, Mr. Wad-

dington Deputy Chairman B & M. He was shown into
the drawing room, Ld. S finished eating then went in
desiring us to follow, we did so soon for we did not
know what might happen. Now what do you think was
the impudent man's proposal, that Lord Stanley should
allow the managing clerk of the R.R. to give orders on
one of our private days !

The Cottontots forsooth prefer the days without a
crowd. The boon would be no double tickets on the
other private days, but as double tickets or not we do
manage to keep them off on those days it would be giving
up a 4th day. Lord Stanley demurred & appealed to us.
I spoke. I said Lord Stanley was *already extremely*
liberal in granting 3 days & that we must have the other
3 for ourselves. "Oh but these wd be respectable people
who would show you respect" I answered I did not
want respect but privacy & that it was perfectly immaterial
to us who the people were, we wished to be quite alone
to enjoy ourselves with our children, dogs, & friends.
The man was pertinaceous. "Would we not try it?"
Impossible, Lady Stanley, Mr. Stanley would not hear
of it. Oh Lord Stanley lived in the heart of the people &
something about the public. I said we had nothing to do
with the public & owed them nothing & after all this
man is a Tory. I was very much put out & Rianette
looked as stern & unbending as possible. Both this
Waddington & Westend are just like Americans so free
& easy. At last he went, Lord Stanley walking with him
through the garden—the fact is Lord Stanley leads so
secluded a life he is glad to see anyone & when he gets
in talk with people is too civil by half.

The Granvilles called & we all met on the Edge,
there we found no damage but the people having wantonly
thrown down a quantity of dirty paper from the rocks all

about the Well, so his L'ship said they were to eat in
future at Stormy Point.   A good many ferns had been
hurt.   I fancy there was very rough work there on Sunday & nothing but the big dogs keep things in order—
Mr. Waddington ended by saying no alteration would be
made this year but next year he will wait on his Lordship,
& perhaps he flatters himself he will get the private day
for the Cottontot *grandees*, but you will be there & no
one can be or is better inclined to defend their property.
Oh Ld. S did tell us one thing he had said he was proud
of : the man asked if the people were allowed to walk
about the woods on which Ld. Stanley said certainly he
should not allow them to interfere with his son's sport &
game.   Fancy Edward's horror at the idea of *people* loose
among his beloved pheasants.

I never saw such weather at Alderley, we walked out
admiring the moon last night, it is too hot for *me* but
perfect for people in a natural state.

Your affec daught   H. M. S.

LADY   STANLEY   TO   LORD   STANLEY

(84)   NORWICH *Sept* 10/43.

The Globe is guilty of a misrepresentation in saying
the Bishop shook hands with Father Mathew on the
platform.   Those who were present say that at that part
of his speech where he greets the Father as a Christian
Brother he threw out his hand *towards* him, but neither
then nor at the end of the meeting did they shake hands.

The result of our observations upon the Father, after
the dinner here was to come to the conclusion that there
was not much in him beyond his *trade*—I do not mean of
a Priest but an apostle of temperance.   His whole power

of mind was engrossed by this one subject & he did not
seem to observe or think on any other. He spoke quite
modestly of himself & any merit he could claim in urging
forward this great national movement, spoke of it as an
impulse which once excited had gone on spreading from
its own internal impetus almost without assistance from
any one & he seemed convinced that the benefit felt by
so large a portion of the community will be sufficient to
keep it up.

I have heard of your rail road persecution in the shape
of a director. I must remind you, in order to confirm
you in hard-heartedness, how very angry you expressed
yourself at first when they advertised the invitation to the
publick [to Alderley Edge] & that you thought it a great
act of impertinence—& really 3 days allowed & a 4th
(Sunday) taken by storm is a very generous allowance.
Moreover the Manchester *gentry* are much more annoying to ones comfort & enjoyment, than operatives as one
can neither hand cuff nor great dog them if they are
intrusive or offensive & for our sakes (as you do not often
go to the Edge) you must always keep in mind how outraged your feelings would be, if you were to see a party
walking across the lawn, tho' they were not to come near
you—& how if you were Henry's age you would be
discomforted as you were lying under the tall pines or
on the rock above the Holy Well reading or sketching
or thinking, if all of a sudden an uproarious party of
Cottontots came upon you, perhaps with some anxiety to
see what you was doing. I have been thinking whether
it might not be desirable to make a sort of log house near
the Stormy Point, it might tempt them from the Holy
Well & they might be made to feed there if they commit
enormities about the Well.

There was a large meeting here yesterday to take

74

further measures in respect to assisting sufferers from the
Storm.   Three surveyors have been engaged in the
estimate which amounts to about 30000£ & without
taking into account glass & minor losses.   The ruin to
many is complete for a year or more, crops entirely
destroyed on some farms—I have seen some orchards
where the trees have more than a winter appearance, not
a leaf or a bud left & the bark much cut.   There were
140 present, Lord Wodehouse presiding, & it was
agreed that besides a subscription on the spot from the
gentry & landowners there should be a collection through
the county on the basis of a Rate, but of course not com-
pulsory, which it is thought will answer very well.   Sir
John Boileau who came here after the meeting said it was
pleasing to see the general good will shown by yeomen
in distant parts, towards the proposal.   Sir John gives
50£, the Bishop gives 30£.

I think I have sent you a capital long letter, now you
must not be curmudgeonly about your letters, but let
poor Hen: have the benefit of them.

Adieu ever yrs affecly   M. J. S.

LADY STANLEY TO MRS. STANLEY

(85)   *Undated.* NORWICH.

I should have written more but the scattered family take
a deal of time & I could have no pleasure in writing
circular letters & I have been obliged to throw a small
bone to his Lordship because Emmy said she had written
to Ri only about *business of Egypt*, that is, not my Lord's
business.   I assure you he sent me an account of Mr.
Waddington's business that was not the least alarming
& he seems to have been highly amused with the spirited

manner in which you & Rianette fought the battle—
but not a hint of being willing to make any concessions—
on the contrary talks of enclosing the Holy Well &
putting it under lock & key.

Perhaps you have not heard that Mrs. Cowper was
opened & it was found she died of inflammation of the
womb—so much for stone & Sir C. Clark's medical or
surgical insight into symptoms.

LADY STANLEY TO LADY DILLON, ON THE
OCCASION OF THE BIRTH OF ALGERNON,
AFTERWARDS BISHOP OF EMMAUS

(86) CROMER HALL *Sept 19th/43.*
DEAR LY. DILLON

I think Henrietta expects she has a patent for produc-
ing children without trouble or delay—if she is not *quite*
satisfied with this performance, which seems to me to
have been quick enough in all reason. And so now she
has 4 couple,[1] a very pretty collection & number, I wish
she would be content, especially as she has had as many
as anybody in the family now, for I know she does not
like to be outdone by any body. My best love to her.
I wrote on Sunday not at all thinking she would be so
correct in her reckoning.

I am much amused by your being obliged to give me
a report of the dairy. The cow in full milk was got
because the other was going off. I do not understand
why she should give such poor milk, probably it is a breed
that makes up for it in quantity which our man knew
would be an object.

This is a beautiful place, sea & woods together are

---

[1] Alive, she had had ten in all.

delightful It is very unusual for Mr. Baring to have
company & I am afraid he suffers from the change in his
habits, generally dining at 2 o'clock. Lord & Lady
Walpole are here & there were a few men yesterday also.
The Bishop turns all his visits to account by combining
with them visits to the Churches in the neighbourhood.

We return tomorrow & alas ! leave Norwich on
Monday for Babraham.[1] Poor Edward & his missionary
sermon ! he must think there is nothing else at Northwich, for I remember just the same *ill luck* attending him
one Sunday last year when he went to Church with Hen:
My love to him & many thanks for his letter

Very truly & affecly yours   M. J. STANLEY
What outlandish name is this *doggy* to have ?

LADY STANLEY TO EDWARD STANLEY

(87)   NORWICH *Sept* 21*st.*
DEAR EDWARD

Thank you for your letter.   If Hen: goes on magnify-
ing every time as she has done the Stanley family will
become much exalted & look down on the two preceding
generations considerably.

Norfolk never was so deficient before in game—
partridges are so scarce that Mr. Baring has put off all
his shooting gentlemen & his son Henry is gone away
in disgust.

In moving from here on Monday we may be said to
be on our way home—but we have Sir John Boileau's
& Babraham & we shall look in at Leamington for a few
days.   I guess we shall not be at Alderley before the
3rd week in Oct:

[1] The seat of Mr. Adeane, Lady Stanley's son-in-law.

Hen: will tell you how she & Rianette have battled for our private days on the Edge & how I have backed them up by my *judicious* observations to his Lordship— I think we are quite safe from any further grants. Simpson writes me word he has seen one of the principal directors & given him to understand that if his Lordship is troubled any more it is most probable the permission for the publick to enter the private grounds at all will be withdrawn & he thinks the private days will be respected without any more efforts to intrude.

Yours affecly   M. J. STANLEY.

MRS. STANLEY TO LADY STANLEY

(88)   WINNINGTON *Sept* 22
MY DEAR LADY STANLEY

We were afraid you would only learn of your new grandson thro' the papers, having forgotten your removal to Cromer.   I can give a much better account of myself— I have now no ailment but pain with nursing which is absurd at my stage of the business.   Thanks to the never-to-be-too-much-praised Carlsbad my digestion is as good as at 15 now I have got rid of the Monster boy— he is the make of Lyulph but they say darker I see nothing but a red lump of flesh.   He is very quiet & gives no trouble.

Edward rode over to Alderley at 7 this morning he shoots today & tomorrow.   Is that not a liberal leave I have granted.

Tho' I do not see Miss Eccles [1] I hear a great deal. Her indolence about walking exceeds all I cld have

<hr>

[1] New governess.

imagined—she has only been outside the door three times in this week of lovely weather.

LADY STANLEY TO MRS. STANLEY

(89)   LEAMINGTON *Oct* 21/43.

Emmy has had a tolerable night—no headache but I see she is not too well this morning & I guess palpitations.

I am very glad to hear so favourable an account of Edward's affairs & I trust he does not heed his Father's crotchets for you know he has them wholesale on most occasions, & living so much in himself he imagines difficulties in everything. But Edward has a way of listening & playing with My Lord's arguments that will do for him ; I am very unselfish in wishing success to E for I am sure he is ten times more amiable & agreeable since he shook off the shackles of Place (such a place perhaps) & Politicks.

We heard in Town of an upholsterer who was sending down a quantity of fine furniture to Ditchley,[1] part bought part hired for the reception of the Grand Duke Michael. Have you heard he's going there ?

MRS. STANLEY TO LADY STANLEY

(90)   WINNINGTON *Oct* 26.

I am very sorry for Lord Melbourne—he had been particularly well this summer & had had gout which one always considers a safety valve.

Blanche is very much pleased with your invitation to Alderley She is very well now that she is dram drinking

---

[1] The seat of Lord Dillon.

with bark, she will not drink wine as it makes her sleepy. Henry's letter enclosed a very kind one from Mrs. Piele to him.   I wonder if it would be possible for Henry to lose all the overflowing loving kindness he has now for all who show him affection—I trust not altogether.

LADY STANLEY TO MRS. STANLEY

(91)   LEAMINGTON *Nov* 2
I have not much hopes from E's nibbles there seems to little chance of success for moderate people or even tolerably moderate ones—those who do not go the whole hog which I hope E is *not* quite prepared for.   The Tory's hate a Whig more than a Radical & will do *all* they can to keep one out.   And as there is no love lost between them, the Whigs are ready to join the Rads to keep out a Tory.   But I heartily wish he may creep in at last, somehow.

What is the baby to be ?   Was not Leonard once thought of.   I am sure I have no fancy for one more than another except that I do not like taking Rowland out of another branch, never I believe having had one of our own.

What story can Louisa have got hold of, about the Queen *misbehaving* at the Ball.[1]

(92)   LEAMINGTON *Nov* 4/43.
DEAR HEN
I really do not see why the profession of parson should bear the blame of Mr. Berry's [Henry's tutor] conduct. If he is wrong it is from not being a judicious sensible

---

[1] At Wimpole, the Earl of Hardwicke's house.

man—of which you had your doubts before—but there
may be two sides to the story, & may it not be *possible*
that he has good reasons for sending away Fox & that
he *may* think him not a desirable companion for Henry
& the other boys, & if this is the case would it not rather
give one a better opinion of his establishment that he
would not keep boys of whose conduct he had reason to
disapprove.   Coming in late for breakfast & making a
mess on the carpet are trifles, but as part of a whole line
of conduct they might become of consequence, &
irregularity at meals, in a school, could not be allowed.
The worst feature I see however is that Henry feels no
respect for Mr. B as he did for Piele & if this is the case
from whatever cause it springs he can do no good under
his tuition.   Henry appears to enjoy a good deal of
liberty.   One thing more strikes me about Mr. B's
conduct—strange to allow a thing he disapproves to be
commuted by *money*.   What a horrible hand Henry
writes.

What a deal of trouble & expence the Grand Duke
gave when at Ditchley for such a short visit.   Are any
of your sisters there ?   I hope nothing will prevent our
setting off on Thursday—we shall have our first talk
over on Friday.   affecly yours   M. J. STANLEY.

(93)   LEAMINGTON *Nov* 8/43.
Do you know Lady Hereford & Miss Devereux ?   I
never heard of greater suffering than the Mother's nor
greater devotion & heroism than the daughter's.   Lady
H. was obliged to have her foot taken off from being in a
thoroughly diseased state—when the operation was
performed the medical man found it had not been taken

off high enough & she was obliged to submit to a 2
operation. The daughter, being resolved beforehand
she would not leave her, & fearing her own courage,
had attended at a hospital to see, & harden, or at least
prepare herself to go through the scene without causing
any additional distress to her Mother.

Very fine day & *here* I enjoy the sun when it shines
as our rooms are South. I shall be very glad to see you
all again, however, though my rooms are North & the
ground does not dry as soon at Alderley as at Leamington.
But I have thoroughly enjoyed the whole of my travels.

(94)   ALDERLEY *Nov 16th.*

I am not at all distressed with fears as to Henry's future
well doing from anything we have now heard. There is
nothing serious & it is fortunate that you have so early
known of his faults, acquired through bad company, I
have no doubt. His very innocence from all bad
thoughts & bad habits, making him the more likely to
be drawn into the snare of Knowledge of Evil. Well it
is no worse, & he no older, before he had to begin to
learn *the world*. I fear he wants strength of character
& may be liable to take the colour of those he lives with.
Yet this is unjust to him—it is too early to form a judgement on his character & there are so many good points
that make one hope firm principles may be established in
him as rules of action. Mr. Berry's injudiciousness may
have been of service in bringing to your knowledge what
is done by many, if not all boys & never known to their
parents. I however quite agree with Mr. Berry that
Eton does much more harm than good, with many
boys.

(95)   *Dec 2nd* WINNINGTON (1843)

MY DEAR LADY STANLEY

I am very glad you have made, without my suggestion, the very same observation I had about Henry. I think he is very much coming on & certainly the opportunities he had while we were together, tho' not many, were made the most of & I hope the time was not lost. I wish his desire for travel was not in Africa but it will be better not to say much about it as whims sometimes get strengthened by opposition. In the mean time he is hard at work with Arabic grammar & wanted an Arabic dic: for his New Year's gift but Ed only found one at 12 gns. He wishes to get ready to learn at Cambridge where there are professors of the Oriental languages.

I think if things remain in the present confused state we shall go to London very early, at least Edward ought & I shall probably go or else follow soon. I wonder if the Whigs will come in—now one feels how very disagreeable it is that Edward is not in Parliament it may make such a difference to his prospects, & his politics have been all along the same about the corn laws. If there is a change of government, that might give him a chance of coming into Parliament ; but I only say this of myself as it bores him to talk about it.

I am afraid I cannot help you to any company, the only visitor I expected, Mr. Buller, [1] has thrown us over as he says it is not worth coming down the time is so short. The fact is Lady Harriet Baring has Ld. Ashburton's house at Alverstoke & that is too agreeable to leave.

Yr affec daught   H. M. S.

[1] Charles Buller (1806–1848), Liberal reformer and wit, a great friend of Mrs. Stanley's.

1844

(96)   ALDERLEY *Jan* 21.

Edward has written I see, but I daresay that will not satisfy you without a bit more. He is gone up to the Edge with O Hutchinson Henry & the dogs—he is very civil indeed & I daresay found much interest in the conversation they had after dinner yesterday as they sat a long time ; but then when he comes out he takes a book & holds his tongue entirely, & a dead man like that in a very small *civile*, who has ears, & of whom the small party is rather in awe, more or less, is an incubus. I wish he would save some of his inquiries or talk for the whole society when together—Hutchinson seems well worth drawing out & when he got aside by the tea table could talk freely enough, but he is very shy & slow in speech, till he gets animated & is the sort of man who pops down on the first chair or stool that stands in his way & says nothing until he is spoken to.

I am sorry you talk of paying *part* only of your Northwich debts you can have been at no other housekeeping expences, except servants wages, for the last half year & certainly 179 does not sound considerable for so long & might be spared out of your income one wd think—Is it you cannot get the money from him or is there none at

84

the bankers. I had hoped the 100 for Henry would have eased you for other things.

It is King's College that Edward means, certainly, at Somerset House which is no great distance to go backwards & forwards to, but if you could quickly make up your minds & quickly meet with a man to take him abroad I suppose you would prefer it, but if *much* delayed & you mean him to go to Mr. Vaughan the end of the summer it would hardly be worth the expence for a short time & be of little use. Kitty says she has written to receive Mr. Vaughan's refusal. I should have little dependence on Arthur for recommending a Tutor besides that he is head over ears engrossed with his book & could not pay much attention to a request to enquire.

I suppose the kitchenmaid will stay her month at least —it is very vexatious you cannot keep her, would a little more wages tempt her ?

Yrs affec   M. J. S.

(97)   ALDERLEY *Jan 25th*.

Mrs. Markham would be ludicrous if it were not that it is just the idea I have of modern education, quite as much solid as can be mixed in with the vapoury accomplishments. An extraordinary Clergyman to have such a governess—if he falls into poverty capital governesses *his* children will make.

My Lord pulled a long face at your message. I think we shall see him forced to succumb & become a Leaguer.[1]

They say Mrs. Girdlestone has got the fever in the throat—I think she must be a bad subject for such a complaint.

I hope Edward will not go on dawdling from day to

[1] Anti-Corn-Law League.

day, it is so desirable Henry should do something soon, but in the mean time he is a great deal out with his father & I heard some jocose passages between them about Iser one day, & Henry has been as much interested in Bingham's China as he was with Mexico.

(98) ALDERLEY *Jan* 28*th*/44

Henry will not like London, & London is certainly not a good place for him to be in, with much of every afternoon disengaged—& you must not think me very prejudiced & wrong if I say I fear his Uncle Gerald's company for him. I do hope you will see & feel the necessity of their not going about together more than cannot be avoided especially to evening amusements. I *believe* it *was* Gerald who figured so unpleasantly last year in a Police Office tho' you thought it was not. No doubt the knowledge was kept from Ly. Dillon if it could be—& I would not force it upon you if I did not think it so important just now that you should watch over Henry & guard him from learning life in London as long as possible. His is a most critical age, & his little silliness about Georgy, so different to last year, shows there is a change in him.

Quiet as Hy & E were we miss them. To be sure E was rather *too* quiet in an evening, but the last 2 or 3 days I think he must have felt in better health & spirits for he talked a good deal more at & after dinner, tho' not in the evening when a book or the Land of Nod occupied him generally.

Lady Holland is quite right to be a tyrant if people are willing to be slaves—& you are very well enclined to *crouch* for the sake of good society at her house.

Pray order the Times to be sent you first—I mentioned it to Ed.

Mrs. Girdlestone is better—think of the foolish woman asking Nightingale if there was any danger of infection from her. We had a new Curate today, they say, that is Jane saw in the Ch:yard one who is engaged— he is an old man with a bald head & preached a very prosy sermon—no improvement in that respect.

(99)   ALDERLEY *Feb 4th/44.*

How is it that you cannot hear of any governess at all— have you seen any ? I am afraid it will be a difficulty as indeed you find it having such a large family. I expect at last, rather than have no help you will be obliged to take a moderately accomplished person & trust to Masters when you can get them or to the girls hereafter improving themselves when older. I am very sorry for your *nerves* & other trials I can well understand them all, but try to bear them & keep to your resolutions of forbearance, as the best policy as well as a duty.

My note to Henry is to enquire if he can give me any information as to his sheets & pillow case having been cut in holes.

In Godfrey's bill there is in Sept: Solution of Morphia & Aromatic Powders of which I know nothing. Rianette is not sure whether it was last year you sent for Morphia can you recollect.

You have now from Lord S 2,300 hard money besides perquisites & from Lord Dillon (I think it is 2000) that is not settled is it ? for I am not sure. Being really as careful & self-sacrificing as you both are I do wonder that income cannot do more, with all the advantages you have—horses kept entirely in the country & other helps.

A snowy Sunday has helped my letter writing very much

Yrs affec M. J. S.

(100) ALDERLEY *Feb* 9/44.

Theory I have a great horror of in education or chance meddling, new ways of finding the road to learning—you will perhaps *not* put on the cap but understand me without at all agreeing with me, but there is a great deal more in Nature than anybody almost admits—& one child or set of children will turn out all one can wish without good, or even against bad management, while others, do what one will are unimprovable. I believe one may as well do as little as may be & trust to Providence.

Fine weather for the frisky Episcopals ! Very well if they escape colds.

(101) ALDERLEY *Feb* 15th.

If O Connell[1] had as much courage as wickedness he would indeed be a most dangerous man, so I am glad if he *is* a coward. How can you believe him a Patriot or *even* a lover of his own country.

Just after luncheon yesterday Emmy had a fainting fit which lasted so long we were quite uneasy about her & she is but a poor creature today.

It has been a great treat to have Uncle Bishop here these two days. I suppose the Court Mourning still continues or if not I hope you will put it on for Sir

---

[1] Daniel O'Connell, 1775–1847.

Gregory Way[1] he is my first cousin & there are several
of the family in town who might observe & be hurt if
you did not.

with much love   Affecly yrs   M. J. S.

(102)   ALDERLEY *Feb* 29*th*/44.

I am very sorry indeed for all your troubles & I am
afraid the boys will not have it [measles] slightly—so
much irritability in Johnny & so much fat in Lyulph.

I am glad you will have seen the Bishop I do not think
he will give a very flourishing account of us, except of
My Lord's looks & they are certainly younger than the
Bishops—but then his legs —!

Is Lena alive & at home? I was charmed to see in
the papers a dog stealer had been fined 20£ for stealing
a pretty Spaniel that recognised his mistress directly in
the office while he was on trial.

(103)   ALDERLEY *March* 3/44.

DEAREST HEN

We are much grieved that the poor dear body could
not keep up to the energy of the spirit which is carrying
you through so many troubles. You have indeed enough
on your hands.

I send this enclosed, with a few words to Edward, that
he may read it & give it you or not according as he thinks
you are disposed to hear a very unexpected event, about
which I can give you very few particulars today—but
nothing shall prevent my placing you amongst the very
earliest informed. Albert Way has proposed to Emme-

---

[1] Lady Stanley's mother was Abigail Way.

line, & after three weeks nearly of much anxiety in this house as well as in his family, Lord S. has given his consent. Arguments for & against have been fully urged & considered & I hope we have judged right for her happiness.

I wonder if you remember his visit here, 10 years ago —& if you then saw an inclination on both sides, which I have ever since tried to prevent increasing or continuing, by very little intercourse & by her being fully aware of the strong objection [1] that there would be against it. During those 10 years, the affection has continued on his side, without encouragement, without hope & few opportunities of meeting & when we found him at Leamington last year I really hoped the feeling was quite at an end—but there it was, deeply rooted. I *saw* nothing particular in his attentions, however encouragement was given, no doubt—unknown to me, perhaps to herself, & they only seemed to be highly interested about old arches & Roman bricks & brasses & never were alone together, not even to walk together when she was with him & his sisters.

An Association of Antiquarians has occupied him much at the beginning of this year about which he wrote to My Lord, who unluckily could not answer his letters & Emmy undertook to write for him. After a few publick letters came a private one. The sisters only have had any idea what was going on—not even Aunt K. No one of us all will be more interested than you, I am sure, in the matter, but the fact must be enough for today. I think you will be one who, weighing the pros & cons will see much to counter balance *the* objection as I have done. Her health in the first instance & his entire absence from any appearance of an excitable character

[1] I cannot find out what the mysterious objection was.—N. M.

under trying circumstances, & his manner of taking the
refusal he got was so perfect, as well as that of all his
family, who must guess & might have been angry &
now Adieu, dearest Hen.   Albert comes on Thursday, I
should like Edward to call on him 131 Piccadilly.   I
have gone through a great deal lately & have had little
inclination to write to you on indifferent subjects.   I am
not the better for all we have suffered, nor Rianette either.
The dear Father has been very quiet & very kind even
while firm in his opinion & nobody could blame him for
that opinion, however as he has not been made ill, & not
seemed nervous & unhappy I think it has *not* gone much
against his feelings, all things considered.

Affecly yours   M. J. S.

(104)   ALDERLEY *March* 5/44.

DEAREST HEN,

My *nerves* are very much relieved by *all* the letters I
have had this morning—kindness from all & great
warmth from some—you first,—then William & even
Edward—I trusted at once to you & am quite content
to bear Edward's little innuendo (heartily seconded by
My Lord) that "all women look only to one side of the
question" for his letter is very kind notwithstanding &
I can assure him I did not make up my mind to be an
advocate without very deeply feeling all the responsibility
we should take upon ourselves in allowing her to follow
her inclinations & what she believed her happiness.   But
we, women, all know better than any man can, how much
there is in her character & constitution to make it very
desirable she should marry, that is that she should meet
with affection & be loved.   But I would not *tell* a

man, *any* man this for he would only see it in a gross light.[1]

Edward may well say he never had any idea of anything of the kind being in contemplation, for we have never given Albert any encouragement to be intimate since the first visit 10 years ago. I daresay you do not remember, what Ri & Louisa do, at that time E. was the first to have a suspicion, & noticed to you that Albert always shook hands with Emmy at night, when the party separated. We have never invited him again, & only very occasionally in London. Leamington revived her liking, for it had not gone farther (& as you know she had looked out for Love elsewhere) & no doubt gave him some encouragement. Their tastes & pursuits were so much alike, at least she could & did enter into his so warmly & *not only* in architecture, that 10 days frequent meeting & conversation had to report progress much more than I suspected at the time, as I had no idea of his still existing regard. Then the correspondance abt. the Ant : Association followed which seemed innocent, his letters addressed to My Lord—till *perhaps* the answers became too interesting, & as soon as he felt it to be so he explained himself, telling her of the constancy, nursed without hope or encouragement for so many years— which you may easily believe set fire to the tinder at once. The letters of his family have been highly flattering to her & few women can expect to be so warmly & even gratefully received by all as she will be. They have behaved so well on the occasion—they must have known the cause for refusal, indeed it has appeared as if they did, but not the least feeling expressed of resentment or displeasure, which many families have felt & expressed when a refusal has been attributed to the same cause. His

[1] Marriage proved to be the medicine Emmy needed, for she lived to 96.

letters have been *beautiful* & I am sure you would love him if you read them, as I hope you will do when you know him. If all goes right in that one way I have no doubt she will be very happy. Their income will be 2000 now & another 1000 or more at his Mother's death, money chiefly in the Funds except an estate of 700 acres in Dorset & something in Sussex. His intention is to purchase an estate somewhere having 45,000 in the Funds ready for the purpose of his own, & 20,000 more the interest of which goes to Mrs. Way for her life ; so they will do well enough in the style of life which will please her best.

This summer she hopes to dedicate to a little English tour not to be in a hurry to fix—& as his occupation, as Secretary to the Antiquarian Socy will require much of his presence in Town he would probably take a house there next winter.

You will easily believe Emmy is overdone with writing at present, but she will not leave you long unattended to. I wish *I* had a secretary to write for me just now. I shall want to hear of Albert's dinner with Alethea today & yesterday he was to meet Mr. Adeane.

Affecly yrs   M. J. S.

(105)   A L D E R L E Y *March* 10*th*.

Almost too perfect to be true—most satisfactory certainly —*not* playing herself an *advantage* I think as she will not want to practise. I do indeed hope you are now well suited.[1]

I thought you would gain all the information you wanted about the happy pair from Ally, but she asks as

[1] New governess, Miss White.

many questions as you do—so she has not been fully fed.
I can't say which of the pair has caused the most joy to
the respective friends by this step. *His* have been for
years so anxious he should marry, & on the other side
all her friends who know her well, especially some who
know something of him, are equally pleased she should
marry at all in the first place, & in the 2nd to a person so
likely to suit her & make her happy. She behaves very
well, quiet & composed, hardly certain yet I think
whether it is a dream or not.

(106)   ALDERLEY *March* 25th.

Very glad you are well pleased with Miss W. hope it will
continue—but I think you praised Miss Eccle's *sense* at
first however I daresay this is quite a different person.

Mrs. Way is very desirous of having Emmy for a few
days (Albert is in Town) as she will not be able to come
up for the wedding nor two of the sisters. They certainly
idolize her.

(107)   ALDERLEY *March* 27/44

I expect Mr. Buller's humanity & philanthropy are very
much excited at the expence of the real merits of the case
by his hoping all this will lend a helping hand to the
League. I cannot see how the 2 hours given up by the
operatives will help much in making them more moral or
religious & I do see that it will be a loss both to operatives
& masters.

I believe you & Buller also look to your political
interests in this case as I said before, more than to any
other motive.

I am glad to hear you are to have the Ways & Scotts
at dinner—Ally gives a very bad account of herself I
think, & I have no great expectations of a living produc-
tion.

(108)   A L D E R L E Y *April* 1/44.
The young ladies went off this morning—I am glad
Emmy is gone for she was fretting herself, taking leave
of everybody & everything & she will be as happy with
Albert's people as she can be anywhere without him.   He
expressed himself very much pleased with his visit to you
& with Edward's manner to him & his conversation—&
to hear of this was as gratifying to me as it appears to
have been to A.

I am very glad you continue to like Miss White so
much, now you have seen more of her—I do hope now
the girls will gain & keep hold of some information &
learn to speak & write *English*.

E M M E L I N E   W A S   M A R R I E D   T O   A L B E R T   W A Y
O N   A P R I L   3 0 T H ,   1 8 4 4 ,   A T   S T .   G E O R G E ' S ,
H A N O V E R   S Q U A R E

(109)   A L D E R L E Y *July* 14/44.
Henry has been eating enormously, feasting after William's bad fare, & devouring fruit by wholesale made him
very uncomfortable by Friday evening—the whole roof
of his mouth was blistered & very painful, he could not
help complaining tho' having the fear of his freedom being
curtailed before his eyes.   Two blue pills & a black dose
& an *entire* rainy day yesterday have set him up again—
he was very good & did not attempt to go out & refrained

from fruit.   You always say so much of nothing disagree-
ing with him, I did not like to stop him in his career of
pea & fruit eating or everything else eating that came in
his way.   We could not do anything for his [17th] Birthday at such short notice but get him an additional peal
from the Ringers by an additional Sovereign & give the
servants some punch.   I think we must keep Rianette's
& Alice's birthdays together on the 30th with Prison
Bars [1] & School Children.

(110)   LEAMINGTON *Aug 20th*/44.
I am much more angry than is good for me—it set my
stomach beating for an hour—how *any*-body, Simpson or
any other, can have dared to use Kitty [2] is beyond my
belief of impertinent officiousness & disregard to superior
authority.

    I have feasted on grouse but I think I was quite as
much or more pleased to have a letter from Ed: besides
—I made my birds last by letting the Poulterer have a
couple to give me others when I wanted them.

MR. ALFORD, HENRY'S NEW TUTOR, TO
MRS. STANLEY

(111)   WYNNESWOLD *Aug 20th*.
I was prepared by your account to find him very young
for his age—& certainly this part of his character is one
which nobody could help observing.   His simplicity &
openness & inquisitiveness thoroughly boyish are upper-
most in all his intercourse with others.   I have every reason

---

[1] A game they always played at family gatherings.   Prisoner's Base ?
[2] An old and favourite pony.

to think from what I have seen that these qualities may be taken advantage of in forming his character. He is fortunate in having fallen in with a very gentlemanly lot of companions who have every kind feeling towards him & will I believe produce on him an effect just the contrary of that which unfeeling ridicule & unkindness would have on him. I fancy I can see also an improvement in the tone & feeling of his questions & he is so thoroughly goodnatured that the little friction which he undergoes in the way of ridicule, now & then, appears to chafe him hardly at all. I feel with regard to him that his character has in it very much that is valuable & truly amiable & this part it is to be our endeavour to fix & mature while all that is undesirable may be expected to fly off in his intercourse with society. He has appeared as yet to be happy & comfortable here & I hope to be on that footing with him that if ever he is not so he will make me his confidential friend that we may labour together to remedy the fault.

MRS. STANLEY TO EDWARD STANLEY

(112)   ALDERLEY *Aug 25th*/44

My DEAREST LOVE,

You will have missed my letters &, I am particularly sorry, one of Mr. Alford's which I think will please you.

I am very glad you agree to Alice being confirmed now. I do not, as you may suppose, attach any value to the ceremony itself but it is a useful time for self examination & for making a fresh start in good things & it wd. not do to put it off for Blanche as then Alice might be in the world & the first year of society is not generally one of much reflection. You certainly need not assist at the ceremony.

Mama came yesterday & will stay here till Monday when she goes on a little tour in Wales till Saturday the 9th when I shall meet her at Winnington. I do not wish to be there quite alone it w'd make me nervous. The 15th is the day I expect the Baby—a Steamer leaves Glasgow [1] at 2 O'clock on the 14th. You will have to buy me a plaid gown, & a couple of *small* Scotch brooches will be acceptable little trifles for the girls.

Your mother has been utterly disgusted with Mr. Milnes who staid at Hurstmonceaux [2] all the time they were there. Lady Stanley is now gone to Sheffield Place [3] & will be at Norwich the end of the week.

Your affec wife   H. M. S.

(113)   ALDERLEY *Sept 1st.*

MY DEAREST LOVE

I had a talk to Simpson yesterday, he had been to Swain with a message from Lord Stanley to say if he did not keep Manchester people off on Private Days he should be removed, & he said he could any day but Sunday when the people sit all along the path from the Hough to Stormy Point. Lady Stanley is very intent upon having all we can fenced round with a wire fence, an estimate is being made & your opinion is to decide.

Simpson told me he thought there would be a great advantage in laying out Chorley as Villas that it wld quadruple the value of that part & improve the whole.

---

1 Edward is in Scotland.
2 Hurstmonceaux Vicarage, with Julius Hare.
3 Earl of Sheffield's seat.

I think 6½ yds. wide width of tartan will do, as for
pattern, what you like will please me, but I like the blue
dark in some, I think called Albert plaid.

Yr affec wife   H. M. S.

(114)   WINNINGTON *Sept 7th.*

MY DEAREST LOVE

I have just heard from Henry that the smallpox is in
the village & Gurney has got it in the house—all had
been vaccinated. I do not feel much afraid of Henry's
taking it as that is not the malady his constitution inclines
to, still it is disagreeable.

I think the Queen's arrangements for Scotland [1] will
be much pleasanter than going to people who mostly
grumbled at the expense & trouble.

I hope you will answer Henry's letters he feels kindness
very much & seems dans de belles dispositions.

I suppose you are delighted at O Connell's [2] release I am
of course but can say little from hospitality to Aunt
Georgina.

It seems they have made a spurious well on Trafford's [3]
ground & there was a great to do on the 2nd in christening the well by the name of Dalton there was a large tent
& 143 R.R. directors dining on the ground where
Walton used to live. I cannot make out the locality very
clearly.

Ever yr affec wife   H. M. S.

Johnny always sleeps with me & we have much talk in
the morning.

[1] Balmoral was first leased in 1848.
[2] O'Connell had been tried for sedition.
[3] The de Trafford's estate marches with Alderley.

LADY STANLEY TO MRS. STANLEY

(115)   LEAMINGTON *Sept* 9/44

DEAR HEN:

Hurrah ! for O'Connell & *Justice*, to him at least—I
suppose you are in raptures. What a stir it will make &
will it not be a great blow to Government ? Will he now
go forward with Repeal or be more prudent for fear he
may be more correctly indicted & sentenced next time.

My Lord is charming—so warlike, & Mr. Waddington not in the favour he was this time last year. Such
plans for defence, & orders to discontinue the leave that
has been granted & really hopes for a Battle on the
Frontier next Monday. The rival grounds, walks, seats
& well are in our favour I think, if we can stand the comparisons drawn between Traffords liberality & our
illiberality. I am most pleased with My Lord's *acting*
independant of his *Grand Vizier* [Simpson]—of Sir
Robert Peel, as Louisa calls him but tho' I think he
would make a much more decided Prime Minister at the
head of the nation I do not wish him to be Sovereign
over us at Alderley. I am sure he has always supported
the Rail Road managers in spite of us & encouraged
them.

Glad to hear so well of Miss White[1]—I *do* hope you
will discourage any intimacy between the girls &
Madame,[2] but girls often take to those who have *not*
authority over them & Mad: appears to be lively &
cheerful & indeed all of *that* religion are very cunning &
artful in pursuit of the object, that ends justify the means

Affecly yrs   M. J. S.

---

[1] Miss White stayed until the girls were all grown up. Cf. "Amberley
Papers."
[2] Madame was there to teach the boys French.

AT THE END OF SEPTEMBER ROSALIND
WAS BORN, AFTERWARDS COUNTESS
OF CARLISLE

(116)   ALDERLEY *Oct* 27/44.

DEAR HEN:

If you come Tuesday you can let me hear whether you
wish to be met—I wish Louisa had come home sooner
that we might have had her Penrhos stories for a day
before you came, but it would be putting you off too long
as she only arrives Wednesday, so you must not be
affronted if we congregate where you are not, as you
know little & care less about Penrhos & she will have so
much to tell us on the subject. My Lord will want to
talk to Edward about the Edge—I was at the Holy Well
yesterday & it is *dreadful* to see the fence there.

I do not think Charley's [1] marriage is a subject of congratulation for any of the family & I do wonder they did
not put an end to it as soon as they knew anything of the
matter being *serious*. No money *at all* I believe, no connexion or rather a very inferior one, & marriage, under
the most favourable auspices must act as a blight & a
clog to him in his career—his pay, called 400 a year, has
to cover all expences I believe, travelling lodging etc. I
am rather surprised that her father listened favourably
—but to him the connexion would be flattering & he
would trust that his daughter would have enough to live
on, & a Banker's profession is so insecure he may be,
any day, *penniless*. Kitty does not seem to like it, says
the Bishop had such a horror at the possible alternative
of the West Indies that it acted upon him like Emmy's
fits.

[1] Son of the Bishop. His fiancée was a Miss Clayton.

Emmy is pretty well, Maude [Adeane] gives a good account of Albert & that he has made himself very agreeable at Babraham tho' he cannot talk husbandry & cattle nor Mr. A. brasses & monuments.

I do not recollect much of the Grasshopper's Feast except that it was an imitation of the Butterflies Ball which was excellent.

Adieu   Yr affec   M. J. S.

---

(117)   ALDERLEY *Nov* 27*th*.

Ally & Co. got to Town safely, she has seen Emmy who has sent up her equipage very smart with a prancing horse, & is very well.

I send you sundry eatables, one fat pig & 2 of Louisa's bantams just brought in & more potatoes, as the cart was here—very right to send it & to do so whenever anything is wanted, the man is paid & the horse kept whether they come or not & it is only the expence of the turnpikes incurred by coming here. I send one pair of plated candlesticks to lend, they must come back when you do, for good.

My Lord kept his 78th birthday yesterday.

---

(118)   ALDERLEY *Dec* 3/44

Will you send on the Atheneum to Lucy when you have done with it. I send you a correspondance between the Rectory & me—what do you think of it ? All the *horrors* of *friendship* rose up in array against the exercise of our Christian charity. Over & above the very unsatisfactory nature of his *apology* he clearly sees no fault in himself. I *saw* the 8 boys, at the Tree, I *heard* Mr.

Girdlestone's easy jokes, just as if we had never ceased to be good friends, & I fancied him at our table, the servants all agape to hear how we got on. It is a quarrel, or rather a separation that had much better continue & you will think the same, or Edward will at least.

Simpson goes to Winnington tomorrow but I write by post in case he should be late—he will take 2 herrings for Edward. They are choice dainties & we have a very small keg, only 12 & cannot spare him more. His father is *greedy* over them. Ewell met with them in Manchester in an Italian warehouse.

Heard from Emmy this morning, delighted to be in Paris but found Albert's presence was quite necessary— she began to expatiate on the superiority of a foreign climate for Wednesday was clear & bright, as it was here. Thursday & Friday were foggy & very cold, as here.

Some time ago Sir Edward [Parry] seemed to wish his 2 boys could spend an Xmas here, & I think in the present state of his health he would be very glad they should but I would ask first if you think your Girls, at least would be kind to them—that they might not feel strange & among strangers—I know Henry however well inclined does not know what to say to boys younger than himself, but they would go different ways probably, the Parrys not being old enough for shooting. Edward, if he has a book, wishes for nothing else—Charles is a regular *boy* & would be up to anything, but I think would not be rough, & if the cousins would patronise them they wd be very happy & I am sure *you* would be kind to them.

Do not send off the Times ever before you have quite done with it.

Yrs affec   M. J. S.

(119)   ALDERLEY *Dec* 6/44.

I am not sorry poor Iser died in Henry's absence—I
think the grief is rather less. I found Fleetwood knew
exactly the spot where she was to be buried & it has been
done this morning.

We are quite pleased that you express yourself about
Mr. Girdlestone's letter *so exactly* in unison with our
opinion. There could not be a letter worse calculated to
work an effect—even if we had been *better disposed* than
we are.

I should never have thought of that small *light house*
for Lady Dillon if you had not named it—but it did look
& feel warm & gay when I looked in tho' hardly space
for her & her maid to turn round each other in. It is
quite as convenient to me as the Tent Room.

(120)   ALDERLEY *Dec* 8th/44

I thought you would like to come before Christmas—
the season would be imperfect without, more imperfect I
should say, for it is a very great imperfection & vexation
not to go to our own Church, en famille, on that day as
we have done for so very many years—all our young ones
following us there in succession, & now I would willingly
see another generation doing the same & *almost*, not *quite*
regret that we ever *seceded*. Though I do not feel *malice*
in my heart against the man, I do feel so much of repug-
nance & aversion to his character & conduct, quite
separate from any Tithe concern that I *could* not feel my
mind & thoughts in the state they should be when
receiving from his hands, & hearing his odious hypo-
critical voice.

I think you might propose the Tues: or Wed: 19th or

20th for the migration being governed in some degree by the weather—but indeed you could not all move in one day. I am not at all afraid of the little boys being troublesome particularly—it is the very large family altogether & especially feeding time that is oppressive for a great length of time but it will be very short this year & I shld be sorry either Ed: or Henry lost any of it. I wish I could explain to your clear understanding, that I am more annoyed sometimes by your own anxiety to keep the boys quiet, & your unceasing attention to them, than by anything they can do—& I would like girls, & all, to be more *natural* than they are with me & that they should not be lectured too much into pretty behaviour & that if I find a trifling fault & say don't do or do do such a thing that you should neither be offended nor yet say anything to *back* me, as if it was necessary. I want not to feel, what I always do, that a daughter *in law's* children are not the same to me as my *daughter's*. But till you have sons & daughters with families I do not expect you to think this otherwise than very silly.

(121)   ALDERLEY *Dec:* 10*th.*

I will speak to the coachman & see if we can get our coach over—if the horses would be as useful in bringing another carriage back perhaps it would be worth while to take post horses for the coach, when loaded, rather than for our or your horses to go backwards & forwards as often as they must do otherwise.

Naughty Henry has not written to say whether he will come to-morrow—I suppose his deep affliction has made him forget everything.

Just heard from Capesthorne, Mr. Davenport is suffering from a swelled & inflamed tongue & much fever, he had had leeches but found very little relief.

Your *dear* Parson has written a very injudicious letter asking for subscription to the Barnston school, alluding to the refusal of his request for land & certainly intimating that it is his Lordship's *duty* to attend to the *wants* of the people & that it is no *interest* of his. I am *sure* the poor man did not mean to be impertinent, but that he is & must be totally ignorant of all his Lordship's feelings on the subject ; & also deficient in *tact* as all Priests are I believe. I got the letter away before My Lord had conned it over much. I wish he had spoken to you & you had advised him *not* writing.

(122) A L D E R L E Y *Dec* 13/44.

Henry is come back such a polemic, au fait of real presence, prayers for the dead, adoration of the virgin [1] etc. & talks as if he had fought a good fight in the cause of the Protestant Religion. I think it is to be lamented very young persons are subjected to hear such disputes & absurdities, but as the subject must be brought before them sooner or later, certainly not later than at the University it may be no harm in having his mind awakened & his thoughts turned to it. He may be the better prepared, bye & bye to give a reason for the truth that is in him. I do not think he is *indifferent* to the subject, all I hope is that the language he hears, here, may not lead him to think lightly of *all* opinions. He & his father have been out ever since breakfast. Henry has left off wine, which I am very glad of—he says it is his

---

[1] Whereas M. J. S. scatters capital letters wholesale on every page, none of these Romish expressions is allowed one.

own choice for that he feels better without. He looks remarkably well says he never catches cold, washes in cold water every day.

The coachman will take the coach with 4 horses. I suppose you will want a larger cart & 2 horses for your luggage, & as all live creatures cannot be conveyed in the Barouche & Coach you will say, when you arrive, what further journeys are necessary.

The Parry boys come on the 17th.

(123)   A L D E R L E Y *Dec* 14*th*.

The poor old Gentleman is still very rheumatic & suffering a great deal not violent pain I believe but constant & wearing. He has no gout yet.

Henry I believe is gone to the Edge—Edward got a headache yesterday from the intense cold.

Girdlestone has been adding a little fuel to the fire of hatred for him in the Parish by refusing to bury a child —The parents, living at Stockport.

The family, being that of Partingdon, have *five* burying places in the Churchyard, with tomb stones, & in one of them three of the sisters of this baby have been buried & by him, this child also was christened at Alderley Church a year ago. He has lately allowed Mrs. Calwood to be buried at Alderley tho' she was not & never had been a parishioner, so there is either caprice or *interest* in the business—or *spite*.

Such a dish of theological disputes in todays Globe

Yrs affec   M. J. S.

MRS. STANLEY TO HER HUSBAND, WHO IS
IN SCOTLAND

(124)   WINNINGTON *Aug* 18*th.*

MY DEAREST LOVE

Algernon is decidedly better—the others well &
Johnny not quite so wicked but he is a naughty boy.
Henry is returned to Wynneswold in great disgrace at
Alderley for his fishing propensities. I have had a letter
from him this morning begging me to prevail on you to
get him a dog.

I have had a letter from Lady Stanley complaining of
our horses, or at least pointing out that they are an
expense. I do not think the horses will go to Penrhos
for Lady Stanley does not wish Clark to go, & John Tait,
Louisa's groom, is not well. I do not think it matters as
four weeks are soon past. I have a request to make.
Clark tells me he informed you that Rebecca's saddle
was done when it was lent to us two years ago, it is now
quite unsafe. He says there is an excellent saddler at
Northwich one who works much for the hunting, & he
would make a side saddle as good as mine for 6gns. for
your approbation. Just tell me what I may do for we
want one & there are no more at Alderley.

The day is not yet fixed for our departure for Penrhos, William & Ellin leave this week.

One of the guinea pigs is missing, we have bought 8 geese

Yr affec wife   H. M. S.

(125)   PENRHOS *Sept 8th.*

I have only today received your letter my darling, as you sagely conjecture I am but moderately grieved at the contre temps that deprived you of Lady Harriet Baring's [1] company as you are always very disagreeable when in her company & I would rather have you with the unsophisticated Mrs. Ellice.

Lady Stanley wrote to Ellin to put away all her things, & to have the house put in the old order & now she finds fault her own orders should have been obeyed. She is in a most irritable mood, finding the day long, the evening tedious & then the meals—such a talk about everything. The one who takes it worst is Blanche for she seems sulky when she has been scolded & her singing is asked for & not liked. Lyulph & Kate in great favour. I long to hear where you are going

Yr affec   H. M. S.

(126)   PENRHOS *Sept 19th.*

MY DEAREST LOVE

I have just received your Sunday letter, I am sure you must have enjoyed yourself very much, & as I said before I am most envious of you. Social enjoyment is not our

[1] Daughter of the 6th Earl of Sandwich, afterwards Lady Ashburton, a great charmer.

bright side here, there is no freedom—all are afraid of being snapped up & that makes Alice frightened & Blanche sulky. This morning I was bathing with all the children before 8 & then took them round by Beth-manach home. I will stay in the water longer than your sisters have been wont to do, & tho' I come out smoking hot yet they think what they have done must be right & no other. I hope you will not forget the brooches. I want one for Maude & a little one for Katie & three plaids as before settled. Ever yr affec H. M. S.

(127) PENRHOS *Sept 15th.*

My DEAREST LOVE

I have written to you every day & begin to fear you will tire of my letters as I have little to say that is agree-able. I do not know why we were asked here it is so evident our presence gives no pleasure. Louisa does what she can but it is impossible to make things go smooth where every action or expression must be moulded to suit the imperious pleasure of one whom nothing can please. The poor girls are quite subdued & it gives one an indigestion.

I heard from Mama from Bessborough she tells me Mr. Horace Pitt has married Nelly Holmes [1] to the despair of his family, what a dreadful thing. Lady Stanley has just brought me in £6. 10. to pay our journey & she pays the coach—I wish she would not be so very cross. I believe she wishes William to come here from Alderley where he & Ellin now are, I should not think he will much wish it. I heard today that Algernon is better, but I fear still very delicate. Rosalind is in great

---

[1] A well-known adventuress.

preservation.   Johnny *very* naughty, disagreeable &
pettish, he is now in punishment for throwing things at
Eliza's head.

I hope I shall hear exactly which day you return to
Win: that I may be there the day before.

(128)   PENRHOS *Sept 27th.*

MY DEAREST LOVE,

I have been fidgetted all the week at not hearing from
you & this morning I have received yr. letter of the 21st.
I wish you would go to Alderley first as I had settled to
leave this only Thursday on account of that being the
day for the best boat, & as it has been settled I don't
think Lady Stanley will like me to go sooner.   But perhaps you will not be at Liverpool before Thursday & we
may meet there—I wish you would leave a note for me
at the Adelphi—I rather trust to your usual procrastina-
tion & hope to get a letter to say you are not coming
before the 2nd.

Henry is still suffering very much, has had a blister
behind his ear.   Dr. Seymour says it is from debility &
recommends sea bathing when he has got rid of the pain
in his ear, but the time of year if nothing else is against
that.

MRS.   STANLEY   TO   LADY   STANLEY

(129)   HOTEL DES BAINS,
            BOULOGNE SUR MÈR. *Nov 2/1845.*

MY DEAR LADY STANLEY

We arrived here yesterday having had the most beautiful steam of only two hours—finding it actually in mid

111

channel too hot to wear a fur cloak. We came with the Lilfords [1] & had no trouble at the custom house. At 5 we all dined at an excellent table d'hote where there was only about a doz. quiet English people—we breakfast & dine with the Lilfords.

Henry bathed 5 times at Folkestone & will bathe tomorrow, he does not at all dislike it. I think he seems better for the change & this place amuses him. We met several agreeable people on board coming over, Sir Alexander Woodford [2] & family, & the clever French lawyer M. Ledru whom I know in London & two officers. Henry made acquaintance with them all & was very conversible & gentlemanlike. I am sure my being with him was of the greatest use for I have made a point of making him make any acquaintance that was eligible. This morning we all went to the Frank Protestant church, it was held in a small drawing room, a few English & several nice women of the country in caps. The sermon was one of the best I ever heard & tho' it lasted an hour & a quarter none of us thought it long.

MRS. STANLEY TO EDWARD STANLEY

(130)   BOULOGNE SUR MÈR,

MY DEAREST LOVE   *Tuesday Nov 4/1845.*

Just as we had sat down to dinner with Col. Arbuthnot & the John Abel Smiths they brought me your letter & I was very glad to find no complaint of gout. I hope you will be well amused & in good humour so that you will not be at all cross with me when I come home. You have been most amiable hitherto & I do think I have been most useful to Henry & he has made several acquaintances.

[1] Lady Lilford was the daughter of Lady Holland.
[2] Governor of Gibraltar.

112

HENRIETTA MARIA STANLEY

The Folkestone boat came in before 5 and yet the insolent Douaniers refuse to clear the luggage till to-morrow & Mr. J. A. Smith is quite furious as he wants to get off very early on his way to Madrid where he is supposed to be going on most important business. Mrs. S. seems much pleased with her intended journey.

Henry & I took an immense fagging walk today. Lena continues to excite great admiration tho' very dirty—it would be too expensive to get her washed, she follows so well that I am not at all afraid of losing her. I am to send this letter over by the Packet & Mrs. Arbuthnot will forward it. I never saw a nicer little girl than theirs who has been staying here. Lady Wellesley & Mrs. Henry Howard are here we have not seen them but hear Mrs. Howard sing. Il sposo is not here.

Ever yr affec wife   H. M. S.

(131)   BOULOGNE *Saturday Nov 8th.*

MY DEAREST LOVE

Henry has had his 11th bath today, one more, Monday, will do for him. He is grown quite fat since he has been here. The Dillons [1] came here last night & were off this morning in a large Berline with Ethel's carriage inside. Poor little thing she looks very delicate—they were to take 3 days to Paris. We have been to the Museum today there is a tolerable collection of birds & a great number of Roman antiquities. The custodian repeated often that Julius Cesar set sail from here for the conquest of England I could not help thinking he regretted much not having a later invasion to narrate. I hear there are 7000 English here, some hundreds are factory people.

[1] Her brother and sister-in-law, the 14th Viscount Dillon and his wife.

I am really vexed not to have heard from you—the Folkestone boat is come so that my last hope is gone— I shall have no letter today. Poor ensnared man you have been basking in the charm of that wicked woman.

Pray write   Your affec & irate wife   H. M. S.

(132)   THORPE,[1] CHANTREY, *Nov 18th.*
MY DEAREST LOVE

We went today to St. Ann's Hill & while walking over those beautiful grounds heard of Lady Holland's death yesterday. From her lingering so long I could not divest myself of a sort of hope she might have recovered—we shall miss her very much.

next day.

I had a note from Oh Buller with the account of Ly. Holland's death which was easy to the last. It was much remarked upon Lord Melbourne being at the play on Saturday. Mr. Buller says Ld. Lyndhurst will certainly die—really every old person seems going.

The Col. went this morning after having been much disturbed by the policeman coming to tell him his labourers had carried off 2 bundles of wood so he is going to prosecute them at the sessions.

MRS. STANLEY TO LADY STANLEY

(133)   *Nov 22 1845*
MY DEAR LADY STANLEY

I believe Lady Holland's will is open. She has left for life an estate at Kensington worth 1500 a year to Ld.

---
[1] The seat of Colonel Scott.

John Russell with a charge of 500 a year on it.   1000 to
Mr. Babington,[1] legacies to all the servants, her fans &
300 to Lady Palmerston, her rings to Mme. de Flahault,
her pearls to Lady Elizabeth Grey Ld. Carlisle's daughter,
her dictionaries to Charles Howard, her H. B.[2] carica-
tures to Willy Cowper[3] & numerous legacies.   I hope
Johnny's is not forgotten she told me she had made it.
Nous verrons.

(134)   GROV: CRES: *Nov 24th.*

Ed. came last night & we are off at 4.   Our visit to
Woburn will not be gay, beginning with Ly. H's funeral
tomorrow.   Lord John, come from Edinburgh to attend,
will be there.   He has all Ly Holland's papers etc. & is
to write whatever will be written.

Lord Holland will get 7000 or 8000 a year by his
mother's death.   The Jamaica property was for many
years 15000 a year & all went to the Fox's therefore Ly.
Holland had had power given to leave money.   500 a
year of Ld. John's legacy goes to Ld. H., after Ld. John
it goes to Lady Lilford's children.   Lady Holland was
perfectly calm & composed the whole time quite aware
she was dying & expressed nor felt, I believe, either hope,
fear or emotion.   It was a singularly cold death.   Had
life been prolonged her sufferings would have been fearful
to think of (from stone)   I dined with Miss Berry yesterday she was pretty well.

[1] Lady Holland's doctor.
[2] H. B. was John Doyle.
[3] Hon. W. Cowper, son of Lady Palmerston by her first marriage.

(135)   WOBURN ABBEY[1] *Nov* 26.
MY DEAR LADY STANLEY

All our gentlemen are gone—the Duchess who read Lady Holland's will last night tells me Lady Lilford had the wardrobe, laces & onyxes left to her—I did not know this before so mention it now. Nothing can be more amiable than the letters the Fox family have written to Ld. John.

I am very glad Alice has given satisfaction, tho' the information would have been more pleasant to me if unaccompanied by strictures on my possible conduct, highly undeserving in my mind as I am not in the habit of speaking to children or servants before company & therefore should not be likely to do so ill bred a thing with regard to my daughters.

We have detestable weather. I have however got the conservatory this morning—the collection of cactuses supposed to be the best in England, but altho' all is in high order I do not believe the present Duchess cares much for the green houses. In a house in which the corridors round the Quadrangle are $\frac{1}{4}$ of a mile there ought to be at least 20 or 30 people, instead of that we shall be 8 tomorrow. I think we shall return home Friday as Edward is rather bored. The Duke & Duchess never take the slightest notice of their guests—the Duke seldom appears till dinner, both however are most kind & unaffected when they do meet you.

Your affec daugt   H. M. Stanley

[1] Seat of the Duke of Bedford, Lord John Russell's brother.

1846

(136)   ALDERLEY *Jan* 26*th*.

DEAR HEN

Your babies are going on remarkably well, Algernon [1] making his way famously, & we do not at all approve of his answer, when asked his name " Ugly Monster " who calls you so ? " Papa ! " I never saw so young a child *amuse himself* so well, the advantage of being at the fag end of a family. I paid Wee a compliment on his good behaviour this morning & her good management, but in my secret mind I thought the nature of the boy did half the work.

As for Alice, I think it wd be all the better for her health, & I daresay it will not at all postpone her marrying, if you were to keep to the old custom & not to take her out at all, before she has been presented.

The Tories have been exerting all their eloquence to induce Ralph [Leycester] to come forward for the County, but he is resolved against it. Tatton Egerton has tried hard to persuade him.

---

[1] Algernon, almost from birth, was her favourite grandchild.

117

(137)   ALDERLEY *Jan* 27/46.

Algernon has come down to breakfast every morning since you left & he has been so good—I am very glad to *make his acquaintance.* My Lord came to breakfast this morning & was not at all incommoded by his guest.

Our Globe failed on Friday, but by a new arrangement at Chalford a few Times of the same day arrive there at ½ past 2 & Mr. Granville was so kind as to bring one here & so we all read it carefully before night; & next morning's post was quite dead & dull. I should not like this often but on particular occasions it will be an advantage to be able to satisfy our impatience. It is Mr. G's doing in hopes to put a little money into the pocket of a poor lame boy. D'Israeli amused us so much, but *poor* Peel—he was really quite *touching*—I wonder if he whimpered in one part—really D'Is was *almost* too hard upon him. I do indeed wish as much as you do that Edward had not been turned out of the County & that, ever since, he had found no other refuge. It cannot be long before he will, one way or another, again enter upon publick life. If Peel should be obliged to give up, there must be dissolution & surely he can never go on under such a constant *baiting* as he will endure.

Mrs. Way [1] has rallied wonderfully, some of her complaints mend others & the irritation of the kidneys & bowels has carried off the water on the chest.

(138)   ALDERLEY *Feb 5th* 1846.

All well, but Algernon disgraced himself sadly this morning at breakfast. There was a little whine followed

---

[1] Emmy's mother-in-law.

by "I've done my job" & a terrible job it was. *Wee* was very shocked as you may suppose & made very anxious for the state of his bowels.

We dined at Capesthorne[1] yesterday—a dull dinner as usual—& he had not brought any news from Town with him.

Louisa has had a letter from Muff today, delighted with Naples. They are in the same house with the Brabazons—Ly B. & the Duchess of Calabretta (was not she a Jenkinson) are the usual chaperones of the Boothby girls.

Thanks for yesterday's letter & account of Alice's début. A girl seldom cares for going out before she has made some acquaintance especially to a ball, unless she is so fond of dancing that all men are much alike to her. By the time she has found out younger brothers are more agreeable than their elder ones & are less bored because they have not the same command of worldly pleasures I daresay she will like balls very much—& tho' you may try hard you cannot invariably keep detrimentals at a distance. What you say of young Egerton is exactly what Henry told us of the few young men *he* knew— how different from the style of young man in my youth, but I suppose everybody has said the same, from the beginning of the modern world at least.

How very amusing the debates [on the repeal of the Corn Laws] are, Sir J. Graham[2] does so wisely to take the bull by the horns & disarm the effect of all extracts by his *honesty* or *impudence*, which you please.

I have been very much pleased to hear of William dining with you so often this year, & that Edward did

---

[1] Seat of Mr. Davenport.
[2] Sir James Graham, one of Peel's most loyal supporters and at this time Home Secretary.

not disapprove his motion. Always tell me when you have him with you & can *testify* to any kind of brotherly feeling [1] for I do feel W's position is one likely to excite some envy & most heartily I wish it were otherwise— E. in & W. out tho' I see the great advantage it is to William to be obliged to come forward as by nature he is more inclined to vegetate in a corner. What sluggish blood there must have been in the Stanleys that so much indolence should have been infused into the males of this generation—for E. has his portion too tho' he also has some idea of exerting himself upon occasion.

The children are all well, unless one can call it indisposition Algernon's frequent inclination to pee.

(139)   ALDERLEY *Feb* 22/46.

Lucy [2] brought a bad headache & went to bed as soon as she arrived here. She came down to luncheon. She seems to enjoy returning to be her *old* self & dwelling on old times without forgetting anything since. The children are lovely little things, especially Luciebella. Theodore [who had some eye trouble] was taken to Travers who says the eye is only weakened muscles & that the *weak* eye must be used more than the other, which sounds odd. You may indeed be *sure* Lucy was pleased with Edward's visit, & especially by his very kind & affectionate manner both to her & the children. She always did love Edward most of any. I am sorry to hear from Lucy Emmy feels the motion of a carriage over the stones so much, *I* cannot wish she should have

---

[1] William and Edward were twins !
[2] This is Lucy Hare's first visit to Alderley since the death of her husband. Lady Stanley writes on black-edged paper during her visit.

children at all—but if she were to begin she could never do well in London.

You will enjoy your two visits very much I am sure, if all's well & Maude [Adeane] particularly will be so glad to have you. I only hope the *London ladies* will not pervert the extreme simplicity of the *country lassies* & teach them to long for London amusements.

How very curious the state of Elections [1] now going on & over. It is really I think rather disagraceful that Ld. Lincoln should so openly fly in the face of his father [2] by contesting the County.

(140)   ALDERLEY *March* I.

There never was such a first of March, southern gales as soft as possible & all the Spring flowers & the hedges are like April or May at least I have seen the hedges *less* green the 1st of May.

Is not Mr. Cobden's a fine speech, & if all his statements are true, very satisfactory as to rents. How glad the House must be it is over, so far, for I suppose there will be plenty more talking to the purpose before the Bill is passed.

What is said of Dissolution—I cannot see *why* there shd be one, except that *you* wish it.

MRS. STANLEY TO LADY STANLEY

(141)   GROV: CRES: *March* 2*nd* 1846.

MY DEAR LADY STANLEY

On Monday I thought I perceived rather more fullness on one side of Blanche's waist than the other, & on

----

[1] Bye-elections.
[2] Duke of Newcastle.

examining more closely she said that was the part where her back ached. I wrote to Mr. Hawkins to satisfy myself—he saw her today & tho' he assures me with care all will be right yet he has ordered her to lie down 6 hours a day, give up drawing altogether, writing as much as possible & to spend her time in the open air & in exercise when not reposing ; she has outgrown her strength, the spine has been weakened & has revolved, not curved. I cannot enumerate all the shower baths, rubbings, steels, port etc. she is to have—still I feel perfect confidence in Hawkins.

LADY STANLEY TO MRS. STANLEY

(142) ALDERLEY *March* 1*st.*

DEAR HEN

It is a most lamentable case. Poor dear Blanche, whose figure I was admiring so much—& so vexatious that one [Alice] should be too short & the other too tall, at least too rapidly becoming so. As to Alice's cold I was afraid *that* would *come* very soon. Did you mean to take great credit for not taking her to Lansdowne House the day after Calomel & James ?

MRS. STANLEY TO LADY STANLEY

(143) GROV: CRES: *March* 7*th.*

Henry has got an Arabic vocabulary I got at Bain only £1. 1. 0. it is enough at present. Alice enjoyed her ball very much yesterday & looked very nice in a black tulle gown & I think people will approve of her quiet & unpresuming manners. Lord Pomfret & Lord Goodrich were introduced to her, certainly they are two of

the most insignificant ugly little mortals I ever saw—
eldest sons do not shine this year.   I am getting to know
many of the infants who frequent balls.

There never was such a state of politics as the present
no one knows what will come next.   Mr. Ellice the
Bear [1] thinks Peel will get through the session by the aid
of the Queen's confinement [2] as no one will like to disturb
H.M. at that time, but others think he will never get on
but be constantly liable to defeats like that of Sir J.
Graham the other night.   Edward called on Mrs.
Cobden the other day with Charles Buller found her a
pretty, quiet little woman.   I think no one dislikes
Cobden who knows him.

Your view of what is best for Henry is exactly mine.
He seems bitten with the idea of Norway & says that it
is a very cheap & beautiful wild country.   I wish we
were going to meet then we could talk it over, not discuss
for we are all of one mind.   Lord Neville who will be
20 in Sept is engaged to Miss Johnson [3]—Ld. Goodrich
who is 19 is on the high road of being entangled by Lady
Dolly Walpole—it is well to keep these boys out of
London as long as one can.[4]

Mama heard that the potatoes that she had induced
the people in Mayo to plant in Nov: by giving them small
rewards have all failed.

If you are tired with my long letters you have only
yourself to blame, there is no one I like to write to better,
you enjoy letters & send in answer such delightful ones.
My love to my babies   Yr affec daughter   H. M. S.

---

[1] Edward Ellice (1781–1863), well-known Liberal politician and host, called
Bear from an early connexion with N. American fur trade.

[2] Princess Helena, afterwards Princess Christian, was born 1846.

[3] He married her in 1848.

[4] Henry, as the result of all this care, ended by marrying secretly and
bigamously a low-born Spaniard.

(144)   GROV: CRES: *March 10th.*

MY DEAR LADY STANLEY

Our dinner yesterday at Sir John Hobhouse [1] was not very well got together, there being too many women. Lord Melbourne spoke a good deal in his usual way now—he gives out what he is thinking of or has been reading lately in a clear good voice, but to me there is something very melancholy in his otherwise absent look. He got up suddenly at dessert & went away. Lady Dacre was there, she had not seen him for 12 years tho' so near a country neighbour. She told me several traits of his knowledge & love for his odd little wife [2] as she called her.

Lady Palmerston's Wednesday was as usual very pleasant. Lady Clanricarde was there trying to bring Lord John over to the Coercion bill which he is rather against at present   She says that Ireland is in a worse state than she ever knew it.   Lord Bessborough is also much in favour of the Coercion—he begins to feel doubts of the Corn Laws passing the Lords, much depends on the Bishops.   Yr affec daugh: H. M. S.

LADY STANLEY TO MRS. STANLEY

(145)   CUNDEN *March 20th.*

DEAR HEN

Kitty gave me an account of your visit & Alice's appearance in Dover St.—She said Alice looked like the Queen at her best & that her dress was very becoming.

---

[1] John Cam Hobhouse (1786–1869), Byron's friend.
[2] Lady Caroline Lamb.

What a gathering of the family K. had—the *house* must have felt *at home* & quite itself.

We had the usual annoyances that are apt to befall rail road travellers in coming here—first an hours wait in a very uncomf. room in Manchester, then arriving at a small station in the snow, where we expected to find a conveyance from Cunden but as *usual* (letters you know never miscarry except when it is important they should arrive exact) Louisa's letter to Mrs. Parker, announcing the time of our arrival & our needs only arrived this morning. After an hour's anxious looking out for a carriage & hearing there was none to be got, we sent off a messenger to Cunden stating our plight & in another hour there came a pony carriage which conveyed us safe through the chill air (& chill it was). The station is only $1\frac{1}{2}$ miles off & as they promised to send, ordering post horses to their carriage I did not take ours as the trans-shipping at Manchester is a bore.

Shall be very glad of a few more books—I should like Reine Margot tho' I shall not approve of having my prepossession in favour of Henri Quatre ce bon roi ce grand roi overturned—but *all* ones *old* historic ideas *are* to be turned topsy turvy in these days.

I was much amused by your & Blanche's criticism of the fitting up of the Opera House—because yesterday Mr. Parker was describing it & saying how beautiful it was. Upon farther enquiry I found he had only quoted his *hair dressers* opinion & had not *seen* it. I hope your stomach behaved well & carried you safely thro' the Drawing Room & that Alice is not laid up.

I am going to see *Miss Clayton* this afternoon, I felt no inclination thereto—but as they live within a mile I thought Kitty & certainly Charley wd take it very ill if I did not. Adieu.

125

(146) A L D E R L E Y *March* 22/46.

I found everything going on well yesterday on my return & we had no unpleasant adventures on the road.

Mrs. Parker took me to see Miss Clayton—oh dear—that Charley should be such a blockhead & his parents much more so to give such ready consent. I forget if you saw her in Town—face tolerably pretty, figure very bad, the family the jest of all the Cunden people, for their vulgarity. She is the best of them. I saw nobody but her—she is so awkward in her movements & such a long thin figure & mincing voice like a vulgar person who wishes to speak *genteely*. The Parkers said the Claytons would feel highly exalted by my visit.

What a number of obscure people, or who would have been thought so 50 years ago, & as quite presumptuous to *think* of Court, were at the Drawing Room. Why does not E. like Alice to go to parties. I think there is more opportunity for conversation than at balls & of making acquaintance—quadrilles give very little time for that purpose.

MRS. STANLEY TO LADY STANLEY

(147) G R O V : C R E S : *March* 27/46.

Catherine Stanley never walks but just thro' the door & feels the fatigue of standing to dress. I believe there is much derangement of health but I think like her she will get well for she has no disease only functional disturbance. The one leg being longer than the other I am told proceeds from the strain when walking on it painfully. She very much enjoys the large quiet room.[1]

---

[1] Lady Stanley had lent her the Dover Street house.

Edward dines to day at the Beef steak club it always gives him a head ache, & I now do not believe there are any great wits there.

I have got the rheumatism from a window opened behind me last night at Lady Londonderry—it was a very pretty ball but Alice danced very little, very few of the people who dance with her happening to be there. There is a great difference in the invitations to dance that young ladies get & I think the love of the filthy lucre of ball giving & feeding parents shows itself as men always ask the young ladies who have parties. We dine on Saturday with old Mrs. Rothschild which will be dreadful. Edward went to Lady Palmerston last night but having been obliged to ask him for money to pay a bill this morg. I have not had much conversation out of him since

(148)   GROS. CRES: *March 30th.*

The story is that Albert is so fierce for free trade that he may put down the aristocracy & when Ed. told the on dit to Lord Melbourne he replied " Ah yes they are very incautious in their talk at the Palace." Ld. Melbourne dined at the Palace the other day but they say the Queen is quite nervous when he is there, he is so easily overcome.

I did not know Alice had confided to you her longing for a dance. I never thought of it as we certainly have not 25 pounds to spare. Now the time is past as people *eat* after Easter, but before do not expect so much,— Lady Londonderry had no supper but sandwiches & such like. Alice always looks satisfied & lives in hope it will be better.

LADY STANLEY TO MRS. STANLEY

(149)   ALDERLEY *March* 31/46.

The brutes of hounds are coming here on Thursday &
have put it in the papers which annoys Fleetwood greatly
—he says he will not allow them to draw the wood—if
they come through it in pursuit it cannot be helped.

Algernon is so different to any boy of yours—he never
asks a foolish question but finds out things for himself &
has so much observation & never shows the least unwill-
ingness that other children should approach his play-
things. He does not seem to have any *evil* in him, no
love of mischief, of teazing an animal, giving it a sly
pinch as *some folks* will. Baby [Rosalind] is good &
coaxing, the ladies' maids doat upon her.

Foolish Prince Albert, I think he will find the League
worse cattle to deal with than the aristocracy—I cannot
guess how it is all to end.

I suppose it may be considered that the Indian warfare
is at an end & after all, tho' one suffers deeply for those
who have lost friends yet the total loss is really trifling in
comparison with what is gained.

Peel seems to me the most pitiable object living &
somehow he makes himself look smaller & yet more
pitiable by his deprecating phraseology.

Have you read La Reine Margot & who recommended
it ? Please answer these 2 questions.

(150)   ALDERLEY *April* 2/46.

You had not mentioned Little Holland House before—
think it must be a very desirable alternative to either
leaving London or going into a small house in it as I
suppose it is rent free. Is it more than a mile from
Kensington Turnpike ?

La Reine Margot shocked *even* My Lord very much.
I have read many descriptions of St. Bartelème in different
novels but never such a disagreeable one—none but a
Frenchman could introduce such disgusting details.

It is an age since Emmy wrote—not for a week I think

MRS. STANLEY TO EDWARD STANLEY

(151)   PALACE NORWICH *April* 8.
This morning I went with Mary to her home for factory
girls where she has also got her Valenciennes lace workers.
It answers well & really the lace they make is quite as
good as that made in Belgium but they will not be able
to earn more than 3 or 4 shillings a week. After luncheon
the Bishop took Blanche & me to the Electric Telegraph.
Blanche is now walking with Arthur he is very fond of
her & talks to her a great deal. He is the most singular
compound of childlike simplicity & mental power &
acquirement. Aunt thinks his sermons will astonish
every one when they come out, so bold & so new. Only
those on Peter as the Founder have been preached. Paul
the Propagator & John the Finisher will take this season
& next. I am *very* happy here, so much kindness &
evenness of temper & so much agreeable conversation.

Your affec wife   H. M. Stanley.

LADY STANLEY TO MRS. STANLEY

(152)   ALDERLEY *April* 16th/46.
DEAR HEN:

I was glad to get your note for I get nothing out of
Edward—I think it would have been a better arrange-

ment to have written daily to me & given me a message
for him only I suppose he would not have been satisfied
with no more, tho' one might think he cared for nobody
nor nothing. I don't know that we are much the better
for his company tho' he is *very* civil. You won't thank
me for this preface.

My Lord goes out in his chair but he will not make
much progress in appearing better until he gets the use
of his feet & his bad hand.

We are very sorry for poor Sir William Boothby, or
rather for his poor girls abroad. He is not expected to
live & they will be in the greatest distress—he had got
into rail road speculations & consequent difficulties—
had a fit & has been gradually sinking.

I wish Arthur would let alone the difficult parts of the
New Testament, I doubt if he will get much fame by
them.

I *hope* Blanche's ailment is not another edition of
nerves in the family, which seems to be the most annoying
of all complaints & the most difficult to cure.

Yrs affec M. J. S.

(153)   ALDERLEY *April* 26th.

I have been so *provoked* with Wee. She & the Donkey
& the panniers were going on so happily together that
she thought she would set off to the Edge. Well, while
she & Margaret were admiring the view from Stormy
Point poor Donkey thought she would rest herself & lay
down—*possibly* preparatory to rolling but that would have
been difficult with the great panniers. Wee seems never
to have heard of a donkey doing such things & thought
she was going into a fit. Of course she pulled Algernon

out on one side—Margt. too much alarmed to pounce upon Baby at once, but she was got out very safely & Margt. was sent off post haste to get water from the Holy Well to revive the poor fainting beast. Wee declares she will have nothing to do with a donkey & panniers again & will not hear of another trial. I am sure she will complain of me. The donkey was not in very good condition & I daresay it was rather tired of carrying the two heavy children so far for Wee said it *yawned* several times. There never was such a gentle docile creature.

If you know of any *proper* French books I shall be much obliged to you but no Reine Margot please.

Emmy talks of coming next week & we shall be very glad to have her & Albert to enliven us.

(154) ALDERLEY *May* 3

DEAR HEN

My Lord is better than he has been since the beginning of his illness [1] he was in bed from Sat. till Friday last groaning & howling—on Friday he got up, had a long talk with Uncle about things in general not at all tired, slept well, & had a long visit from Mr. Granville yesterday afternoon when he *enjoyed* the whole story of Mr. Jones & the Girdlestones & had it out to his hearts content—very well today, Dean says *quite* well.

You have perhaps heard of the death of Mrs. Wm. Way (I am quite tired of mourning but I think it need not eclipse Alice at all & you very little, except, for the sake of the additional Way connexion a little black may be necessary)

[On the 26th June, the night on which Peel's Corn

---

[1] He had been dreadfully ill with gout the whole spring.

Bill passed in the Lords, the Irish Coercion Bill was
defeated in the Commons and Lord John Russell formed
an administration for the first time.]

MRS. STANLEY TO LADY STANLEY

(155)   GROS: CRES: *July 4th* 1846.
MY DEAR LADY STANLEY

Edward was sent for yesterday by Lord John & was
offered the Under Secretary of the Foreign Department
as being the only place he could give him while out of
Parliament. I believe it was offered at the suggestion of
Lord Palmerston who has been most friendly to Edward.
Ed. stated to Lord John it was not a place suited to him,
nor is he suited to it as he certainly can neither speak nor
write French. He is gone now to Lord Palmerston &
will then take his answer to Lord John. The whole
thing has been most mortifying as Lord Bessboro' wished
particularly for him to have been secretary for Ireland
if he had been in Parliament. It is too provoking to
think how easily he could have got in if there had been
no objection to his pledging himself to the total & immediate [repeal of the Corn Laws] which he never objected to
& which has come to pass.

Ed. just come back from seeing Lord Palmerston who
wishes him very much to take the place—the fact is he
wishes for Ed. to be in the Govt: It is much lower than
the places he has occupied, in fact going back to what he
first was. Ed. hardly knows what to decide but I think
he will accept as it is better to be connected & he will
stipulate it does not bar higher claims. He is gone to
Ld. John—Belgrave Square is a short way to have to
make up your mind.

Alice is gone to Lady Oranmore at Richmond till Monday, Ed. will write to Alderley when anything is settled—it seems that Lord John & the others told it as certain last afternoon at the H of C that Ed. would be U. Secretary of Foreign Affairs.

I forgot to say I saw a cook likely to suit but she preferred seeing you. Our brown horse lamed itself in the stable, your horses are in physic so we have been on foot.

Edward has accepted as they all pressed him to do so —Lord John said it would be a convenience to the Government & would not be in the way of higher office.

Your affec dau: H. M. S.

MRS. STANLEY TO EDWARD STANLEY

(156)   WINNINGTON *Aug 6th/46*

MY DEAREST LOVE

Johnny looks very pale, is very thin, & is much more selfish & naughty than I ever saw him before. Speaks to Lyulph & indeed to all the little ones as if they were dogs—it makes one more unhappy than even his health. Williams even complains of him. Lyulph is a very good boy, Algernon a beautiful child with the most lovely curly head, Baby is a dear little duck.

My garden looks very nice & Walton seems inclined to work & be civil, certainly the eye of a master is rather wanted.

How perfectly happy I should be with you in the country.

Yr affec wife H. M. S.

133

(157)   WINNINGTON *Aug 9th.*
MY DEAREST LOVE

I was sure you would be grieved to hear of Johnny's delicate state of health—I observed last night when saying his prayers how short his breath was. Dean came yesterday & said the heart had too much action & unless care is taken of him the seeds of consumption will be laid. He must have been fearfully ill, 9 days in bed.

Do you think you could give Miss White £20, we owe her a quarter. She did not ask for it but I saw she was in distress & Alice told me that her brother wanted £20 & could not get it from some people that owed it to him. If you could send it her she would I am sure be thankful.

I am very glad you miss me a little & still more flattered at your saying so. When it is my happy lot to go into the country with you & the children to a decent place & not a dirt hole like this I shall forget London & be among the most impatient to depart.

Your affec & devoted wife   H. M. S.

(158)   ALDERLEY *Aug: 13th.*
MY DEAREST LOVE

Your Father seems well tho' much aged. I am very sorry Lady Stanley is coming today for she must feel the cold & damp & I am sure she will be very uncomfortable here as I see very well that Rianette does not think her as ill as she is nor feels softly for her, which is what sick people require. Both Rianette & Louisa have grown very hard & I think selfish, & Louisa having been for 3 weeks in London is considered quite a sacrifice.

134

Your Father has been finding great fault with the Govt: about the Irish arms bill, & I had thought they laid themselves open to great fault finding by their own friends & thought how much better for them if you were in the Cabinet & more able to tell them what the world does think.

I am very glad you wrote to Henry—I do not wonder at his getting a foot into Italy I am sure I should. Addio my darling.

(159)   A L D E R L E Y *Aug* 16

Your mother arrived tired & ill with her cold & wind on the stomach. She slept badly & I have been sitting with her this morning, she has been complaining very much of weakness & malaise. I am afraid she will be very uncomfortable here for they are not very pitying to her. . . .

Lady Stanley still says I was hunting some young lord —they continually try to find out Alice's favourite partner—she is much more frightened here than in London & never opens her mouth.

I am sorry to find that only £20 of the money comes to me—Miss White has not received hers.

                                     Yr affec   H. M. S.

(160)   W I N N I N G T O N *Sept* 22*nd*

I have had a letter from Henry at Ischel 12th Sept. he was again walking. I conclude he will soon come home —he is insatiable, he had had some fishing too.

I cannot agree Lady Harriet is not dangerous, for you seem to have been entirely occupied with her—to the extent of making you give up your favourite pursuits, but people who have only to amuse & be amused have great advantages over unfortunate women who have as many children to see after as I have—all the same I shall be very happy to see you & it will be 8 weeks since we have met.

Johnny is well but thin & very naughty—pray remember it is his birthday on the 30th he wishes very much to have a chest of tools.

Yr. affec: wife   H. M. S.

Lady Stanley asks if I am jealous of Lady H. B.   I am glad we shall see Mr. Buller.

EDWARD STANLEY TO MRS. STANLEY

(161)   GLENORCHY FOREST HOUSE

Sept 25/46.

MY DEAREST LOVE

I had settled everything for leaving this today but Breadalbane pressed me to stay on for a large drive they are going to have for Lord Sefton who is still far from strong.   I have therefore agreed to remain.   Sunday I shall go to Edinburgh, Monday perform your commissions & start for England either by steamer or rail.   Lord & Lady Sefton & Fred Craven came over the hills yesterday from their shooting lodge in Glen Lyon.   The day before yesterday I killed a very good stag of 17 stone but yesterday I went out with Landseer & neither of us got a shot.   Goodbye   Yrs affecly   E. J. S.

[Typical of all of Edward's letters at this time.]

LADY STANLEY TO MRS. STANLEY

(162)　　　　　　　ALDERLEY *Sept 26th.*

As you did not find fault last time I have again opened a letter of Henry's—how happy he must have been to follow his Trade again, I think not with much success as his numbers are not large & I suppose a grayling to be only a trout.[1]

I hope you have got Edward now—surely you do not mean that you have had no letter about his return.

I *ought* to be in mourning, for George Way, but I think I shall only mourn in *black wax*, which you shall see *next* time not to *alarm* you now.

I heard of Lady Dolly from Mrs. Hibbert, pretty doings indeed of aristocratic young ladies

　　　　　　　　　　　　Your affec　M. J. S.

I must say another word.　Aunt K. says the report of Ly. Dolly cannot be true as she is going to balls in the neighbourhood & riding every day.　But that does not *prove* she has not *miscarried*.

Have you seen the article which alludes to Alford[2] in all but *name* as the first corrupter of Morris & that he went to college a *Roman Catholic* in his heart.　Keep me au fait of Henry's doings.

MRS. STANLEY TO EDWARD STANLEY

(163)　　　　　　　WINNINGTON *Oct: 30th.*

MY DEAREST LOVE

　　I cannot express half my sorrow at your having had so inconvenient a headache, I also much regret not having been there to nurse you.

[1] She is wrong.　A grayling is a grayling.
[2] Henry's late tutor.

The state of our stud is not encouraging :—

Finella is very bad
Merlin better
Rebecca beginning with the same
Nora's corn again troublesome
Clarke [groom] very cross.

I am the most vexed at Finella being so ill—she has been
ill used by Johnny.

I hear from Mama that Mrs. Damer [1] is in town she
is a lucky woman to have so long a " season " which I
know she considers desirable, & her house will be a
great resource to you.   Miss Berry is also again in
Curzon St., but nothing will ever replace Ly. Holland,
what an opening for any one.

Your affec wife   H. M. S.

(164)   WINNINGTON *Nov: 6th.*

MY DEAREST LOVE

I had not seen G. Fox's death & am sorry to think we
shall never see the ugly face again.   Your account of
London is not brilliant & I wish I was with you, unen-
cumbered—how glad I should be if Alice were to marry
next year & I should have a free winter.

I am really quite ashamed of Ireland, how their want
of principle shows, or is the Times too hard on them ?

I am very grateful for the offer of so agreeable a visit
as that to the Grange [2] would be but I think I shall best
tend to my comfort by not accepting.   I look back to the
many painful hours I have passed this year due almost all
to your reproaches to me for spending money unneces-

---

[1] The Honble. Mrs. Dawson Damer, a great friend of the Stanleys.
[2] Seat of Lord Ashburton.

sarily. I am therefore firmly determined not wittingly to merit that reproach again for when the moment of paying arrives you always are angry with me. Next year we shall begin with a larger income & I hope that you, who are the H. of C. [of our ménage] & vote the expenses will not find fault with me, the administrator. If you do I must take the usual ministerial exit, & resign.

How very soon Lady Elgin has been married, it will save her trouble as she will not now want a chaperone. When does Lord Elgin go to Canada.[1] I do not think it sounds comfortable to be married & then have the Atlantic between one but I do not suppose it is a love match.

I read the boys extracts from Sterne, Johnny was touched but Lyulph laughed at the mingling of tears in Maria's handkerchief till I thought he would have gone into fits. If it were not that you are not with me I should be perfectly happy.

LADY STANLEY TO MRS. STANLEY

(165)   LEAMINGTON *Nov:* 10*th*/46.

DEAREST HEN

I am very glad you know all—while there could be a doubt, not only of success but of the fact, which I could not help feeling, considering the number of years,[2] I thought it best to say nothing. I can hardly explain to you how conflicting my own wishes, even, have been or how much all my ideas have been *bouleversées*, so that, at first I scarce knew whether I was glad or sorry; but

---

[1] As Governor-General, married as his second wife a daughter of the Earl of Durham.

[2] Emmy was 34.

139

now I can truly say, I think most of the disappointment poor Albert & Emmy are feeling. Indeed, delicate as she is there might be great doubts if all would have ended well, for her, I mean, had it gone on.

I am afraid Henry[1] has rather too many visitors & engagements might it not be desirable you should recommend him to *sport oak* as I have heard called, closing the door to miscellaneous visitors & thereby give himself more time for reading, & be less frequent in his excursions. Rianette gathered that he had many engagements tho' they seem to be of the best & soberest kind & happily he has not a turn for either gambling or drinking—he said there was a good deal of the former going on in the evening parties. Many visitors in the course of the day are objectionable because one may be sure it is the *idle* & the *least valuable* men as *friends* who dispose of their time in this way.

You must not let the young ladies read the Roman Traitor. I have just got Cesar Borgia by the author of Whitefriars—a period of history & a character which enable him to luxuriate in *horrid* descriptions of barbarity.

Yrs affecly   M. J. STANLEY

EDWARD STANLEY TO MRS. STANLEY

(166)   F. O. *Nov* 7/46.

Lady Mary Lambton was married this morning to Lord Elgin & I met all the people coming out of the Church in Eaton Square on my way to the Office.

Lord Brougham has arrived at Paris full of ire against Palmerston—very French & I believe the only man not a Frenchman who approves of Louis Philippe.

[1] At Cambridge.

I went to Mrs. Damer's whom I found at home with
Blanche, the fat Miss Dawson & Miss Seymour.   That
melancholy dull Sir Boothby always in Blanche's pockets
& Ld. Ebrington [1] looking silly at nobody in particular.
I hear the Wharncliffes are so poor they intend to let
both Wortley & the house in Curzon St. & go abroad.

We had a pleasant dinner at the Palmerstons Ld. &
Ly. John Russell, Ld. Lansdowne the Greys & Clanricardes to meet the new American Minister Mr. Bancroft
& his wife.   He is rather solemn & prim but intelligent
& inoffensive—she is rather a pleasing looking woman—
on the whole I think an improvement on the general
breed of American Ministers.

Lady Emily [de Burgh] [2] is looking very well both in
health & beauty.

MRS. STANLEY TO EDWARD STANLEY

(167)   WINNINGTON *Nov* 10*th*.

MY DEAREST LOVE

My cold is so bad I can do nothing but sneeze & cry—
I believe it is all owing to my cold bed, I really cannot keep
warm alone.

The only places I wish to go to are Woburn &
Bowood.[3]

Sir Brook Boothby has not one shilling besides he is
old [4] & ugly & I should not think would be dangerous—
certainly if ever there were young ladies who had their
fill of flirting they are Mrs. Damer's.

Is Emily de Burgh having any profitable flirtation ?

[1] Eldest son of Earl of Fortescue.
[2] Daughter of the Marquis of Clanricarde.
[3] Marquis of Lansdowne's seat.
[4] Thirty-seven.

At your leisure pray return me Henry's letter, Aunt Kitty says she thinks him much improved, I am sure college will be *the* best thing for him just now. a 1000 kisses to you   yr affec wife   H. M. S.

(168)   ALDERLEY *Nov: 15th.*

I believe you heard when here that Arthur Davenport had been flogged.   Mr. D. has written a most abusive letter to Dr. Vaughan [1] telling him he will show him up in the Times & only dating his letter *South of France* so that Dr. V. shd. not answer him.   I am sorry to say that both Vaughan & the tutor in whose house Arthur is say they can do little with him he is so sulky, morose & ill disposed.

Henry says he is making gun cotton which I must try to prevent him doing—so dangerous.

General & Mrs. Scott arrive tomorrow.

Nightingale says that with Johnny it is the Mysenteric Glands that are amiss & he has prescribed very small doses of Calomel twice a week, great warmth & *dry air.*

Maude [Adeane] has been very ill but has not miscarried so she may expect her 12th in due course.   I am *quite* safe.   I will conclude this at Winnington.

Winnington   I find all well here & am going to devote myself to my cold.

EDWARD STANLEY TO MRS. STANLEY

(169)   F. O. *Nov 19/46.*

You will see by an article in the Times that Russia, Austria & Prussia have decided on destroying the

---

[1] Headmaster of Harrow, afterwards the husband of Katherine Stanley.

independence of Cracow. This is a bold move that
would never have been attempted if the Northern Powers
had not taken advantage of the present state of feeling
between England & France.   It is a gross & flagrant
violation of the treaty of Vienna to which England &
France were parties but yet all I suppose we can do is to
enter our protest against the act.   It still seems doubtful
whether France has not given an understanding that she
will not interfere in the matter.   It will however be a
dangerous move for Guizot to run in the teeth of all the
French feelings on this subject as he will be accused of
having done so to conciliate the Northern Powers in
consequence of his difference with England.[1]

With regard to your male cubs I shld. recommend a
wholesome application of the birch.   Their increased &
increasing malignity will not make the house full in
London more agreeable.

I was at Mrs. Damer's last night, the old Boothby still
there but as you say, not really a danger.

MRS. STANLEY TO EDWARD STANLEY

(170)   ALDERLEY *Nov 26th.*

Your Father is very well & merry on this his 80th
birthday.   Alice Kate & I came here before luncheon.

Mr. Girdlestone tells everyone he is better than he has
been these 20 years but the people say he looks at death's
door.

I am getting very weary of my widowhood I have now
been alone three months out of four—I shall be so glad
when the time comes for going to London, I have quite

[1] Over the Spanish marriage.

settled in my own mind how I shall locate the children without you being aware they are in the house.

(171)   WINNINGTON *Dec 3rd.*

I would give a little finger if not a larger portion of myself to bring to pass the bright vision you have set before me.[1]   Italy offers such a field at present.   Do make some démarche.   Oh the very idea makes Winnington appear more odious than ever—the blessing of being independent away from all control & the advantage to the girls & in another way to Johnny who by the by looks thinner & more pinched than ever.   Oh but this bright prospect I can think of nothing else it wd. be too heavenly.

(172)   WINNINGTON *Dec 4th.*

I am sorry my observations on your love of a Bachelor life annoyed but certainly it does not alter the fact that I have been a desolate female most of the autumn.   How pleasant that would make Florence, you could not get away.   I shall be glad if you would send me some money this is the third time of asking.

We have all frequently relieved the mulatto woman who was my nurse[2]   I never knew her name was Andrews, only Black Mag—I will give her something when I go to town as she has had misfortunes & lost all her savings.

Your mother came here this morning I am dreadfully nervous, feel all of a tremble, but I trust all will go on pleasantly.

[1] Edward Stanley has asked how she would like it if he were sent to Florence as Minister.
[2] Mrs. Stanley was born at Halifax.

The Scotts will be obliged to stay [at Alderley] over Christmas as she cannot travel it is a great disappointment having lost a boy.

We have been all the morning giving clothing to the poor—I have been obliged to expend 2 5/– of your money to eke out—there is much distress this year.

I & half a dozen of the children have colds.   I never suffered so much from cold as this year, I wish you would get a small Arnott stove or I shall die of it.

(173)   WINNINGTON *Dec* 16*th*.

Poor dear Blanche has had a *most painful* operation on her toe performed today—so painful I will not harrow you with the details she behaved perfectly except that in her agony she bit Wee's shoulder.   She is so very brave she never screamed or offered any resistance.

The children all behaved well during Lady Stanley's visit.   I feel very nervous about the large Christmas party at Alderley—with so many it will be noisy work.

EDWARD STANLEY TO MRS. STANLEY

(174)   PANSHANGER[1] *Tues: Dec* 15/46.

We have just come in from shooting in one of the most freezing days I ever was out.   It was however a fair day & we killed about 200 head altogether.

The party is composed of the Granvilles, the Marchioness & Lady Emily, Ld. & Lady Sidney, Miss Eden, Henry Greville, Spencer Cowper & Morpeth. Lady Emily is the only young lady & except Spencer Cowper there is no one to flirt with her, she however

---

[1] Seat of Earl Cowper.

takes her part right well in conversation with any body & seems to me to be very sharp, intelligent & agreeable.

I shall stay over tomorrow & go back early Thursday evening.

MRS. STANLEY TO EDWARD STANLEY

(174A)   WINNINGTON *Dec 17th.*
MY DEAREST LOVE

I have had much to fret me the whole day—Johnny's knee is swelled & stiff, Blanche of course is suffering very much, Lyulph has got a boil on his leg where it was hurt with the rocking horse. Alice's cold is worse. All these worries have worn me out but not one has vexed me so much as the tone of your letter from Panshanger. I wrote a letter to you this morning about it but have put it in the fire & will only say that I wish you may for the future let your own daughter share in the advantages you see the good of to others. Emily de Burgh has been constantly put forward in every way & *her* father would not have proposed that she should be sent upstairs when there was company to dinner & she has therefore become agreeable & conversible which it is impossible for a girl to be who is only allowed to appear at balls & interdited from all places where she is likely to hear any rational conversation.

I am glad you have been so very well amused at all your visits but I had better say no more & be content to enact the part of nurse & housekeeper without meeting with help or sympathy.

I have been far from well lately & am sure it is that I feel so hurt at your caring so much more for all the people you live with than you do for me or your children. It withers my heart & I feel, too late to repair the evil that, in sacrificing my own happiness to the good of my children, by remaining away from you, I have allowed myself to become quite a cast off.

It is impossible I am afraid for you to understand the chill I feel in seeing you so gay & engrossed with strangers while I am unremittingly harassed by the many cares I have had lately. I am quite worn out with anxiety about Johnny & I am sure he is seriously ill.

The housemaid [at Grosvenor Crescent] has sent me this bill, pray pay it as she says she is in great want of money.

I am so unhappy pray come to Alderley sooner instead of going out visiting again.   Yrs affec   H. M. S.

EDWARD STANLEY TO MRS. STANLEY

(175)

MY DEAREST LOVE

On account of your troubles about the children which may justify your vexation, I excuse your attack upon me which I think unjust & unfair, & my only security against such assaults is never to speak of any person I see or of anything I do. If I express myself in favour of a married woman you are jealous, if of a girl, I am a Monster to my own children. Whatever annoyance you may have had or however much you may complain you have no right at this time to accuse me of having kept you in the country as I asked you to come to Town & rather wished you to do so than not, so that it was your own act & deed to remain where you were.

Ld. Palmerston goes down to Broadlands next week

so it will be impossible [for me] to go as no one else will be left in the Office.

I hope to get a better account tomorrow of the children & also of yourself. I have paid the Housemaid.

Yrs affec   E. J. S.

MRS. STANLEY TO EDWARD STANLEY

(176)   WINNINGTON *Dec* 18*th*.

My sick list increases but I am just returned from a brisk walk & feel in better heart & will even forgive you the second dose of admiration you give me today of Emily de Burgh.

When I get low & am feeling unhappy a gay happy letter from you jars but I am determined I will not again give way to it but trust you do sometimes think of us poor country folks tho' not so beautiful or so very agreeable as Lady Emily seems to be.

I find great difficulty in getting to Alderley but hope we have at last got an omnibus. William & Ellin, General & Mrs. Scott & 2 little girls are there, on the 23rd Mr. & Mrs. Adeane 2 girls & 2 boys come & on the 2 of Jan. Lucy Parry & her 2 brothers.

MR. GIRDLESTONE TO LORD STANLEY

(177)   ALDERLEY RECTORY *Dec* 21 1846.

The Revd. C. Girdlestone presents his respects to Lord Stanley of Alderley & wishes to inform him that having received the offer of a vacant benefice in Staffordshire he expects 'ere long to vacate the Rectory of Alderley. Having made this communication at the earliest possible

opportunity, simply with a view to the convenience of
Lord Stanley as patron, & proposing with the same object
to apprize his Lordship as soon as he knows when the
vacancy will actually take place, Mr. Girdlestone cannot
conclude without expressing a hope that before he quits
the present sphere of his duties he may be allowed to
exchange some token of reconciliation with friends
whom it was ever far from his intention to offend.

LORD STANLEY TO MR. GIRDLESTONE

(178)   ALDERLEY PARK *Dec* 21/46.

Lord Stanley presents his compts. to the Rev: Mr.
Girdlestone & has to acknowledge the receipt of his note
informing him that, having received the offer of a living
in Staffordshire he expects 'ere long to vacate the Rectory
of Alderley & that Mr. Girdlestone will apprize him as
soon as he knows when the vacancy will actually take
place.

MRS. STANLEY TO EDWARD STANLEY

(179)   ALDERLEY *Dec* 22*nd*.

MY DEAREST LOVE

So you forgot my birthday well peace be with you it
is only one small one to the heavy list of your sins.

I confess I heard with a great mixture of fear that Mr.
Girdlestone vacated—the difficulty of choosing his
successor will be immense. I wish very much &
advisedly you would be quick in suggesting some one
for your Father will give loose reins to his imagination
& I do not know who he may not think of—Lady

Stanley told me but sous le sceau du secret " Sir Brooke Boothby " do you like him I know you do not but I said very little only that if Arthur [Stanley] was not the man you would wish for a man who wd. not hereafter interfere with your own sons. Lady Stanley has written to the Bishop as Lord Stanley will not make a direct offer [to Arthur] unless sure of being accepted, this I fear will not be & Lady Stanley I think does not wish it very much.

I think you are very unkind to Blanche in not being sorry for her suffering.

Pray tell me where you dine, you can surely mention people without praising them.   Yr affec wife   H. M. S.

EDWARD STANLEY TO MRS. STANLEY

(180)   F. O. *Dec* 23/46.

I quite forgot the date of your birthday but as you know I am always shamefully ignorant of these matters, & do my best to try & forget my own.

Many happy returns however I now wish you & beg pardon for my omission.

With respect to a successor for Mr. Girdlestone it is extremely hard to know what to say but if Arthur does not wish to have it I shld. certainly object to its being given to anyone whose age was such as not to make it possible there would be a vacancy before one of my children was old enough to succeed, or who would not consent to give it up when whoever might be our Rev: child was qualified to take the living.

As to B. Boothby I think him a tedious bore & certainly should not wish to have him there.

I have been afraid to mention who I see but as you ask

I may perhaps venture to say that I dined yesterday at the Rothschilds, today with the Edens & tomorrow with St. Aulaire

MRS. STANLEY TO EDWARD STANLEY

(181)   *Undated*

MY DEAREST LOVE

I was so disappointed though I had no hopes of Arthur accepting. I think you will find your Mother most anxious to meet your views. Now to the all absorbing New Year's Gifts. Your selection seems excellent. Do you mean to give Mme. de Trey the watch if not I suppose you will give her the shawl & I the Pensées de Pascal but she has worked hard with an additional child, Kate, & never had any increase of salary & has no watch which is very inconvenient. Henry would like Eastern Europe perhaps it could be got half price, for Alice the envelope case. Have you got Blanche shawl pins she will be disappointed if she does not get them & she has got you a very handsome present. Maude I have fitted for you with a sketch book. We shall have books enough with the 2 you bring, Battle of Life is said to be bad. Who are the Waverley novels for, such a large sum—Henry would not care for them—did you mean them for Alice ?

Lady Stanley is so amiable & soft you will be surprised. She has been talking a great deal to me.

(182).   CHRISTMAS DAY 1846.

You can hardly think my dearest Love how very much your children miss you this day. It has been a beautiful

clear hard frost & I have walked with Alice & the boys
in the wood—Henry is skating. Nothing can be more
harmonious than the whole party & the young ones
agree perfectly & except Johnny all are quiet. The
poor fellow is in a very excitable state, eats bread &
butter for dinner & has a gland very much swelled.
We shall be 19 at dinner today & 27 at dessert. We
have put off our pool of commerce [1] till you come.

(183)   A L D E R L E Y *Dec* 27*th*.
The children are all very happy & there is no noise
except when allowed or when Johnny makes it. All sigh
for you & Henry says it is so dull without Papa.

Girdlestone gave out 5 young people of riper years
were to be baptized this afternoon & it is reported to be
John Trap & his brethren ; the story goes they expect
an inheritance & fear, not being baptized, they cannot
obtain it. I hope you are thinking of someone to propose
Edward Dawkins was mentioned en l'air he is 55 a quiet
inoffensive man not very bright, then your Father thought,
who do you think, Cruttenden [2] ! ! ! ! ! ! the *prince* of
bigots.

EDWARD STANLEY TO MRS. STANLEY

(184)   F . O . *Dec* 30/46.
I am very glad to hear of the marriage of that polite
young nobleman Don Francesco de Ebrington with
Minnie Damer it is a very good match, he is respectable

---

[1] Commerce, a simple card game, is still played regularly by many of Mrs.
Stanley's descendants on Christmas Eve.
[2] Cruttenden it was, however.

& well behaved & if she does not think him a bore why
I hope she never will.   As for Mrs. Damer she must be
in the seventh heaven & having accomplished her object
so satisfactorily may exchange notes with her great rival
match maker Louis Philippe on terms of perfect
equality.

LADY STANLEY TO MRS. STANLEY

(185)   ALDERLEY *Feb* 2/47.

DEAR HEN:

We had a very full church on Sunday for Mr. G. gave it out in the Parish that Mr. Cruttenden was to preach for the collection for the singers indeed I believe we helped the reports having been told he had *asked* him; but I suppose Mr. C. thought it better not, situated as he is at present between the two incumbencys, & Girdy did all the duty himself—gave us a little humbug about leaving the Parish " where so many had been very kind to him " & told us that next Sunday in the afternoon he should preach his last sermon in that church. The collection was 5—8—0—not so large as last time. His voice was very weak & I thought he looked more ill than usual. *Perhaps* the man has *some* feeling which may be painfully called forth at this time—I wish I could fancy or believe it to be a feeling of sorrow for the conduct he has adopted or the least shadow of repentance.

One of Mrs. Townley Parkers sons is in the same regt. with Major Deedes at Clonmell & I have got the direction that I may write to Deedes for particulars. I have heard that a very beneficial change in the feelings of the poor Irish has taken place in many parts, seeing how

much the Protestants & the Military feel for them, & do
for them, more than the Catholicks.

How have you settled Henry's college payments ? I
hope it has not been necessary to take all or nearly all
his ready cash or it will lead to a beginning of being in
debt which may be difficult to recover.

LORD STANLEY TO EDWARD STANLEY

(186)   2nd Feb 1847

DEAR EDWARD

I send you the proxies signed & sealed, but before
you hand them over to Lord Lansdowne you must obtain
an assurance that they will not be made use of in support
of any bill in which a provision is contained for the maintenance, encouragement, or exclusive education of roman
Catholicks in Great Britain & Ireland, nor a provision
for the relief in future of the poor of Ireland out of English property, nor an exemption from any payment of
taxes by holders of property in Ireland to which the holder
of property in England is made liable.

I should not wish formally to withdraw my proxies on
any particular question when I dont agree with the pro-
positions of my party, I had rather it be sub: silentium.
I cannot persuade myself it would be right to give way
for political considerations ; if roman Catholicks will be
roman Catholicks, with their doctrines of infallibility of
a Pope & prostration of all intellect & reason I would
have them persecuted for their blindness & absurdity.
I must be, notwithstanding the charm of the word Tolerance, intolerant of what they call their religion. If it is
bound up in any way with morals & true belief it is

perhaps better than an absence of all religion which can in any way keep men from vice & immorality ; it is on the whole however such a mixture of bigotry fraud deceit & hypocrisy thrown upon the world, that I view it as an enemy & would crush it as a serpent if I could.

With regard to the maintenance of the poor in Ireland, I cannot but think that an act of injustice to the English land owners, if in addition to the obligation of maintaining the poor on their estates Irish landowners were allowed to be free from a similar obligation. It is said that perhaps it would be a wise policy to keep landowners in Ireland in good humour with England by favouring them. I cannot accede to such a doctrine. An act of gross injustice to England can never be a good policy as far as England is concerned.

Guizot & his master Louis Philippe have put me out of sorts with politicks, all high principles seem to be lost sight of by those who call themselves statesmen, but Louis Philippe will as I hope & believe be caught in his own net. The Cracow business or iniquity it should be more properly called will I also hope meet with its deserts, trifling as it is to power gained it seems to be opening eyes to the chances of future robberies of more consequence.

My love to Henrietta   Your affectionate father

STANLEY OF ALDERLEY.

LADY STANLEY TO MRS. STANLEY

(187)   ALDERLEY *Feb 5th.*

Herring is the name of my dog doctor & he lives in the New Road opposite those collections of vases &

animals. I must tell you that I have been told Herring is sometimes disposed to say a *dog* is *dead* if it is valuable & not immediately inquired after when put under his care—but as you may only intend to consult him & not give up Lena to his tender mercies, or if you do as you will certainly require to see her corpse if he makes such a report to you, I do not think you need be afraid. I liked him very much & he was very reasonable.

Nothing very new in the Alderley world except that they say Girdy's voice is so entirely gone he will not be able to preach his farewell on Sunday.

(188)   ALDERLEY *Feb* 7/47.

Girdy found voice to preach his evening farewell. There was an over-flowing congregation—whether they assembled to do him honour or to enjoy the feeling that they saw & heard him for the last time I cannot say. He told a *lie* or two about the tithes, saying that he had nothing to do with the increase of them as it was all arranged and settled long before he came. The only thing he said which was to the point & proper to say was that if he had offended any he begged their pardons, & he was most willing to forgive all who had spoken ill of him. I was not there, could not have sat quietly through it I am sure.

(189)   ALDERLEY *Feb* 14th/47.

Just returned from Church & heard Mr. C's first sermon nothing could be better—just enough allusion to his new position & not a word *too* personal. Text

Romans Chap. 15 V. 30., & he laid a proper stress on the words *Strive with me*. He has not yet met with any Curate.

I heard from Major Deedes. He says the people about Clonmell are not *so* badly off as in many other places tho' bad enough & much distress had been occasioned or at least failed to be relieved by the shameful delay there was in paying the labourers on the Works. Near Ld. Lismore's, close to his park, he saw a gang employed on a road on whose features were depicted starvation & real misery. He asked them when they had been paid last—most of them said they had received 2/6 only for 20 days work & the overseer pointed out one man who had fainted from sheer exhaustion 2 days before. We have seen many more letters from other places with details too horrid to believe possible. Major Deedes says the prospect is fearful for the time between this & harvest, supposing seed *is* put into the ground.

I am sorry for Alice's, or rather *your* disappointment but I do not think you could expect a second season to be so successful as the first. There is a great deal in novelty & the wish of friends to introduce a débutante. I never expected A. would make her way like many & I doubt if one dance in Grosvenor Crescent would make much difference. I am afraid you will be obliged to bring her again out of Town without a husband which I *guess* you expected the first season. You had better make up your mind quickly, expect nothing—either husbands or partners but let her enjoy her dances as well as she *can* & as she *will* if she does not see you *too* anxious—for depend upon it she knows well all that passes in your mind, & very few girls dance a great deal at every ball they go to.

A horrid fog   Adieu   Yrs affecly M. J. STANLEY.

MRS. STANLEY FROM MRS. ADEANE, WHO
HAS LOST HER HUSBAND ABOUT A MONTH
PREVIOUSLY

(190)   BABRAHAM *June* 25 1847.

I have had so many letters I was obliged to write that I
have been able to write but little to those I cared for.
Mr. Pym & Mr. D. come on the 5th when I hope things
will be more settled, for till the will is proved no money
can be got.   It has been a long time owing to my confinement for things to go on unarranged—but it must
still be very long before all is new modelled as it must be.
I hope the little ones will go to the sea in August that I
may not have the whole family at home in the holydays
I do not think I could stand it.   Poor little tribe of
mourners it is indeed a sad lot to provide for.

It is very difficult to care for anything—all seems so
indifferent.   I am best in my own room, out of doors
all has lost its interest.

The girls hope to see yours as they go through London.

The pangs at times that strike through my heart are
dreadful but at others I can feel *really more* than resigned
I can rejoice in his safety & happiness, & thank God
it is I not he who has this sorrow to endure.

Your affec sister   M. ADEANE.

LADY STANLEY TO MRS. STANLEY

(191)   ALDERLEY *Aug* 21st.

I think I have not told you that the Bishop of N comes
on Wed. next week till Monday, but spends Sunday &
sleeps with the Cruttendens.   How pleased they will be.
He joins K & Catherine & they go to Havre, Caen &

Paris home on the 17th to receive the *singing* girl Jenny [Lind]—surely it is too comical.

Poor James it is a release to him—a memento to the *five*, nearly of the same age, who had gone on together in near connexion so many years—longer than the century is old, ourselves, Long, Moomie & James.

Ally is at Bourn Mouth & she likes the place very much, so quiet & good bathing & Poole, their post town, so primitive. She has the two eldest girls & the Gen. with her, says he is very happy tho' he can get no gossip at all.

We are much pleased with Henry's letter & very glad he has fallen in with Arabs & his writing improving will I hope soon slide into a free, gentlemanlike hand.

EDWARD STANLEY TO MRS. STANLEY

(192)   GLEN QUOICH[1] *Aug* 19/47.

There was a report at Liverpool when I arrived there that Louis Philippe had been shot dead at last but papers of a later date have arrived here so that there can be no truth in the report, though if they continue to persevere even Louis Philippe & a snipe may at last be brought down.

I hear they gave the Queen a great reception at Inverary & Walter Campbell brought over from Islay 150 naked savages to greet the Royal party.

I do not believe there would be much difficulty in getting Henry attached to the Embassy at Paris, but it will be time enough to consider the matter hereafter & in the mean time let him try to write like a Christian.

---

[1] The Ellices' shooting lodge.

MRS. STANLEY TO EDWARD STANLEY

(193)   COMBERMERE *Aug* 21/1847.

MY DEAREST OF LOVES

Had you been here you must have died of it so I must
even rejoice at being deprived of my soft heart.   The
house is a wretched lath & plaster affair tho' there is one
fine old room said to be the refectory.   The company is
El Conde with two followers his brother the Infante Don
Juan who came unexpectedly yesterday, Sir Baldwin &
Lady Leighton, Miss Bentinck, Miss Mainwaring, Sir
Harry's younger daughter, & ourselves.   Oh dear *how*
dull it has been the Spanish princes like dancing & even
old Ld. Combermere stood up—what shall we do
tomorrow Sunday.

I had made Alice a wreath of red geraniums & she
looked so pretty & so distinguée—tout à pure perte.
Verily such visits are awful affairs.
Later The Lake is a great resource & the Spanish
princes are wild about it.   I am so interested in a book
upon the epidemics of the Middle Ages.

Your affec wife   H. M. S.

EDWARD STANLEY TO MRS. STANLEY

(194)   GLEN QUOICH *Aug* 30/47.

MY DEAREST LOVE

The weather does not improve & the Queen will have
had a nice time of it.   I hear the footmen & servants
were running wild about the hills the night of their
arrival as the storm had blown down their wooden houses.

Albert is reported to have shot one stag & one dog
when he went out grouse shooting.

I bought a Terrier yesterday with a pleasant physiognomy, I found him on the road with a shepherd & got him at once.

What a shocking tragedy this seems to be at Paris, I hear the Duc de Praslin is a little chétif animal & the Duchesse a large powerful woman but they say he is certainly guilty though no sufficient motive appears as yet.[1]

Goodbye   yours affec: E. J. S.

(195)   GLEN QUOICH *Sept 8th/47.*

I got your letter from Penrhos announcing your arrival, but as I feared after a very rough & disagreeable passage. However I am glad to find you got safe through though I am quite sorry to hear you suffered so much.

I am afraid there is no chance of getting a small Scotch Terrier as they are all too large to jump on people's laps & the general breed in the country are very ill favoured beasties with harsh stiff hair & ugly faces.

What a complication of horror there seems to be at Paris & to crown all this dreadful tragedy of the Praslins. The eldest son is said to have destroyed himself—much still remains inexplicable.

I hear the Damers are quite done up, at least for the present, are going to let their house in town & go abroad.

MRS. STANLEY TO EDWARD STANLEY

(196)   PENRHOS *Sept.*

We feel very grateful for your tender thoughts of us on our passage.   I *know* you love me but it is very pleasant to see it sometimes.

---

[1] The Duc, apparently, murdered the Duchesse in the most horrible circumstances and committed suicide before he could be brought to trial.

We have heard this day that Mr. Davenport [1] died on the 9th he had never been so well since he went to hear Jenny Lind in Manchester—a very wild thing for him to do. It is a sad thing to see a man with such talents, benevolence & good principles pass away unlamented & unloved all from his fearful temper.

If you could get a cheap bracelet for Alice's birthday present it would be acceptable.

So you have had your love Lady Jocelyn,[2] well you have had a very dull time of it before so I do not so much mind, but I am beginning to get more weary than ever of my solitary autumns.

Lady Stanley though perfectly well in health does nothing but lament over the dullness & the length of the day; luncheon dinner & tea hours are continually changed to shorten time but that most inexorable of tyrants will keep on its even course & bed time is still as far off as ever. She had tried to get some people to dinner to eat the venison but has only been able to get the parson & apothecary. It is not lively but the place is better for interest than many, certainly than Winnington.

Theobald [3] is very anxious if he could to get a place of Queen's messenger for two or three years. If you thought there was any chance I would ask Lord Palmerston myself.

EDWARD STANLEY TO MRS. STANLEY

(197)   AUCHNACARRY [4] *Sept* 23/47.
The situation of Queen's messenger is not fit for a gentleman nor is a gentleman fit for a Queen's messenger.

[1] Of Capesthorne.
[2] *Née* Lady Fanny Cowper, a Lady-in-Waiting to Queen Victoria.
[3] Her brother, afterwards 15th Viscount Dillon.
[4] The Earl of Malmesbury's shooting lodge.

Induced by the good pay many are anxious for the employment who are idle & useless members of society & think they are notwithstanding good enough for the service of the country. I shd. think there would be no chance for Theobald even if I was to apply, at all events I shd. not like to do it & equally object to you doing so. His knowledge of French & Italian wd. go but little way in qualifying him as everyone knows French, & Italian is of no consequence.

I can hardly believe that Mr. Davenport has left 4000 a year to Mrs. D.—it is more than is necessary but she will make a good marriageable widow.

I am glad Charles Buller declined the Indian appointment as it would have shelved him & done him no good. His enthusiasm for Robespierre & apology for Marat are exaggerated, but Robespierre seems to have had the merit of honesty & integrity & have been sincere & consistent in his objects. Marat was a bloody butcher & I do not see what can be said for him.

The Castlereaghs arrived here last night, she still pretty & graceful but the mark on her mouth disfigures her & I am afraid they are disappointed at not having any children.

The Ashleys are expected here but what is to be done with Ashley [1] remains a mystery unless he gets up an agitation about the filth of Scotch cottages to which the worst abomination of the worst horrors is a joke.

I go to Breadalbane on Monday & I know nothing of who is there except Fox Maule & perhaps the Duchess of Montrose but I shd. be better pleased with her absence than her presence. I hear she goes out shooting & leaves the Duke at home.

This place is beautiful & only wants a sight of the sun

[1] Afterwards the great Lord Shaftesbury.

164

to make it delightful. Love to the children. Yr
affec   E. J. S.

MRS. STANLEY TO EDWARD STANLEY

(198)   PENRHOS *Sept 30th.*

We heard from Aunt Kitty about Jenny Lind at the
Palace, her reception was enthusiastic & she has won all
hearts.

I am afraid Mama is not well, Margaret says she frets
about a pain in her heart it makes me very uneasy.   She
is so very badly off for money—that worries her.   Charles
has let Ditchley very well only for the winter to a bachelor
for the shooting & hunting.

I am very happy in the prospect of being with you on
next 7th Oct. which you ought to remember is our
wedding day.

I will write tomorrow & leave a note at the Adelphi
on my way thro' Liverpool.

EDWARD STANLEY TO MRS. STANLEY

(199)   BLACK MOUNT *Sept* 28/47

I got here yesterday in time to go out with Breadalbane
but taking Duchesses on to the hill does not improve the
chance of success.

The house is quite full the D. & Duchess of Montrose,
the Seftons, Fox Maule & Arthur Kinnaird.   The
Duchess wears plaid trousers & short petticoat about
half way down below her knees.   She seems good
humoured & unaffected but I fear may cause that worthy
man the Duke some uneasyness as she is quite at home
amongst the hornéd beasts of the Forest.

(200) BLACK MOUNT *Sept* 30/47.

We had a splendid day yesterday & killed ten stags, three of them were brought to bay by the hounds & the Duchess shot them all with her rifle which has made a proud woman of her & a famous paragraph in the papers when Her Grace will probably find some observations on her dress as well as her pursuits.

The Duchess informed us of two marriages, Lady Dolly Walpole [1] & Mr. Nevill who she describes as a religious man with 8000 a year, an odd choice on his part unless he wishes for practise in conversion, & the other is Miss Leila Jones & Mr. Joliffe a young man of 20.

(201) FOREIGN OFFICE *Oct* 29/47.

I am sorry to say that affairs in the city are rather worse again there are rumours of more failures & the Funds have dropped again to nearly what they were before the temporary rise. Altogether the prospect is not pleasant & I am afraid there cannot soon be any material improvement.

I saw Mrs. Damer & the Clanricardes last night at the play. Lady Emily was not looking well & they are going out of Town.

(202) FOREIGN OFFICE *Oct* 30th/47.

I dined with the Clanricardes yesterday & went in the evening to Lady Palmerston who had had a dinner;

---

[1] As Lady Dorothy Nevill she became well known as a hostess and friend of Lord Beaconsfield.

there were the Jocelyns, the Ashleys, Mr. Broke the Rajah who seems the great Lion of the day & a pleasant & intelligent person. I think Lady Pam. has set herself to effect a marriage between Ld. Anson & Lady Emily de Burgh but they neither of them seem much disposed to promote the alliance.

I have no objection to your coming to Town when Parliament meets provided you leave the children in the country.

MRS. STANLEY TO EDWARD STANLEY

(203)   WINNINGTON *Nov 2nd*.

Thank you for your invitation to London it is not pressing enough to make me decide upon coming—if you *wished* for me I should not so much mind being away as then I should feel secure my place was not usurped.

Mrs. Smith Barry came to see me yesterday she is just returned from Ireland & gives a bad account of the people, so emaciated & the dysentery so bad.

(204)   WINNINGTON *Nov 5th*.

Poor Lena died at 2 this forenoon we never got any effect either from the castor oil or injections. She never moaned—the cause is quite a mystery. I have sent the body to Fleetwood that he may tell me & it is to be buried near Iser. I am very sorry to have lost my little pet that I had five years but I do not wish another dog, where is the use of preparing griefs for oneself—

I have put Demoniacal affairs in another note.

EDWARD STANLEY TO MRS. STANLEY

(205) FOREIGN OFFICE *Nov* 6/47.

Parliament meets on the 18th & one of the first discussions will be as to the admittance of Rothschild into the House & whether it is to be met by a resolution or by a bill is not I believe yet decided.

I only just got your letter by the afternoon post & am much grieved at hearing of poor Lena's death. I should think it will be found there is some internal injury.

I will pay your bill at Howell & Jones though it is an operation I detest.

LADY STANLEY TO MRS. STANLEY

(206) ALDERLEY *Nov* 6/47.

DEAR HEN

How poor Lena must have suffered, there was a large stone in the bladder—how it could be Fleetwood cannot guess. The whole of the inside was in a terrible state— I think it is surprising she did not show more signs of suffering. They say you wish her to be buried by Iser, I think Henry will not *quite* like it he seemed always to wish to have the place *sacred* to her but of course it will be done.[1] I know how very sorry you are tho' not a real general dog lover but she was so fond of you & you have given her so much nursing lately—she was an affectionate animal to those she liked.

I must send you Emmy's letter as I am in a hurry & you will be glad to hear both of her well doing & *prudence*.

I think the least expence must be considered in doing up the Pew the oak panelling should be examined—if it

· [1] Lena's grave stands alone.

is good certainly it would look handsomer (tho' rather gloomy) than paper.

EDWARD STANLEY TO MRS. STANLEY

(207)   F.O. *Nov 9th*/47.

MY DEAREST LOVE

This your last misfortune is indeed most grievous & puts all others in the shade. What can you have been doing to account for so juvenile a proceeding, it comes very opportunely to disturb all your family arrangements & revives the nursery & Williams in full vigour. I only hope it is not the beginning of another flock for what to do with them I am sure I know not. I am afraid however it is too late to mend & you must make the best of it tho' bad is best.

I do not understand which you wish now, whether to come by yourself or with Alice. When do you wish to start Blanche? Is it lawful to do so before being presented. To my mind it is not lawful until the elder sister is disposed of. Ld. P. goes to Windsor tonight & I have been very busy all day   Yrs affec   E. J. S.

MRS. STANLEY TO EDWARD STANLEY

(208)   WINNINGTON *Nov: 9th.*

DEAREST LOVE

A hot bath, a tremendous walk & a great dose have succeeded but it is a warning.

We suddenly thought we should like the music in the Octagon room & lo! in an hour it looked habitable & from henceforth we mean to make it our evg. room for our concerts, the singing sounds beautiful, also I do not hear the duets in the morg. A wee lamp in the gallery gives a mystery to the approach.

I feel not too well which makes me idle.

Your affec wife   H. M. S.

EDWARD STANLEY TO MRS. STANLEY

(209)   F . O . *Nov* 10*th*/47.

I hope you are not going to do yourself any harm by your violent proceedings, for though it would be a great bore it is not worth while playing tricks to escape its consequences. If however you are none the worse the great result is all the better.

I really think there can be but little object to bring Alice to Town just now for there can be but very few parties. As to yourself it might amuse you though with no Lady Dillon & no daughter you will find yourself like a new married lady just beginning the world.

I send you a story about Rothschild at the late City elections. After his return when he was thanking the Electors he repeated rather pompously that he was the choice of the People on which the mob called out " So was Barabbas." This story will I hope be acceptable to your anti-Israelitish feeling.

I am afraid the account of Walter Campbell's ruin is quite true, I know his debt was enormous & matters have been brought to a crisis by the famine of late years, for he received no rents & had to keep his people.[1] I am extremely sorry for him as is everyone.

Yrs aff   E. J. S.

---

[1] Walter Campbell sold all his islands to pay his debts. A very few years later immense mineral resources were found on them which made the fortunes of the White family, who bought them.

MRS. STANLEY TO EDWARD STANLEY

(210)   WINNINGTON *Nov. 10th.*

I was sure you would feel the same horror I did at an
increase of family but I am reassured for the future by
the efficacy of the means. Emmy is now advanced pros-
perously to a safe period having been in her bedroom for
the last three months—I wish one could sell one's
beginning to those who covet such things.

They have sent me from Alderley the stone found in
poor Lena, it weighs ½ an oz. I miss the dog very much
—I wish there was a child like her.

We have had the wretched Pedagogue down some
evenings but he has such a frightened imbecile manner
it is only from humanity we do it.

Is it true that Campbell of Islay is bankrupted for
600,000 how was he in trade ? I should be so sorry for
him.

EDWARD STANLEY TO MRS. STANLEY

(211)   LONDON *Nov 13/47.*

I saw Mrs. Damer yesterday, she has come up to Town
but goes away for a short time & returns a little after
Parliament, I suppose it will end in their remaining in
London.

The Queen will not open Parliament in person &
there is nothing very pleasant in the prospect before us
to make her very anxious to do so. The state of Ireland
is monstrous, worse than ever, neither life nor property
secure & in one respect different from all former occasions in there being no political feeling mixed up in the
outrages. I suppose strong means will probably be
found but I know nothing as yet for certain.

I heard today that Walter Campbell's debt is £750, 000 & that the whole estate will not pay it—how he managed to obtain such an immense amount no one knows. He has crossed to France & intends to remain some time at St. Malo.

I saw the Bishop of Norwich today who has come up to Town with his wife & daughter. I suspect he thinks he would have made a very good Archbishop [of York] but no Govt. can make Archbishops out of people who say there is more religion in Jenny Lind's fingers than in half the clergy of his Diocese. Dr. Musgrave has been elevated to the See because he has held his tongue, acted sensibly & will do no mischief. Hampden [1] however has none of these qualities & is I think an unwise appointment.

I will think about the money but your voracity is endless & the more you get the more you ask for

Yrs affec   E. J. S.

MRS. STANLEY TO EDWARD STANLEY

(212)   WINNINGTON *Nov 13th.*

I suppose I must say nothing tomorrow [to Lady Stanley]. At our time of life it is better not but indeed I do not feel a day older in the love I have for you, & even after my long experience that tenderness is not given to me I often feel my heart overflow with love & the hope of living some day together in a place that will allow us to share the same employments & pleasures. At present we are never together without the great world en tiers, rather a trial for any wife but we shall see what the tête à

---

[1] Just appointed, in the face of much opposition, to the See of Hereford.

tête we are to have will do. I cannot bear not going when you wish for me for fear anything should happen if I did not.

(213)   ALDERLEY *Nov* 29*th*/47.

The adhesive envelopes were from Asprey (late partner with Kennedy, now 166 New Bond Street) who has my die as above.[1]

I hope you did not feel any objection to Alice's sudden engagement, all the household was of opinion she should go, & she appears to have had a very pleasant evening & danced a great deal with unobjectionable partners, & had the amusement of seeing many quizzes as to dress among the Yeomanry wives & daughters. Sir Wm. Warre's son, & Charles Egerton were the most agreeable of her partners—the former has been far in America among the Indians & the latter could give an account of New Zealand so they had plenty to talk about.

We heard from Mrs. Hibbert that she seemed to be very well amused & looked very well. Nobody could have been turned out to better effect I am sure, her hair was so smooth & well done. She gives a good account of the Buchanan who we *think* is flirting *seriously* with Louisa Parker. He was at Birtles[2] when we dined there but there is such a bad style in that house I only set eyes on him at the dinner table—all the young ladies adjourn instantly after dinner to another room & all the young men pass thro' the drawing room the moment they leave the dinner table & the elders see no more of them.

[1] The address is never printed on the notepaper, which merely has a monogram.
[2] Seat of Mr. Hibbert.

MRS. STANLEY TO LADY STANLEY

(214)   GROV: CRES: *Nov* 29*th*.

MY DEAR LADY STANLEY

I am glad Alice was so well amused as she did go to the ball but I have, as well as her Father a strong objection to her going out without me or some very near relation. I do not admire the manners you describe at Birtles & should not like Alice to go there alone.

We had nothing very agreeable at the dinner at Lord Palmerston's—a dinner of 14 is too large for general conversation & nothing else is really agreeable. In the evg. I had a good deal of pleasant talk with Fonblanque who raves about Jane Eyre which I have not yet got. We got Arthur's sermons [on the apostolic age] what I have read I like & I think it well he has published something as his reputation is very indifferent, one man thinks him materialist, another neological, another pantheistical—I beg all to read his book. I wrote to Arthur to send a copy to Lord Melbourne, but at this busy time I fear that other statesmen will hardly have time

Yr affec dau: H. M. S.

LADY STANLEY TO MRS. STANLEY

(215)   ALDERLEY *Nov* 30*th*/47.

DEAR HEN

I suppose you will have many & full accounts of the irruption into the woods yesterday of the Trentham Hounds & of Blanche's great regret that she had not been there or she would have seen the spirited young man who alone arrived at the end of the chase, out of 36 in the field—I was so sorry Fleetwood did not learn his name—he was young & on a very fine horse. The huntsman was Maiden, Sir Harry's old one in Cheshire & he never expected to be brought to his old quarters again. The fox took refuge in the sand hole near Foxley Hill & went to earth in the sand which fell in & buried two of the hounds with him so that they were obliged to be dug out, but the fox could not be reached. Poor hounds ! They were ill rewarded for their gallant long run, 7 miles beyond Newcastle, for they found themselves in the midst of *traps* & some were caught but not much hurt & the huntsman was quite satisfied when he found F. never put poisoned bait—indeed I hope not.

I had heard the cry of the hounds, from the lawn & thought they were our Cheshire pack at first but was puzzled by hearing cries of pain which were afterwards accounted for. The gentlemen gave Fleetwood a sovereign for his trouble in digging for fox & hounds & they did not seem displeased at the traps, only one of the people said the Cheshire gentlemen were a shabby lot & did not pay gamekeepers high enough for preserving the foxes.

Mrs. Smith Barry fixed the attention of the ball room. I am sorry to say, for I had liked all I knew & had seen of her—her behaviour with Ernest Fane was *shocking*, both in her romping, polking & her aside flirting between whiles, her husband not there & her child ill at home

Yrs affecly   M. J. S.

MRS. STANLEY TO LADY STANLEY

(216)   GROV CREST *Dec.* 20*th.*

MY DEAR LADY STANLEY

I think you will be surprised to hear that Henry has become an official person. Lord Palmerston has most kindly appointed him Assistant Précis writer with the salary (£300) which Lord Anson cannot take, being in Parliament. This place has always been one most coveted for young men as it is the best opening into public life & gives them an opportunity of learning business— like habits, & they can show their ability if they have any by the way they do their work, which is chiefly to make abstracts of dispatches. I have not seen Edward so pleased with anything for a long time. I shall be most impatient to hear what you & Ld. Stanley think of it.

I saw Sir Brooke Boothby at Mrs. Damers—he is for Hampden & the Jews—there is a very strong reaction against the Roman Catholics from the villany of the Irish Priests—really that Mc Dermott deserves the pillory.

I am very sorry Mrs. Barry should be such a fool but I do not believe her to be any more—it is generally the consciousness of that which makes people act so very improperly. Poor giddy thing, she has not much in her but she is good natured & very fond of her husband & I am very sorry she shld. act as I hear. Yrs. affecly H. M. S.

LADY STANLEY TO MRS. STANLEY

(217) ALDERLEY *Dec* 21*st*

There can be no doubt what *we* think of it or how very glad we were to hear the news—there cannot be a better introduction to publick life, much better than attaché on many accounts. It is very flattering to Edward & some little also to Henry as I think Lord P. has seen him several times. As he is now *independant* I should suppose what we allowed him cannot be better bestowed than upon the education of the junior branches of the family & I hope it may induce you to think of sending Johnny & Lyulph to school, you will be glad of their room rather than of their company perhaps.

Mr. M.[1] is as *safe* a man I should think as could possibly be turned into a family of girls, but I cannot help thinking a family of young girls are better without a young man of any kind, tame in a house & *I* cannot quite admire Maud learning Latin of him tho' you may indeed laugh at his being an Abélard or Maud an Eloisa but it is a sort of bond of intimacy better disposed with, in my mind.

Rosalind comes while I am dressing & amuses herself very well—Algernon is *too dull* I can make nothing of him—no doubt he will be a profound *theologian*.

[1] The boy's tutor.

1 8 4 8

MRS. STANLEY TO EDWARD STANLEY

(218) ALDERLEY: *New Year's Day* 11 *o'clock.*
MY DEAREST LOVE

I must have a few words with you this night the first
of the year tho' I have had so much to do I am quite
tired.   Johnny had a restless night & was so weak he
fainted when he got up—so did Kate [1] but all picked up
enough to be able to be taken down to the Tree tho'
three came muffled in shawls.   Mr. & Mrs. Cruttenden
dined with us—the Tree was small & had no presents on
it, but the table looked very well, & everyone was pleased
with their share.

Henry will be with you in the afternoon he will dine in
Wilton Cres: & be ready to go to the Office on Tuesday.
Very impatient to see you   Yrs affecly   H. M. .S
Sir Edward Parry has come here with his three children.

LADY STANLEY TO MRS. STANLEY

(219)   ALDERLEY *Feb* 3.
We cannot make out if you had *two* dinners or only one,
e.g. if the dancing was at the Jews'.

---

[1] All the children had influenza.

178

I went to see Emma Mainwaring yesterday who was full of her intention to be delivered without knowing it. She has been collecting information from many quarters & been encouraged by several medical men as well as by Mrs. Middleton Biddulph who has practised it with the greatest success. Mrs. Russell is another. I think in her case she *appeared* to suffer, & screamed, but had no recollection of anything afterwards & recovered particularly well—but in general people wake in about 10 minutes after all is over in perfect ease & comfort.

Mr. Dean & Mr. Harrison of Chester who have both attended Emma in her confinements strongly advise her to try & I think she told me that Dr. Locock either had made use of chloroform or had expressed approbation of it as a boon not to be rejected. She has large children & always suffers very much in her labours. She expects in a fortnight, & had an alarm lately that it was all over, but by lying up hopes to go on. What a pity she & Emmy could not have changed lots—for Emma is as unwilling to have an addition as the other Em is anxious to begin a family. I think Emmy doing so well is in consequence of her system having been so much set up by Homeopathy, but I do hope she will keep to the common doctor next time.

I am glad you have seen as much of Maude, she is just what you say, *very* inconsistent about her children, totally without method & firmness in the management of them & I am afraid they will be great plagues to her.

(220)   A L D E R L E Y *Feb 9th.*

I shall be very glad to hear tomorrow that [Blanche's] pain is quite gone. I do hope you will not *indulge* either her or *yourself* in letting her go out unless you are

sure she is well, there is something wrong about her which
calls for the greatest care & watchfulness.   It is so vexatious just now & I don't wonder you are proud of showing
her, but do deny yourself the gratification.   I am glad
it was a comparatively quiet thing on Saturday.   I
daresay she did not look *awkward* from being shy, I have
much greater fear she will look *affected*.

I should have thought Lord Lincoln a bad subject for
experiments [1] & cannot imagine how any people can like
to make it a matter of amusement in parties, by experiments on animals.

Fonblanque has followed instructions & been very
civil to Mrs. Fry, [2] taken Mr. Cresswell's words I think,
nearly.   The Spectator is rather more satirical I think.
How can anybody say she was not a vain woman when
they read all the minutiae about the trifling civilities of
Kings & Queens—& can any rational judging person
not see the ridiculous & the humbug in all the calls of the
spirit to go to one or another scene of display, all along
seeing plainly she is neglecting her family ; & if she was
not blind indeed, must she not have felt, at every falling
off from the sect that she *might* perhaps, by a different
conduct, have kept them firm in what she thought the
right path.   Then how reconcile the universality of her
tolerance with her keeping aloof from the marriage &
baptismal ceremonies of her children, so *affectedly*
recording her *praying* aloof.   I must say I am astonished
you should have been so taken with the book tho' there
is much to admire in her character but chiefly where
she seems disposed to throw off the trammels of sect.
Sir Edward's fears seem to be more lest the *religious*
world should disapprove her views & liberality—I do

---

[1] With chloroform.
[2] " Memoirs of the Life of Elizabeth Fry," by her son-in-law, R. E. Cresswell.

not see why he should be afraid of any criticism on that head in the Q[uarterly] & Ed[inburgh] Reviews, I should doubt the latter taking any notice of her at all, the Q., you see, has given a short article to her.   Yrs. affecly   M. J. S.

(221)   ALDERLEY *Feb 15th.*

A very disagreeable circumstance has occurred here which will keep us in hot water for some time—a dog came into Fleetwood's yard & bit the large black dog Lion twice. Fleetwood was in the yard but never thought of the dog being mad & only warded him off from his Missus with a broom. The dog has been traced to several places & has bit a great many dogs, one at John Wyatts which went raging mad yesterday. Fleetwood says our big dog had no skin broken therefore he thinks he may be safe but of course he will keep him up closely.   I don't hear that any person has been bitten.

I should not think there is a very desirable society for Henry in the Authors' Club—I wish he could enter the Travellers. I should be very glad to hear of his going into society in an evening & talking to miscellaneous people— does he ever address a (young) lady ? However you should not mind *that*—much the most *convenient* extreme.

I have found in the library Arnold's Sermons of Prophecy, with notes. I like them particularly—they clear the subject very much in my opinion & they set aside the idea that, in order to fulfil prophecy, the Jews must return to inhabit the Holy Land. Rianette says this is Keble's view—but *not* hers—nothing will do for her but the return of the Jews to their own country, in the splendour they once had—but how she reconciles her ideas with the Christian World which has in fact taken the place of the Jews, as God's people, I cannot say & *do not care* as far as she is concerned—I daresay she is perfectly satisfied with her own opinions & they can do her no harm.   Yrs affecly   M. J. S.

I have got another word to say—& won't cross—I had only read the Examiner's Mrs. Fry when I wrote, but yesterday I finished it.   I think Cobden must have made use of a *fair friend* to induce Fonblanque to say all he has done in his favour.   My Lord was much exasperated at that & several other of his articles which he thought all in the wrong.   The Spectator is a far better paper & its criticisms very superior whether on literary or political subjects, but no wonder as to the former, now we know how they are *composed*, & I have heard just the same in regard to his [Fonblanque's] puffs for Lady Blessington, & that he would speak civilly of any work for a good dinner.   I wish you would cast him off.   Do you know the Editor of the Spec:

I have been reading Plunket [1]—how I do fume & splutter about the French—& *tremble* in every limb for the future—yet I *will* not doubt the spirit of the English nation, in spite of Punch, & Cobden's endeavours to crush it, should it ever come to a life & death struggle.

Think of the foolish Ridgeway family—it appears none of them were ever vaccinated any more than baptised. They did not live where they do now, when the boys were infants, & so never were included in one of my *batches*.

I must seal with black for Bell Way for fear I should forget I am in mourning when I write to Emmy.

---

[1] William, first Lord Plunket.   At this time there was a great agitation about the weakness of our defences.

(222)   ALDERLEY *Feb 20th.*

DEAR HEN,

It would seem you do not communicate your dispatches
to each other at breakfast.   In a letter to Ed: I mentioned
Harry Ridgeway's illness—I don't think it was then
known to be small pox but something very bad & he was
quite off his trapping ; & poor fellow since, in his
delirium he has talked so much of ferrets & traps & all
the difficulties he imagined relating to them.

Did you ever read of such diabolical characters as those
in Wuthering Heights ? In some really scarce a ray of
redeeming qualities & such women ! I cannot believe it
is by the same hand as Jane Eyre, or any one akin to that
author tho' the periodicals seem to wish us to think so.

I knew Leonora was Tasso's Leonora but am curious
to see how Ly. Boothby will treat *any* subject for a novel.
If the pamphlets on chloroform are not voluminous you
might order them at Bains for me, or any other tracts &
pamphlets you recommend as worth having on any
subject.

(223)   ALDERLEY *Feb 24/48.*

DEAR HEN,

I do not like chloroform for teeth, I have heard of
several cases where the experiment has been a very
disagreeable one for the bystanders, & Alice's preserving
a sort of consciousness throughout & being alive enough
to *talk* rather makes me believe more than I had done in
the account we read of some Edinburgh *experiences,*
where the young lady calls her dear Charles to come to
her arms—& elsewhere I have heard that it is very
desirable every body should have a friend with them &

one who *may* hear anything that *may* come out during these trances.   I think it a *cowardly* thing to use it for tooth drawing only, & dangerous perhaps for nervous people.   I think you certainly should not allow Blanche to try it.   It is a very curious discovery & most valuable in some cases, & doubtless there will be a great improvement both in the preparation of the chloroform & the manner of applying it.   I think the most extraordinary part of the business is this partial consciousness, & Uncle confirmed it by an instance he knew of amputation, where a man talked of the operation all the time, like one looking on, yet felt no pain.

Emma Mainwaring was delivered yesterday *without* chlo: & had the best & shortest labour she ever knew. She had been dissuaded from trying it—had she done so how they would have given all the credit of her good time to that.

The Episcopals leave us tomorrow for the Rectory *one* night.   It is said that Ld. Stamford was going to be married to his bed maker's daughter at Cambridge.

Yrs affecly   M. J. S.

(224)   ALDERLEY *Feb* 29/48.
I believe the French Revolution [1] has put out of my head to tell you Louisa & I are going to Delamere House today till Friday.   If you can write *tomorrow* pray direct there—your running news is such a treat.[2]

My Lord had said yesterday I wish Carlyle was in Paris that he might write the account of this Revolution, but from your account he may perhaps do it as well in

[1] Fall of Louis Philippe.
[2] Unfortunately from this time on there are practically no more letters from Mrs. Stanley to Lady Stanley.

England, for it is not the events, but his observations *on* them & manner of narrating which gives the value to his work. But for my part I daresay I should have been in a rage with him, as I had been with My Lord who enjoyed *shamefully* the desecration of the *throne*. *He* thinks only of Louis Philippe—*I* think of monarchy in general for which I have a much higher respect & regard than for a democratic & revolutionary republic.

No doubt there will be a series of revolutions whether the first established form of government is monarchical or republican, but *hitherto* the spirit of the people seems less ferocious than formerly. How La Martine speaks like his book—I don't *quite* understand why the red flag & ribband is adopted instead of the tricolor. This last was only adopted on compulsion by a Bourbon & the tricolor remains the standard of the first revolution as La Martine says. Pray tell us all you can learn of the poor emigrants, especially the Queen for whom I think everybody will feel.

(225)   ALDERLEY *March 5th.*

DEAR HEN,

I have written very little this week for really my visit to Delamere House was worse than nothing to write about—he is more prosy than ever & she is so behind-hand with the world in knowing nothing & caring less for nothing that is going on. Only think of it, the letters & papers are brought by an old woman—three hours after they might have arrived easily—& they all seemed quite indifferent about the matter.

I want anecdotes, not politicks or an account of the progress of the revolution which the papers give—but I

should think you must hear so many, from the many
people & foreigners you see. I hope there will not be
too much fuss made about Louis—let him sink into
oblivion which is the best lot for him.

How can you & Edward meet Cobden after that last
speech of his which I hoped had quite cast him down
from his pedestal & took away, in my mind, every mörsel
of good opinion from him—you do not say *where* you are
to meet him—is it Mrs. Grote [1]—who else can harbour
him ?

Major Kaye has married a woman without family,
fortune or beauty, very much to the discomfiture of Ly.
Amelia—but she is too kind hearted not to make the
best of it. We called to see her [from Delamere House]
which helped to fill up the day ; & chess always comes
to my relief.

I want a french newspaper for a little while & want to
know which is the best. I have a fancy for the National
from the extracts I have seen. I think I shall consult
Henry as he always patronises the foreign press.

Will there ever be a Bishop of Chester ? I thought
our Bishop was a little grumpy & referred it to disappointment of Archbishopric ; & he was so more than
ever *disloyal* in speaking of a certain lady that I thought
perhaps he might think *she* objected to him. Beg pardon
for crossing.   Yours affecly   M. J. S.

(226)   ALDERLEY *March 8th.*

I do not like to see people calling upon these exiles
as they do—there was a great deal too much fuss with
the ex King in Sussex. I think it is very *comfortable* after

---

[1] Wife of the historian of Greece.

all our alarms of invasion to see how *very* difficult it is even to land one small boat's crew & how a steamer may toss about before it reaches any English harbour.

Tell me stories of the foreign princes & princesses. The Infanta is quite right to reject her French alliance now it can do her no good—I wonder if she considers her husband a useless incumbrance.[1]

The émeutes [2] are not very alarming at present but there is a large party probably who will admire the advantage gained in France by confiscating the civil list & the crown jewels. But surely things cannot long go on so quietly there as they do now.

One of our old coach horses died yesterday—he had a fit & died very soon which I consider an advantage for now I *must* have another pair. We are going to Toft today till Sunday.

(227)   ALDERLEY *March* 10*th*.

DEAR HEN:

I liked my visit to Toft, Mrs. Leycester was in a very agreeable humour & not so lackadaisical as she is sometimes. Sir T. Arbuthnot was to have been there but of course could not leave Manchester, tho' we have not heard of any outbreak yet. I believe it is thoroughly understood there that if it should become necessary to order the soldiers to fire it will *not* be over the heads of the mob. His determined spirit is well known. In the last disturbance there, when there was a riotous meeting assembled in a large building of some sort, he planted a gun opposite the door, took out his watch, & sent word

[1] Duc de Montpensier.
[2] There was a small and unsuccessful Chartist rising at this time.

to the people that if the place was not empty in five minutes he should fire, & in three minutes it is said to have been clear.

The names of parents you mention who have children at Mrs. Walker's & are satisfied is a sure guarantee of her worth & competency to the business. I hope Johnny will not inform Master Wilberforce of his father's [1] various nicknames.

I was sorry to find that Algernon had had a feverish day yesterday—here comes Nightingale promiscuously, not sent for so I will go on to something else & insert Rianette's report afterwards.

We shall not be in Town certainly before the 27th, I am very anxious Emmy should stay [in Dover St.] for as long as the doctor wished her. From what K. said I understand she came to Town in a very weakening way —*never having stopped* & the country doctor had persecuted her bowels with aperient pills.

The report of Algernon as good as possible. Another of the Ridgeways caught the small pox & I am so afraid it will spread ; the people are so stupid, on enquiry I find several small children in that neighbourhood have never been vaccinated & some think it *too much trouble* to have it done now.

I had made up my mind to 140 or 50 for the horses, pray desire Clarke to look out in another week or ten days.

I suppose you heard the interesting anecdote of Nemour's [2] child left in the Tuilleries—What a pack of selfish cowards the royal family seem to have been, each only taking care of him or herself. I hope Louis P. will be délegué somewhere farther off than Claremont—

---

[1] The Bishop, usually known as Soapy Sam.
[2] Duc de Nemours, a son of Louis Philippe.

Holyrood House I heard named would not that do for
him ?   Yrs affec   M. J. S.

(228)   ALDERLEY *March* 12/48.
Emmy sends me a very indifferent account of herself,
but now she is taking bark I hope her strength will
return. From what she says she seems to be very much
as she was long ago, before she married. I am afraid
the trade she has started in is one that does not suit her.

Where is the use of laws unless there is somebody
appointed to see they are obeyed ? Three children in the
Welsh row were reported in the small pox, I called at the
door a week ago to ask the Mother about it & she said
it was only chicken pox. I saw one child with a very
spotted face & another lying on the settee. Four days
after we heard one child was dead ; Nightingale pronounced it small pox & upon enquiry found that 3
children had been vaccinated according to the law, but
it was the eldest child that died. Unless somebody
exercised *compulsion* in making the common people attend
the vaccinating days I am sure not one parent in a hundred would avail themselves of the opportunity. They
do not like the *trouble* in case the children are poorly
with it. Several children have been done this week &
more will be next for I shall look them out & insist
upon it.

I see by the papers that a regiment has marched from
Brighton to Norwich—so Uncle's *alarm* has perhaps
gained the advantage of some officers for the young
ladies—what a fuss he was in, going to the Home Office
& wanting to have a man of war stationed at Yarmouth.

What excellent articles there are in the Examiner now
—Fonblanque must have taken the reins quite into his

own hands I think—or else he has several very clever writers in his service.

I am very glad the girls enjoyed their ball so much. I am sure Blanche would thoroughly—Alice always takes things quietly & the novelty is passed with her. I should like to see Blanche in full swing. Adieu.

Yrs affec.   M. J. S.

(229)   ALDERLEY *March* 14*th*.

Algernon & Rosalind have been out twice & much better for it, but their legs do look so long & their arms so small. South West today & bright sun.

I gathered up six children yesterday for vaccination— Nightingale has been so stupid about it all. I had no trouble in persuading the woman at The Haggs to bring her 2 children or any other person. One of The Hagg inmates is in great disgrace & I shall probably send him about his business—John Ellam has thought proper to get a donkey to carry Nanny's washing home, which lives in the lanes, moreover he is accused of getting fern & heath at night from the Edge.

I have written every day on account of the chicks, I don't think I shall tomorrow if they go on mending.

Yrs affec.   M. J. S.

(230)   ALDERLEY *March* 19/48.

DEAR HEN:

I am sorry as Edward has consented he will not do it handsomely & take an interest in it—Blanche says it is a taboo subject with him. I really shall be sorry & think I have done a wrong thing in giving our aid to what he very much disliked, for more than expence which he told me he did, but added (which gave me encouragement) that as I had said, the wishes of his people were strong & the example of recent revolutions dangerous—which satisfied me that he had taken it good humouredly as a *hard necessity* that he could not avoid.

If you talk of white soups, chickens & cucumbers I am afraid the 20£ will not near hold out—for I cannot help you in kind scarcely with rabbits—for those Fleetwood gets are not good, with young or *nursing* but he shall try. You will remember white soup takes cream as well as stock. We have nothing like a cucumber & no chickens or fowls of any sort. When *we* had what I thought you meant by a thé dansant & not a downright ball we had only tea, bread & butter, cakes & sandwiches with some wine & ices. But I suppose you will smuggle something out of your private hoard. If you want some inferior white wine for cup I think we might spare you some out of our cellar & there is some champagne, not fit for dinner company which, if it was only dull & not sour *might* perhaps, with icing, make a figure on such an occasion. The sherry would certainly do for what you mention & it would be a pity to use Gordon's for negus or cup.

I wonder who you will fix upon for Lyulph—I have a prejudice in favour of Seawell from all we heard from Henry, but that is long ago & all institutions are liable to decay.

Let me know if you want the inferior wine & I would send you the cellar key & have no objection to do so.

Yrs. affecly M. J. S.

(231)   ALDERLEY *March 26th.*

I am not *surprised* for I know you are not *particular* as to your acquaintance, provided they are *fashionable*, but I am *sorry* that Mrs. Montjoy Martin shld. be on your visiting list now you have daughters grown up & out. However I daresay she is not worse than many others, & that *they* (the girls) are quite innocent of knowing her character, tho' I think they must be pretty well acquainted with the fashionable world & what it is composed of.

I am very glad to hear how well E. takes to the business. I said nothing of quantity as to the wine wishing you to take as much as you wanted. *If* the champagne *can* be used it is a famous opportunity which may *not* recur & there is plenty of that sherry you know *you* will not drink at luncheon *if* you can get better.

Is Clarke making inquiries for me about horses—I shall be on the pavé when we get to Town without.

I have got the " National ", there are very ugly articles in it today about England. I suppose a french paper cannot be sent free by post like an English one. Can it ? or I should have liked to send it you.

[The whole family now adjourned to London for the summer, during the course of which Edward Stanley was given a peerage, taking the title of Lord Eddisbury of Winnington.]

LADY STANLEY TO LADY EDDISBURY

(232)   ALDERLEY *July 23rd.*

Imprimis—because I shall forget it if it is not put down while in my head—send me all my keys except the jew: box.

EDWARD STANLEY
FIRST LORD EDDISBURY, SECOND LORD STANLEY OF ALDERLEY

2ndly. Here is a fine warm day, the first I have had &
it is very enjoyable.

3rdly. I wish you would remain with Edward & send
me Alice & Blanche I should be very glad to have them
& I am sure they have been exhibited enough for the last
six weeks (twice a day at least) for any good purpose
London is expected to answer, & it would be excellent
for them to be turned out to grass & simple pleasures.
If I were you I should certainly be very unwilling to
leave Edwd. & London in these busy times one day
sooner than quite necessary.

We rejoice in the energy that has carried through the
Irish bill in one day & in the active measures Lord C.
[Clarendon] is taking & the stronger ones he will be now
enabled to take towards crushing the rebellion in that
unfortunate country.

I congratulate Ly. Dillon on the well doing of her two
children—& *you* in having attended upon the lady—I
was with dear Bella,[1] the only labour I ever witnessed, &
I am sure I felt I had much rather be the performer than
the spectator. It is a very disagreeable affair however,
anyhow, & I rejoice Ly. D. is relieved from this anxiety
which was hanging over her & that she has not had a
couple of pair of twins, considering the size of the ladies.

I have many more observations to make but have other
letters to write so adieu

Affecly yours   M. J. Stanley.

(233)   Alderley *Aug 13th*.
Dear Hen,

I cannot impress upon you too strongly the great
necessity of watchfulness over Johnny's actions, & the

[1] Lady Parry.

articles he supplies himself with for his amusement & the injury of others. He had got somebody to make him a *pike* as he called it—tomorrow I shall make a close enquiry to find out who could have been so blamable, but a more dangerous weapon I never saw—& luckily he tried it first upon John [Louisa's groom] & not upon Lyulph, flourishing it in his face in the offices (as he was looking for Clark to prevail upon him to put it secretly in the carriage). John put out his hand to save himself & it was very much hurt by the *three* sharp pointed little *daggers* that were inserted into the stick. I keep it to show you the first opportunity, they were more pointed than any nails & I cannot imagine how they were put in, the ends that are out being so sharp—it is a most fortunate thing it was seen & taken from him before more mischief was done. It makes me shudder to look at it & think he meant to take it among the young children. He is more than mischievous or he would never think of such a weapon. Pray take *preventive* measures or you will repent it—Lyulph's *nose* would not have required a plaster if you had taken away the *sword* the day before when the danger was pointed out to you.

Yrs. affecly   M. J. S.

Of course I do not mean he *intended* to hurt John—no doubt it was play but such play & with such a weapon !

LADY EDDISBURY TO LORD EDDISBURY

(234)   WINNINGTON *Aug* 14/48.

MY DEAREST LOVE,

Johnny was not very well yesterday but is today as riotous as usual. I had a long letter of a discovered

enormity today from Lady Stanley—he had had a spear
made, Ly. S. thinks he *meant* to hurt someone—I think
it was only his usual mischief.

Lady Stanley has decided upon going to Penrhos the
24th & Alice & Blanche go with her as she thinks it dull
with only Louisa. I am sorry to be without them but I
think they like the local of Penrhos best so I give them up
& shall have all the smaller house.

We have lovely weather, it makes this shabby old place
bearable. Blanche tells me there are bronze candlesticks
at 5/– a pair in the Lowther arcade, I wish you would
get them for me   Ever yr. affec. wife   H. M. E.

LADY STANLEY TO LADY EDDISBURY

(235)   ALDERLEY *Aug 16th.*

DEAR HEN,

I was extremely surprised when I found Dumoile had
given Johnny such a weapon I never could have imagined
he was such a fool for if it *was* for the purpose of spearing
fish, as the boy said, any body with common sense wd.
see the impropriety of helping him to such an amusement
as dangerous from leading him to pond sides. But
Johnny was thoroughly well acquainted that such
weapons would not be allowed—for he had got his
brother's spear with which he had torn the housemaids'
gowns in hunting them upstairs & Pearce had watched
for & found it, hid it in the shrubs, taken it away &
locked it up in the store-room, & after this he got this
weapon made, *quite* aware that you would not allow it.
Upon this discovery I made farther enquiries into his
conduct & Fleetwood, when I asked him, at once said
he had never met with such riotous, unruly boys & that

he should not have taken them out again without speaking to you—that he was so frightened by their behaviour that he was obliged he said, to be master, & could not succeed in being so till he had flogged them both. I suppose he meant a few thumps. When Johnny went to look for him he made such a riot in the house, throwing everything about, he thought all in the house would have been broken to pieces. I believe they were equally troublesome at Moomie's tho' she does not like to be accuser, seizing her axe, throwing about the coals, stuffing up the spout of the pump & cutting her flowers. Johnny is the torment of everybody in the house, they say Lyulph imitates everything the other does. It is quite right you should know all this, for if nobody will complain how should you. I daresay *you* do not know Johnny uses very bad language. I do hope you will require your servants to report the truth, however unpleasant, if the young gentlemen continue so boisterous —it will be the only way to check them. I was very sorry we could not keep it from My Lord's knowledge for he took it very much to heart—pondering over the character so displayed. There will be some catastrophy if those boys are together alone & unwatched.

I wonder in what almanack you found that Monday was the 19th—was Ed. to come down Saturday or Monday—you said *Monday the* 19th.

Yrs. affec.   M. J. S.

LADY EDDISBURY TO LORD EDDISBURY
(236)   WINNINGTON *Aug.* 16th.
MY DEAREST LOVE,

It is impossible I think to find a much naughtier boy than Johnny, his mind is filled with filthiness

& evil speaking. He swears, says every improper thing he can think of to his sisters & glories in all the beastliness he has learned in Gulliver. He will do nothing in the way of work & it will be a mercy if he does not seriously hurt some one when in his rages.

Henry seems cloué to London by the interest he has in public matters.

I am afraid there is no gainsaying the truth of it being wiser [for economy] to give up our visit to Rhyl & I have put it to Maud in that way but it is a disappointment to us all for we all like the sea side better than this place. However it may enable us to leave Wing: when the cholera comes, &, good out of evil, I shall have money to pay the bills here.

I wish you would get me any information you can about the gratuitous Emigration—I have a protégé here just suited for it. He is 14, strong, active, becoming the best character for honesty & truth, & the boy has not slept in a house for 6 years but only in winter in the salt works. He is the sharpest creature I ever met with at the same time the most completely ignorant. His anxiety to learn to read is so great he has learnt the alphabet in 4 days. They wanted a boy to weed in the garden & he has worked there very well. I have got him some clothes which will be paid for by his wages, for I do not wish to take him from his self dependance, but if I saw any chance of his emigrating he cd. go to school. He is a very interesting boy & *not* an Irish man.

Yrs. affec.   H. M. E.

Do not put off sending me money.

197

LADY STANLEY TO LADY EDDISBURY

(237)   ALDERLEY *Aug 22nd.*

We have had such a stormy morning, everything in the garden blown to pieces, Louisa in despair over her geraniums on the walls.

You mentioned slightly a wonderful outcast you had met with, highly interesting, a sort of Orlandino I supposed—but you did not say you had made a pet of him & put him in the gardens, so pray tell me something more of the case. Have you carried your philanthropy so far as to lodge him in the house—I hope he will not take to crook-ed ways as I hear his name is Crook.

The General is at Inverness I think Ally must quake for his rheumatick tendency.

What charming touring & sketching weather for a party without their own carriage & *no* man servant, which is Mrs. Hibbert's case. How she could undertake such a tour I cannot think.

Is your change of plans caused by the low state of your finances ? Have Edward's fears of being dry at the banker's caused it ? Having advanced the 500 we can do no more for you now, but you may look forward to 100 for the boys when the rents come in. We must have money enough in Gosling's hands to pay all the allowances & interests we have to pay.

LADY EDDISBURY TO LORD EDDISBURY

(238)   WINNINGTON *Aug 30th.*

MY DEAREST LOVE,

Johnny is naughty as ever, I have just now been obliged to bring him in, having made Kate's nose bleed.

He is more insolent than anything I ever saw.   Pray
pay his school bill as it is most stringent etiquette to do
so before he returns.

As to your movements, if it is your convenience to
come by Winnington I shall of course be glad to see you—
if you come this way from a wish to see me or Lyulph
I shall feel flattered but do not come to *please* me inde-
pendantly of yourself.   I cannot wonder you shld. shrink
from even spending one day in this place for a more
odious disagreeable one I suppose all England does not
offer.

I heard from Alice the journey to Penrhos was tedious
& the girls had their carpet bag exchanged for another
belonging to a man & without a direction.

I have borrowed all the money each individual has in
the house to pay Clarke.

The Ashburtons do not seem the better for their
accession of wealth, then they never knew what it was to
be poor.   I can trace *all* the troubles of my life to want
of money, not for superfluities or fancies, I do not ever
think of them, but for things essential to that position in
which we are placed.   Certainly having a sufficiency of
money appears to me at present the ne plus ultra of
happiness & as far as I am myself concerned esteem
bodily pain very slightly in comparison, but we cannot
choose & doubtless the real secret of happiness is in
contentment with our lot whatever it may be—but that
contentment cannot exist if there is not love & sympathy
from those from whom one has a right to expect it.
The weather is very fine   Your affecate   H. M. E.   I
advise you to read The Discipline of Life.[1]

[1] By Lady Emily Ponsonby, 1817–1877, daughter of the Earl of
Bessborough.   She wrote sixteen novels, most of which were published
anonymously.

LADY STANLEY TO LADY EDDISBURY

(239)   PENRHOS *Sept 9th.*

DEAR HEN,

I am very sorry I was so *hasty* as to bestow my 40£ on Edward for a horse before he had got one—he might have recollected he pocketed the money & let you have it for the sea side—or if I had it still in *my* pocket you should have had it.

I am rather surprised that you should have liked The Discipline of Life so well & especially that you recommended it to the girls—Alice might read it safely enough & pass as cool a judgement on it as I have done, but to Blanche the all powerful influence of love, & love at first sight too, has a mischievous effect & *she* likes the book extremely.   It is more like the work of a clever girl of 18 than a stayed virgin of 40.[1]   She certainly *intends* to prove that it is most desirable & proper to regulate feeling & to act on principles but in reality she holds up to ones view that it is next to impossible not to give way at once to every fresh impression.   Isabel & Col. Maxwell would have been in *great danger* even had they been married & by way of contrast to Clarice, Ly. Emily has made such a fool of poor Evelyn, & of her governess, that it is not wonderful Col. M. should like a woman with more mind & equal beauty when he met with such a one.   Everybody will say I am sure that Ly. E. must have had some very severe disappointment—if not I am equally sorry for her that she should *not* have experienced the warm passions she can describe so forcibly & feelingly.   I wonder how you would like the Bee Hunter I was carried on by the interest of the story tho' the missionary is very absurd.

[1] Actually she was 31.

How illnatured of the Q.[1] to slip by all the places where they wished to show her honour by illuminations & fireworks without giving notice of her being near.

Yrs. affecly   M. J. S.

LADY EDDISBURY TO LORD EDDISBURY

(240)   WING: *Sept. 13th.*

MY DEAREST LOVE,

Lady Stanley still hoops at you not having bought a horse with the £40 & says she would have given it to me to go to the sea.

We returned here yesterday & if we much prefer the exterior of Alderley certainly the indoors of this place is far pleasanter to us all.

Your Father is very well but more testy than he used to be & Rianette is more of an old maid than ever.

Aunt Georgiana came yesterday, she is not much of a companion but it is such a comfort to her to have a gîte & she is so fond of all the children that I am very glad to have her.

The girls do not seem to have very good weather at Penrhos & I do not think Louisa seems too amiable. The new horse she has got for her groom does well to carry a lady, but she did not relish Lady Stanley's proposal that Alice should therefore ride one of her horses sometimes. Alice says that in many ways they seem to forget that they are no longer babies.

Charles [2] is much better. Inflammation in the lungs turned to abscess in the bladder. It might, Seymour says, have produced paralysis & that another such attack must be fatal. He was on his way from Cowes

---

[1] Queen Victoria went to Balmoral on the *Victoria and Albert.*
[2] Lady Eddisbury's brother, Viscount Dillon.

to Ditchley but the illness seized him on the R.R. & he went to bed in London.

I heard yesterday that there *has* been cholera in London. I have ordered some opium & black pepper pills which were recommended by an Indian Officer in the Times & am trying what I can do with the people to cleanse their dirt holes. I have met with a very useful publication The Family Economist, a penny mag:—all in my line about ventilation & emigration & such like philanthropic pursuits.

I shall be jealous if you meet the Duchess of Montrose at the Forest. What a long well written letter I hope you are properly grateful for it. I think of you the last thing each night can you say the same Jeanot?

Ever your own H. M. STANLEY.

LADY STANLEY TO LADY EDDISBURY

(241)   PENRHOS *Sept. 13th.*

DEAR HEN,

How unfortunate the poor Boothby's are—Cecil has been shot in the eye at Lord Craven's & the utmost hope that is allowed is that he *may only lose that* eye. Ld. & Ly. C. are great friends, very much attached to him. They have got all the sisters there besides Sir Brooke & he has had the best advice, Hodgson from Birmingm & Laurence from London. Muff is in great distress, indeed they all are for they idolize this brother particularly.

I think it would be better for Jem Crook to go to school for a time which *I* should think *much* more desirable than

that Maud should turn schoolmistress to a boy of 14.
I cannot admire such a pet for a girl of Maud's age. I
am very willing to help you in your benevolent scheme
for the poor boy & to give you the 3/– per week to keep
him at day school. I have always intended writing to
you about him but had forgot it until Alice told me this
morning that Maud was his chief instructress.

I wish they, Alice & Blanche, were not here, they cheat
me of a proper quantum of your letters & are not very
free in their communications, & I have often thought you
show so much how you miss them that it was almost to
be regretted they came.   Yrs. affecly   M. J. S.

(242)   PENRHOS *Sept. 20th.*

DEAR HEN,

Your account of Jem is really very interesting & I am
particularly pleased with his in-aptitude in comprehending
Original Sin & the very cute sensible reasoning reply he
made to you when labouring this very *ticklish* doctrine—
which I am as slow to receive as Jem can be. It is very
clear there is a most distinct difference from birth in
different children, so much so that I am almost ready to
believe that some are *predestined* to a greater *struggle in*
life agt. the evil spirit than others by a greater degree of
evil in their natures, while some favoured beings are sent
into the world guiltless till they are taught what is wrong,
even then making their way with ease free from violent
passions or *innate* wickedness. Pray get Jem a pair of
trousers for me.

We have no right to complain of the weather after 3
such glorious days but don't you think we *do* complain,

having appointed to go on board the Affonso[1] at 12 o'clock & since breakfast the rain has come down in the most determined manner.   Louisa & Alice found out the arrival of the said Hero of the Navy when they rode to Holyhead yesterday, Louisa of course was in the 7th heaven of excitement & Alice not much lower.   They had been as near the vessel as they could, on the shore, & at all events they have brought away an idea of her & seen the boats which did such noble duty in the hour of need & horror.   Yrs. affecly   M. J. S.

LADY EDDISBURY TO LORD EDDISBURY

(243)   WING: *Sept. 23rd.*

MY DEAREST LOVE,

What a bad wicked woman that Mrs. Norton is [2]—I am sure she is always false & wishing to do someone a mischief—I hope she will not be allowed to molest poor Mrs. Herbert.

Alice has written a very good letter describing their visit to the Affonso.   It seems Blanche danced the polka with a young Lisboa.   They came in for the giving of the medals, some struck on purpose " a woman holding up her child to the poop of a vessel " & " Lord save us or we perish " ; 4 medals had been sent to some particularly brave fellows—unfortunately one had since deserted & so lost his medal.

I have got emigration circulars & ventilation tracts & am amusing myself in that way.

---

[1] Brazilian steam frigate whose crew had a short time before behaved very gallantly in saving many lives from the *Ocean Monarch*, which caught fire off Liverpool.

[2] Granddaughter of Sheridan, sister of Lady Dufferin and the Duchess of Somerset.

I am very sorry I ever said anything about myself, when one is not understood it is better only to deal in generalities & I shall not mention myself again as it only gets me unpleasant rebukes & you forget that a harsh letter from you colours my whole day.

Yrs. affecly   H. M. E.

LADY STANLEY TO LADY EDDISBURY

(244)   PENRHOS *Sept. 24th.*

The young ladies, including Louisa, are subsiding. They watched the departure of the Affonso in the morning (& were serenaded by the band) seated below the battery. The three days have been very enlivening & I wish you had been there but you *must* lend your help to get some of their *heroes* to Alderley & young [name illegible] too who seems a very *nice young man* & the Queen of Portugal has been graciously pleased to grant the reversion of his father's rank of Vicomte to him, which the old Corvo told me was a great favour—titles not being hereditary in general.

Lisboa is innocent enough being rheumatic & deaf but very gentlemanlike & there would be no harm done by Lucco & Teïve in 2 or 3 days.

I shall stay till the 8th but there will be an excellent opportunity for the girls to return a few days sooner for the Bishop will come on the 2nd for 3 days & he could escort them to Chester. I do not think they could go *alone* with their maid & without a man to take care of them in the passage of the Menai.

Yrs. affecly   M. J. S.

(245) PENRHOS *Sept. 27th.*

DEAR HEN,

We expect William & Ellin tomorrow.

I have *nearly* come to the conclusion that *necessaries* are not only *un*-necessaries but increasing the evils you deprecate—unless there was a power exercised to oblige owners & *do*-ers to empty them every three months at least. The open air, which is certainly the favourite locale in Holyhead soonest disperses the effluvia. Instead of not being interested in your sanitary & educational expeditions I assure you I rejoice in them & I think you may be more successful in the latter than the former, but in *both* you may do a great deal of good. In this very instance you see the difference between a gentleman builder & owner & a mercantile one. If these houses had been built by his Lordship every one would have had his *petty*, at all events dividing the odour & also having a chance that *some* of the occupiers would clean out—but a *common* occupation is nobody's business, unless the owner of all the buildings takes it in hand.

Out of pure regard for you I have read several articles in the Times relating to poisoning the Thames by the filth of London sewers—there are *plausible* observations, but as one part of the argument states that the lowlands of Essex are *at present* full of stagnant ditches, I cannot understand what advantage, in such case, can ensue from bringing all London's sewers to aboutir at that point. Poor Essex seems poisonous enough already, in the dispositions of its inhabitants—

I must tell you of a most ridiculous report which the girls are *very* anxious should *not* be repeated to Henry— that he is going to be married to Miss Greville. Blanche says she is *so* young & has scarce seen Henry unless he

has been *sly* since you left town—not very likely. *Can*
you trace it to *any* the slightest foundation ?

Yrs. affecly   M. J. S.

(246)   WINNINGTON *Sept. 26th.*

MY DEAREST LOVE,

I congratulate you on having killed your deer.

The girls seem to have been highly delighted with the
Brazilian heroes as they call them. They had all been up to
Penrhos & had gone out, with Louisa as chaperone in a
boat besides walking about alone so I was not sorry to
hear of the Affonso having left H.H. for Liverpool
where she remains 3 months. Lady Stanley seems very
sorry that William & Ellin do not come & now wd. have
liked to have me there—I certainly would have had no
idea of going all that way for 10 days & I do not doubt
I shd. have been considerably bored with all the fuss
they have made over all their Lions. This odious month
is nearly over.

I agree with you about Mrs. Norton, she always looks
patte de velours, & I would almost believe that the tears
she shed about her son, & which made me so soft to her,
were false.

Yesterday I did a good days work & persuaded parents
to send 12 children to school. One woman who was
keeping a " chance child " from charity, a fine boy of 9,
said she would like to send him but cld. not afford 2d a
week as she paid 1d for a burial club for him " poor
fellow he was so desolate like in the world & it was
comfortable to be sure to be well buried ". But all this
will bore you in the midst of your fine ladies—but it is

the thing I care for most, I mean the amelioration of the working classes.

I hear it reported that Lord Burghersh is to marry Miss Locke [1]—she is barely Maud's age & very lovely.

Emmy is in London to stay there until her confinement in March.

I dream of you all night   Yr. affec. wife   H. M. E.

LADY STANLEY TO LADY EDDISBURY
(247)   PENRHOS *Oct. 1st.*
DEAR HEN,

Tho' you say how much you wish to have the girls before the end of this week you have not *particularly* answered what I said of the great unfitness of sending them with only their maid.   I fully expect Uncle will not stay with us longer than Friday which would do very well, but in case he did not go so soon I wish to know if you wish them to be sent off with their maid *earlier*.

You seem to think I want them which is not the case, any part of the time, but for their own advantage & pleasure.   But as *I* think the maid an unfit one even as their maid only (I think you cannot know exactly what sort of woman she is) of course, without your positive order I cannot think of sending them off before unless it was with the Bishop.   Yrs. affecly   M. J. S.

LADY EDDISBURY TO LORD EDDISBURY
(248)   WINNINGTON *Oct. 1st.*
MY DEAREST LOVE,

Moomie came here this morning she thought the change might do her good—it is a great pleasure to me

---

[1] He did so in 1849.

to be able to be of use to her & I think she enjoys being here.

So the cholera is now at Hull.

I enclose a letter from Johnny—I am sorry he should be so caned.

If I have ever been cross in my letters to you, about you not returning home, do not mind it. It is when I have been ill & low but I am now better.

Yr. affec.   H. M. E.

LADY STANLEY TO LADY EDDISBURY

(249)   PENRHOS *Oct. 3rd.*

What a diet you are put upon ! *No* drink but cold water, morning noon & night ! Life is not worth having on such terms—I hope it is not to last long.

The number of visitors Emmy will have this week will be rather a trial—the more glad she will be to see them all the worse for her perhaps but she will indeed be very glad to see so many as have met in London.

I am more than satisfied that it would be very improper to send young women alone—the Bishop was squeezed so in an omnibus with company *he* did not quite like & it would have been very awkward for girls without a protector.

LADY EDDISBURY TO LORD EDDISBURY

(250)   WINNINGTON *Oct. 9th.*

MY DEAREST LOVE,

Your letter I received this morning made me so very unhappy. Indeed you are very careless & unkind, & if you knew how unwell I am I think you wd. come. Dr.

Lee says I am very weak. The Cholera is rife at North-wich. I wish you would come home & you know how I hate you going to the Duchess of Montrose. I believe you only do it to vex me. I shall now have been two months alone so pray come home & do not make me unhappy.

Emmy has been near dying with a miscarriage but was better when I last heard.

Pray come soon you don't know how low I am

Yr. affec. wife   H. M. E.

6 *O'clock*. A merry tea drinking, 107 girls of the National School all good—they are walking home to the tune of We shan't go home till morg:. Nice sensible people & I have seen so many happy faces I forgive you.

LADY STANLEY TO LADY EDDISBURY

(251)   ALDERLEY *Oct.* 13*th*.

DEAR HEN,

I am surprised at not hearing from you today & con-clude therefrom that I have won my 6d from Blanche & that Edw. is not returned—

There was a poaching battle on Wed. afternoon between three men in Chorley, Harry Ridgeway & his dog. The poor dog was shot for the second time & Harry very much beaten & jumped upon. The dog's ear was shot off but they hope he will recover. Harry seized one of the men by the help of his dog & the others ran away, but finding that nobody came to his assistance returned & ill used him as I have said. Harry would not allow that he was rash in attacking three men—they killed & picked up some partridges in his sight & he said he *could* not stand *that*   Yrs. affecly M. J. S.

(252)   ALDERLEY *Oct. 17th.*

I think you will like to see Aunt K's account of Emmy. It seems a rational explanation of failure but will it not always be the same thing?

Lucy started from Chelford yesterday in company with Dr. Holland's son who was just returned from O'Brien's trial & was before that in Norway consequently he would be only *too* agreeable as talking is not very pleasant in a R.R. carriage.

The poor dog is still living—the Ridgeways are so very unwilling to part with him but Fleetwood says his shoulder is shattered & if he recovers he can never be of any use.

[The Eddisburys and all the children spent the last ten days of October at Alderley, after which Lord Eddisbury left for London.]

LADY EDDISBURY TO LORD EDDISBURY

(253)   WINNINGTON *Nov. 3rd.*

MY DEAREST LOVE,

The house is fearfully cold & full of wind.

Mrs. Hostage tells me they want to establish a dead house at Northwich for the instant removal of the bodies.

What a bore for W. Cowper[1] & Miss T. your being on the train, poor people. It is very pleasant to be making love & it is desperate cold sleeping alone these bitter nights.   Your affec. wife   H. M. E.

1 The Honble. William Cowper married Miss Tollemache as his second wife on the 22nd November, 1848.

(254) WINNINGTON *Nov.* 7th.

MY DEAREST LOVE,

We have a bright beautiful day that cheers ones heart.

I rejoice in my children & thank God I am placed so as to have all my energies called forth in such a heart filling work. Your mother said I ought to have done greater things considering the time & thought I have spent on education but it is not given to us to judge of what good is done at so early a time & I do think each in their general capacities are improving. I am most unhappy about Maud who has such a discontented spirit that she told me yesterday she wished she was dead. It is very sad to see temper spoiling these happy young years. There goes Blanche singing along the house she is perfectly happy tho' perhaps there is a little too much expectation in her happiness—Alice has just passed by the window with her child Kate. She too is brimful of womanly feelings, but they take the maternal line & I doubt if in her dreams the lover is not lost in the father of her darlings. And here am I pouring forth all my heart to a stern man of realities, but I daresay you spare me the time it takes to read my effusions.

Had the Cambridge reforms been in force while Henry was there what a difference it would have made to him. Let us hope Lyulph will reap the benefit & take honours in the Moral Sciences as I am sure Henry would in the Natural.

I have had a very touching letter from Lady Wharncliffe, she says Mrs. Damer was quite aware of her state tho' not expecting her summons so soon. It is very sad to be losing those one has loved so long & with whom

all one's common interests have grown up—what a loss
to her girls—I do not believe a kinder hearted woman or
better friend ever lived & she will be most sincerely
mourned for.

Yr. affec. wife   H. M. E.

LADY STANLEY TO LADY EDDISBURY

(255)   ALDERLEY *Nov.* 13*th.*

DEAR HEN,

If one could have foreseen such a perfect day I should
have urged your coming over—I wish you had been
dashing enough to volunteer with the young ones when
you found how fine it was. My Lord sat in the drawing
room window seeing the people file by enjoying it very
much. If you had but seen Richd. Ridgeway—in full
uniform, when not performing on his *piccolo* as I think he
called his flageolet, beating time— & after a mug or two
seeming quite up to the first footman's situation in
London. I asked him if he should not be sorry to leave
the band & he said oh yes—very sorry—but—& a very
expressive *but* it was, without farther explanation. I
really think he will do, he looked so smart & upright in
his red jacket.

Is not Emmy a goose of the first magnitude ? She is
dissatisfied with Dr. Lee because he tells her there is
nothing very seriously the matter. Yet I do not think I
am quite satisfied either, saying nothing of the heart &
no directions agt. another time—but I shall like to know
what you think of it.

Yrs. affecly   M. J. S.

LADY EDDISBURY TO LORD EDDISBURY

(256)   WINNINGTON *Nov.* 13*th*

MY DEAREST LOVE,

Lady Stanley went yesterday after luncheon.

I suppose if Emily de Burgh married Lady C. will bring out both her daughters. Margaret is near 18—tell me any gossip & news we are very dull here & the days are cold & dreary & we are very weary—this day 8 weeks I shall be in London but 8 weeks is a long time. I have a callender like the school boys.

Poor Henry I am afraid you damp & snub him & then wonder he is not talkative—merry he never was, it is not in his nature, but I assure you he would be very willing to talk if you gave him any encouragement, do try like a kind man. If you put on your severe looks it is enough to frighten anyone, even I am sometimes quite scared ! I feel sure Henry will improve very much but you must have patience with him, he is an animal of slow growth. There is Maude Adeane who would be too happy if Bob wd. take after Henry's pursuits instead of *his* idle habits, or would you have him hardly able to read like Arthur Davenport ? It is not given to everyone to join the good abilities & painstaking qualities to the butterfly ones & I for one wd. be far better pleased with you if you had not such a desperate hankering after those said frivolous people Ch: Buller is always reproaching you with haunting. *You* are exceedingly clever & witty in society but I do not know that your fireside is often enlivened by your jeu d'esprit. Henry is very good tempered & considerate of other's feelings. Good gracious, considering one side of his lineage you ought to bless your stars he has not a Dillon tongue.

Alice has had a long letter from Emily de Burgh she

is at Welbeck where she had hunted for 6 hours under
the escort of Lord Powis.   She does not mention Ld. P.
having proposed but seems in high spirits.   Her letters
are always *strained* in my opinion.

I am so glad to hear Margaret [Hamilton] has a girl
she wished for one so much.   Yrs. affecly   H. M. E.

LADY STANLEY TO LADY EDDISBURY

(257)   ALDERLEY *Nov.* 18*th*.
DEAR HEN,

Very glad Margaret has done her job & so well, got
what she wanted.

Did you find the black puddings under the flowers ?
Strange bedfellows !

The Ridgeways are a soft witted family & nobody
here is surprised tho' nobody would say anything beforehand not to injure him.   It is exceptionally provoking—
so kind as you was in wishing to give him a trial.   This
is folly beyond the usual Alderley folly but the catlike
attachment to the customary hearth is wonderful.   I
should like to have him well flogged & sent to New
Zealand.

If you cannot bear to lose sight of Henry for a few days
we shall be glad to see you but his visit will not be the
same thing if you & Blanche are here also & I should
have thought Blanche was better at home than coming
out in the character of an interesting invalid laid on a
sopha.[1]   Do as you like.   I shall be very glad to see
Henry anyhow.   Mr. Cruttenden will like to talk to him
about Aden & Madras.

1 She had sprained her foot.

What a pity it is Jem is not slightly more learned for *he* would fully appreciate the good fortune Ridgeway has slighted.

Loves to all   M. J. S.

LADY EDDISBURY TO LORD EDDISBURY

(258)   WINNINGTON *Nov. 18th.*

We had a great commotion in the house from Richard Ridgeway who only came late on Tuesday night running away; he said he wd. in the morning. Bob brought him back & I & Henry spoke to him, he had nothing to say & an hour after he was off again. Everyone runs away from Winnington which is rather curious.

Henry has brought no books I suppose you have kept them all at Gros: Crest:—Blanche begs I will not scold you she says it makes you low. I have not such an opinion of your sensitiveness.

(259)   WINNINGTON *Nov. 19th.*

MY DEAREST LOVE,

When Henry came here I found he intended to stay *here* all the time but I advised him to go to Alderley & wrote to Lady Stanley to propose I & Alice & Blanche should go with him as his whole visit is so short. I enclose her reply [see letter 257]. I need not add that we shall not go. Henry will go for 2 days but would much rather not for they bore him with their squabbles. I told Lady Stanley that Blanche now walks about quite independent so it is gratuitous to have said anything abt. interesting invalids.

This morning we had quite a beautiful sermon abt. women as wives & mothers—I never felt before how right it is the clergy should marry.

Dr. Lee told me that *mumps* are no longer considered infectious but epidemic, & that Johnny could not bring them home to his sisters.

Pray answer this letter & tell me if you do not think it is ill natured abt. Alderley.　　Yrs. affec　H. M. E.

(260)　　　　　　W I N N I N G T O N *Nov.* 21*st.*

Henry wishes you would sometimes talk to him on politics.　He does not know, some time hence if there will be any medium way between conservatism & communism & seems to think H. of Lords will go, in England.　I do not give you his thoughts as oracles, only I wish he was shown it is not necessary to be either a Tory or Radical, in short I wish you would imbue him with your ideas.　He goes to Aldy. Friday morning for breakfast.　I have not been written to so I suppose I am in disgrace—I write just the same.

(261)　　　　　　W I N N I N G T O N *Nov.* 22*nd.*

I am very much troubled to find that Henry's African expedition is more at his heart than ever & I fear if not treated gently he will certainly carry it out.　I find by what he says to Blanche that he only cares for my consent, that he thinks you never cared for him or even spoke to him abt. any of his plans so that if he came back successful you would be satisfied & if he died easily consoled. I certainly have known of his ideas since he was at Eton but have always looked upon them as a childish dream &

am much pained to see they have become second nature. I do not believe combatting such visions ever answers but I should hope if he became interested & attached to another profession he would be weaned from his sable love. Certainly this mania has kept him from the ordinary temptations of young men but it is going too far & I would gladly compromise for a few follies. What ever you do, do not speak harshly to him for he has done nothing to deserve it—I believe he means to stay as long as he can in his present office & then on his savings go to Africa !

I have not been hearing any family news—Lady Stanley wrote for grapes as she had a dinner party, the Bishop of Madras I believe.

Pray make time to write, your letters are my life

Yrs. affec   H. M. E.

LADY STANLEY TO LADY EDDISBURY

(262)   ALDERLEY Nov. 25th.

I don't think Henry looks well—his complexion *streaky* & his eyes *very small* & he does not seem in good spirits. His life cannot be a good & healthy one, so many hours visiting & so much Club in an evening & no other society. I have heard there is a great deal of gambling at the Coventry—he is the last young man I should have suspected of that vice, but prolonged ignorance of the world is not always a security against a *stumble* when the *threshold* is once crossed & the Tree of Knowledge open before a young man as it *must* be when living among experienced youths. He liked talking to the Bishop of the Eastern World.

LADY EDDISBURY TO LORD EDDISBURY

(263) WINNINGTON *Nov. 26th.*

MY DEAREST LOVE,

This is your Father's birthday, 82.

I never read so disagreeably toned an article as that on Lord Melbourne.[1] It is evidently written by a Tory & will be very painful to his friends. I never liked Lord Melbourne myself,[2] I thought him so selfish & heartless in his opinions of people, still he is one of that bright circle we met so often at Holland House & they are fast disappearing.

Henry was bored to death at Alderley—besides the two old Aunts, Dosey Leigh & Muff Boothby do not make it lively.

Blanche had a letter from Constance Graham giving an account of much gaiety, they are at Lord Dufferin's & Lady Londonderry is giving thé dansants at Mt. Stewart. Is it true that Lord Castlereagh is getting rather strange, very much excited?

I can get no work for Jem could you tell me when a Government Emigration ship is to go. I have a knack of falling in with little boys I found one so like Johnny quite as pretty—poor little boy he has been set up in trade by having a basket given him by which he can get 6d a day cinder getting. What an idiotic letter to be written to a great statesman but I have nothing more to say.

Your affec. wife   H. M. E.

[1] Died 24th November, 1848.
[2] This sentiment was reciprocated as far as Edward Stanley was concerned. Cf. "Queen Victoria's Letters," Vol. 1.

LADY STANLEY TO LADY EDDISBURY

(264)   ALDERLEY *Nov. 27th.*

I should have wanted to know what you thought of the memoir [of Lord Melbourne] which we were much dissatisfied with but had come to nearly the same conclusion as Edward that there was truth in some of the criticism tho' justice was not done him, & throughout there was such a denigrating spirit. It was also very bad feeling & taste to allude to the *moral* error of his past life.

Henry was off at 10—he seemed better yesterday but he rubs his eyes terribly. He asked me so many questions about Grandpapa's early life Iceland etc.,[1] seeming to be in perfect ignorance of many points of family history, that I set him upon examining My Lord himself & they had a long chat after dinner yesterday & he got a deal of information on these topics. He declared he never knew Grandpapa had been to Neufchâtel & to us it is *the* part of his life he always talks of with so much the most pleasure that I liked Henry to pick up something about it. One really does not sit down to relate family history to the rising generation without something to lead to the subject.

I am agreeably surprised to find that Sopley the k. maid is as good a cook as Woodfield—she dishes up the entrees in a more knowing way, I think, & her second course & sweets particularly good & pretty. I want to know how Thomson makes the crumbs stick on the cutlets if they are boiled ?

You are counting the weeks before London like

---

[1] This must have seemed very strange, as there is a tradition in the Stanley family that My Lord never talked about anything else.

schoolboys their holiday time—but I hope you will make the interval more tolerable by coming here before long.   Adieu   Yrs. affecly   M. J. S.

LADY EDDISBURY TO LORD EDDISBURY

(265)   WING Nov. 28/48.

I am very unhappy at the account you send—I always think Doctors say the best, Charles Buller is so very delicate [1]—I shall indeed be most anxious to hear of him tomorrow.   I cannot bear to think of his danger, we never can have a friend like him.   It seems a very curious case but Henry was quite delirious one night after the splinter had been taken out of him.   I wish they had Seymour he always does him good.

(266)   WINNINGTON Nov. 29th.

I feel there is no rational hope & yet I cannot believe we are to lose so dear a friend, & that one so bright & full of life is to be taken away—how fast our friends are departing, Mrs. Damer I had expected but this blow is so sudden.   I wish I knew more of his own state, is he conscious, does he suffer, or is it that dreadful low muttering delirium ?

(267)   Nov. 30th.

MY DEAREST LOVE,

    I thought I had no hope & yet the sad reality is dreadful.   I can hardly believe it—from thinking so

---

[1] " He underwent an operation which brought on erysipelas, and the erysipelas was followed by typhus.   This happened through the blundering of an unskilful surgeon."—Froude.

much of him the last few days his voice is ever in my ears
& his image before me.   What a grievous loss, not to
ourselves alone but to the country.   To us the loss is
irreplaceable & very long indeed will it be that we shall
feel his absence.   I am so grieved, for himself, for ourselves, for his mother, for the sad circumstances of his
death—not allowed to see his friends till too late.   Did
you see him at last ?   I hope you will be able to follow
him to his last resting place, it will be a comfort to me
to think you have—poor fellow we shall never have a
friend like him.   It is only this day month we lost Mrs.
Damer.   I am so grieved you are alone—do you think
you would like me to go to you I could easily manage, but
only as you like.   I suppose the Ashburtons are not in
London, they will grieve like ourselves.   I am so sorry
I am away from you my love.

Yrs. affecly   H. M. S.

LADY STANLEY TO LADY EDDISBURY

(268)   ALDERLEY   *Nov. 30th/48.*

DEAR HEN,

I am very sorry indeed to hear your bad news—tho'
personally I knew much less of Charles Buller than I
could wish, I can fully enter into E's & your feelings in
regard to such a friend as he has long been to you both—
& the more valuable as he has cultivated so few intimates.
There is scarcely an individual in either of your families
who will be so constantly missed or could be more deeply
regretted.   How I wish you were with Edward now, your
perfect sympathy with his feelings would be such a
comfort, such a relief to him.   I do not think you *will*
venture on an unexpected visit to town but if you did I

should be so glad to have the girls here in your absence if they would like it. My Lord desires his kind love to you.   Affecly yrs.   M. J. STANLEY.

LADY EDDISBURY TO LORD EDDISBURY

(269)   WINNINGTON *Dec. 1st.*

MY DEAREST LOVE,

Being away from you & knowing you unhappy adds much to the wretchedness I feel—I said yesterday I could easily come to you if you liked it but I know, my love, you dread bustle so I mean to tell you what might be done supposing you wished to see me. . . . you did say the other day you would be glad if I were with you—you know I should—but I do not wish you to do anything merely to please *me*. I do not wish to say anything approaching to unkind but you remember that after having asked me to come last year, you said you had been driven to it. I should not have offered to come now but for your opening & that your mother has urged it.

The article in the Times is beautiful, not so the Mg. Chron: I am sure Lady Ashburton will be deeply grieved, who is not—I think sometimes I feel more for you than myself, his softness made him just the friend for you.

I have felt very low for some time I much fear there is a very unpleasant cause for my malaise, & tho' I conclude it will come to an untimely end the remedy is a bad one.   Yr affec. wife   H. M. S.

[Lady Eddisbury went to London shortly after writing this letter but not so much to see Lord Eddisbury as to nurse Johnny who had a very bad attack of mumps at his school at Brighton.]

LADY STANLEY TO LADY EDDISBURY

(270) ALDERLEY *Dec. 5th.*

DEAR HEN,

Many untoward events have made me wish there was no party in view next week—the difficulty of collecting people is one & the wish you should not be hampered as to time is another—but I hope it will all shape well & that the girls will have a pleasant ball for it seems there will be a great many people there & good company. Birtles has been busy they have got the Custs & a *haul* of officers from Manchester.

The Parkers are people one shall feel quite at ease with & they will know I have done my best, tho' I have failed in making a large party.

Grandpapa was very glad to hear all alarm was over for Johnny.

Yrs. affec. M. J. S.

(271) ALDERLEY *Dec. 8th.*

I cannot imagine why any English Protestant can wish to have the Pope [1] in England, or even in any part of her dominions—but by this morning's paper it would appear he *is* going to Malta. Surely the head of the Catholick Church ought to take refuge in Catholick countries especially when the Bishop of London is giving a mark of distinction to Mr. Sewell [2] & would perhaps kiss the Pope's toe next if he came here. Wonderful times indeed

[1] Italy having been shaken, in common with nearly every European country, by the revolutionary spirit abroad during this year, the Pope had been obliged to fly from Rome to Gaëta, where he stayed under the protection of France and Austria.

[2] Founder of Radley, where the fasts of the Church were strictly kept, see letter 4.

224

& hitherto what a favoured country England is as to her position among the nations of Europe & present security against internal convulsions politically—But what a fearful state as to her *people* in many respects.

The girls have just arrived. Yrs. affecly M. J. S.

LADY EDDISBURY TO LORD EDDISBURY

(272)   ALDERLEY *Christmas Day.*

MY DEAREST LOVE,

We have been to Church—Algernon behaved like a young Bishop. Lyulph was discovered with Queen the young mastif in his bed by his gr. mama which made a great stromash. It is most sad not to have you, so to make up I am going to church again.

Next morning. Last night we had our game of Commerce, Kate appearing for the first time—she went to bed at 10 leaving me two lives with which I won the pool for her. All went off well until, after we had come up, Lyulph had a tremendous passion about getting Williams to put him to bed first, he was perfectly frantic & I had to have him carried into his room where he is now in punishment.   Yrs. affec.   H. M. E.

(273)   ALDERLEY *Dec* 28/48.

MY DEAREST LOVE,

I am overjoyed at the prospect of seeing you here.

What an extraordinary people the French are—Louis Napoléon [1] I dare say will aim at being Emperor & then there will be another row. Fancy the Parisians finding out he is a joli garçon.

[1] Elected President 10th December.

Robert Adeane came yesterday much improved in looks but quite a school boy in manners or rather in thought for his manners are gentle.

I am going to tea with Moomie so shall not be able to write more.

Yrs. ever   H. M. E.

EXTRACT FROM THE JOURNAL OF EDWARD JOHN STANLEY, BISHOP OF NORWICH

December 31, 1848.

In a few hours I shall have attained the three score years and ten ! ! and closed the 11th year of my Episcopal life. The train of reasoning and thought passing within my mind is little more than a repetition of what has been already detailed. The same doubts, the same fears, the same dissatisfaction at much I am compelled to witness and to notice, and the same painful feelings at the silence of those about me, acting like a dead weight upon my views, and checking me as I plod my course, the cheering gleams being very far and few between. What would I not give for some few words of encouragement assuring me that I am not altogether unworthy.

In all probability the approaching year will be the last of Mrs. Gibson's life, on which so much of my worldly interest depends, as far at least as related to those for whom I may almost say alone I wish to go on for a few more years. At all events, if I am spared long enough to wind up her affairs, there are no sufficient reasons why the curtain should not close upon my earthly stage, come when it may. I should like indeed to see Owen and Charlie once more, and our family circle assembled ; but with so many possible or rather probable intervening causes, I dare not too confidently look forward to so ardently desired an event.

Seventy years of my life have passed and gone their way ; forty-four of them in a profession dedicated to the service of God, of which the last eleven are the most especially important from the position in which circumstances so unlooked for and so unsought for have placed me. And though these latter years have been accompanied with much labour and pain and sorrow, more and more alive as I am, to the difficulties presenting themselves, still I feel satisfaction in what I have been fortunately instrumental in doing. How many parishes have I supplied with resident clergy, in which no pastoral care had been for years and years manifested. How many churches have had the full measure of services prescribed, in which for time immemorial the most scanty administration had been administered. And how many schools have been established, for the benefit of the thousands who had been with most culpable negligence permitted to remain brutalized and uncivilized and perishing for lack of knowledge. To my impartiality in awarding preferment, I cannot but think my most bitter opponents will bear testimony. To the majority of vacancies I have appointed individuals differing from me politically and religiously, and from some of whom instead of gratitude I have been treated with a want of common courtesy and respect ; too surely proving how little trust can be placed in men professing to be exclusively the supporters of their Church.

When I am gone, it will obviously be utterly immaterial to me what respect is paid to my memory, or how far I shall be regretted ; but for the sake of the honest, and I would hope the Christian course I have pursued, I must confess it would be gratifying to me to think that some testimony should be given in favour of my principles, and that course, which, if I may judge from my own experience and observation, have in few instances been carried out so fully and so strictly by those who had it in their power to do so ; and now, oh my God, whose eye is upon me and who canst search my heart to the very inmost, hear the prayer I would offer in sincerity and earnestness on my entrance to probably the last division and scene of my mortal life. The three score years and ten have passed, and the remaining years must be but few in number. Grant then Thy Holy Spirit may enable me so to act in the right and responsible vocation in which thy providence hath placed me, that my declining days may be devoted to thy service, and that in all my doings and intentions, the advancement of thy Holy Religion and the true vital interests of the Catholic Church of Christ may be my prominent object, end and aim.

1 8 4 9

LADY STANLEY TO LADY EDDISBURY

(274)   ALDERLEY *Jan.* 10*th.*

DEAR HEN,

Lyulph had a good night but waked complaining that his throat *snored* & he could hardly cough. Wee gave him an emetic & he has been a different boy since—very happy all day. Mathews cuts out capital houses with doors & windows that open & he has been quite content to stay upstairs. I think there cannot be a doubt he will be ready to travel on Monday.

Mrs. Leycester & Miss de Burgh came to call, much disappointed not to find you & the girls—what a disagreeable dawdling girl Miss de B. is.

The Times seems determined to *do* for Lord P[almerston] & who can stand such attacks as that of Tuesday last, followed up as I suppose it will be by Lord Stanley when Parliament meets.   Yrs. affecly   M. J. S.

RIANETTE STANLEY TO LADY EDDISBURY

(275)   *Jan.* 16*th*/49.

MY DEAR HENRIETTA,

I enclose Chattertons bill. Tell Blanche & Maud I have paid their debts—the Happy Homes was 1/6.

I do rejoice with you dear Hen that poor Henry has yielded at last. It has not been a struggle to laugh at & I am sure you have treated him most judiciously & kindly. What argument do you think made him give up? However foolish & déraisonné we may think him in cherishing this wild visionary idea,[1] to him it has been as real, as long dwelt upon, & as feasible as the most straight forward journey to another man, & the giving up I feel convinced as great a grief as the giving up a long cherished affection one feels can never be realised. But I hope he will now be happier with the feeling he has thereby given pleasure to his Mother. Will he go to Paris soon? Ever yr. affec. Sister M. M. STANLEY.

LADY STANLEY TO LADY EDDISBURY

(276)   ALDERLEY *Jan.* 21*st.*
DEAR HEN,

Tho' I am as sorry as I can be for your *position* yet I am so happy to have Algernon & Rosalind safe (I hope) here & if we had kept Lyulph till this disaster appeared what a vexation it would have been on acct. of placing us again in the state of taboo we endured when Louisa was ill. Tho' you are now a thorough going *non* contagionist yet I daresay you will *keep your powder dry* & take all the precautions in your power.

If you can make any use of Dover St. pray do—would it be any help that Henry should lodge there or would there be the *danger* of his finding a separate abode more agreeable.

I do not know of a single case of scarlet fever in the neighbourhood.

[1] His project for a journey to Africa.

Adieu, I hope you will keep well yourself in all respects.

Yrs. affecly   M. J. S.

All well here & the little ones *most* charming.

(277)   Undated.

I have a very long acct. of Jenny [Lind']s week from Aunt Kitty—Jenny spoke *positively* that she should not return to the stage[1] & had had a great battle with Lumley[2] about it who made use of all the most cogent arguments to persuade her, but she professed obduracy. We shall see—I have great doubts of either her sincerity or her power to resist temptation—I really think you may do her the justice of believing her refusal to sing with other people, a few excepted, is because there are *so few* good characters on the stage.

(278)   ALDERLEY *Jan. 28th.*

I am very glad the dear boy is so well, but it seems to me you run a great risk by nursing him yourself so much.

It is wonderful mild weather—the children are quite well. I see them in the Park. They are the dearest little animals & *I* think *both* the sharpest & cleverest of the whole lot.

I had a letter from Henry in answer to one of mine in which I said how happy it had made me to hear he had given up his favourite project to gratify those who loved him truly & affecly—his answer is as cold as can be, *no*

---

[1] She gave up the stage in 1849, and it is generally supposed that she did so under the influence of Bishop Stanley. She married Goldschmidt, a conductor, in 1852.
[2] Her manager.

allusion to this. You may tell him I always pay 2d for his letters tho' the name of Palmerston is as large as life in the corner.

I must tell you a story of Maude Adeane—Jenny was saying how kind the Queen had been to her when she was obliged to beg her Majesty 1000 pardons but she could not sing with Grisi, as she had been commanded. Maude who was sitting opposite with ears & mouth open exclaimed in a tone of wonder " Is not Grisi a nice person ? " which of course occasioned some amusement to those present.

Goodbye   Yrs. affecly   M. J. S.

(279)   ALDERLEY *Feb.* 11*th.*

I have been busy this morning seeing a fine lot of rhodendrons planted below the log house—I got 100 very fine plants 3 feet high for 20/–.

We have had a beautiful day & everything is foliating.

It is true Jenny is engaged but does not mean to marry at present, as far as one can depend on what she says, & Aunt saw a letter which proved she had positively refused to engage for the Opera. I do believe that her present intention is only to sing at concerts for another year & then retire from publick life.

Goodbye   Yrs. affecly   M. J. S.

(280)   ALDERLEY *Feb* 13*th.*

Carlyle *could* not like Macaulay's style, nothing can be more different to his own. His *eloquence* might easily induce you, & perhaps others, to think there is some truth in what he said, but I cannot think Macaulay *super-*

ALDERLEY PARK

ficial his statements are surely founded upon much observation of character, but his being so *fair* in judging character may lead Carlyle to say he is not an *earnest* man. I like his character of Cromwell much better than Carlyle's.

Your invitations do not appear to be very tempting.

What a fever Lady Bridgewater's death will put the Egerton's into, I suppose you know the circumstance of Ld. B's will, leaving all his property to Ld. Alford [1] if he is made a Marquis if not it goes to the Egertons. Will the Q. be so dictated to in the exercise of her privilege ?

Emmy gives a poor acc. of herself. I hope she will get to the sea in the course of the Spring, it is a pity Albert dislikes it so much.

(281)   ALDERLEY *Feb 25th/49.*

DEAREST HENRIETTA,

It will be a great relief & satisfaction to you, as it has been to me, that the father has taken the communication most patiently & seems entirely satisfied by your letter. He does not insist on more particulars if he suspects I know more—the truth is that he was too well prepared by the estimate he had been able to form of Henry's weakness of character, not only the absence of good principles of action in him, but the presence of wrong & bad ones which even in conversation Hy. had let out. He said boldly one day before him that he did not think a father, mother, or grandfather had any right to check a young man's inclinations in regard to marriage, & many

---

[1] Eldest son of Earl Brownlow, his great-grandfather was John Egerton, whose surname and arms he assumed.

233

opinions equally erroneous & mischievous, in consequence of which My Lord has often looked into the
future with an anxious eye & foreboding mind. He
made no outcry about Africa, & I believe *felt* that it
might be imperative to send him somewhere, he could
only say he would be safe *no* where. I could only say I
hoped this early lesson would be given in time to ripen
his understanding & lead him to form a better code of
principles. It is clear he does not think of more than a
mistress at present & that his eyes are quite open to the
fears of greater entanglement.

I am sorry you are so poorly & worried about Johnny.
Will anybody tell Williams Henry is gone, & where,
with or without comment—or shall I ?

How riches shower upon those who do not need them
having already so much. The Egertons gain 300,000
by Ly. Bridgewater's will & perhaps eventually the whole
property if the Q does not comply with Lord B's condition of making Ld. Alford a Marquis.

Rianette & I go to Penrhos on Thursday Adieu
dearest Hen,

Ever affecly   Yours M. J. STANLEY

(282)   ALDERLEY *Feb.* 29*th*/49.

I have told poor Wee as much as you would wish her to
know & she is indeed very much grieved. I am afraid
it has sunk deeper into My Lord's mind than I had
hoped at first, he looked very low & miserable all yesterday, all the worse I think for seeming not to *wish* to *talk*
about it. It was impossible to prevent him being told
what was told him by you—if he had heard bye & bye
that Henry was gone abroad & he had not heard it at
the time he would have been very angry, & nothing he

could be told would have been so bad as what he would
have suspected from its being hushed up.

Surely Lucy is not such a *Pharisee* she could not do an
act of kindness on a Sunday, I cannot imagine how she
could let a day pass without seeing Johnny.

How does Henry get to Marseilles? Adieu
Yrs. affecly   M. J. STANLEY.

(283)   PENRHOS *March 7th.*

I expect Henry will not make a long stay in the islands
without his trunk—I suppose he must return to Marseilles.

I apply to you for a piece of information—shall we have
to go to war with Russia? *Must* we not if she forces the
passage of the Dardanelles? May you not give your
own opinion from the general *on dit* of society without
being suspected of being in the *secret?*

Could we manage Johnny if he was *on honour* to do as
he was bid & never take an absence without leave? As
you say he ought to go to the country for a week.

How the names Blanche & Alice have become general
—I am not sure whether the Egertons or yours are the
eldest but they have as good a right to *Alice* as you can
have—Blanche seems to be quite a modern English
name.   Ever yr. affecte   M. J. S.

(284)   PENRHOS *March 9th/49.*

We have just heard of the death of Mrs. Gibson[1]—I
thought she would die soon when I got a coloured poplin
from Ireland the other day.

---

[1] Lord Stanley's sister.

I *have* read Vanity Fair & how anybody can like to associate with the author astonishes me—tho' I daresay his conversation may not be like his book exactly but I should so dislike the man who could give such a work to the publick.   Where do you meet with him ?

Nothing more to say   Yrs. affecly   M. J. S.

(285)   A L D E R L E Y *March* 11*th*.

We came by the early train in order to have some time at Chester for shopping, (my mourning having been quite expended.)   Mrs. Gibson has left a remembrance to Rianette & Louisa, about 200 each & 100 to Lord S. I do not believe she had much less than 20,000 so Uncle will have a pretty windfall.   She is to be buried on Wed: in Chester—I hope Kitty will come here for a few days.

Algernon is certainly not a quiet or a dull boy—I am afraid he will not benefit by Johnny's & Lyulph's company whenever he returns to it, he shocked Louisa yesterday by talking of *snobs* he told her J. & L. often talk of them.

Somehow Henry's letter does not please me—I do not think you need fear that his past conduct will distress him too deeply or too long.   The same weakness of character which made him fall into the snares of wicked people, & which is always shown in his very uninteresting letters, will I fear often put him in danger again.   I cannot put my finger on any sentence particularly, but it is not the tone I should expect in a man who is under such a cloud with his parents.

I don't know who dined with you & I like to know who you have, but perhaps you think I might object to some of them as you see I do object to your friend Thackeray.   Yrs. affecly   M. J. S.

236

(286)   ALDERLEY *March 15th.*

I am very glad you told me you had had letters from
Henry in a depressed state of mind, I was afraid *all* might
have been in the same matter of fact style, upon common
occurrences.   I fear you flatter yourself too much in
still considering his character as undeveloped & that
there is only a want of *animal* vigour ; unfortunately
this vigour has developed itself much too strongly &
the fear is that there is no fund of mental vigour to be
develloped. Certainly there never was a youth more unfortunately exposed to temptation—without a domestick
home for so many months, left to seek & shun his
own companions as he liked.   I do so dread his return
to the same life—I hope something else may turn up.

You say " I do think the General is very well " but I
am afraid you ommitted " not " as you add Ally has
bought him a respirator.

Tell Blanche if you give me a list of the dinner party,
she must of the evening set.

Do you remember a little sopha which I believe is
your property that Sally had—I am sure you will let me
lend it to poor Sarah Toft of Gatley Green who I found
gasping for breath on three chairs so uncomfortable.
The poor woman is not absolutely in a decline but in
great danger of such.

(287)   ALDERLEY *March 18th.*

Johnny is going on very well—he looks as you say
bloodless & the slightest emotion gives a beautiful colour
to his cheeks which is a sign of weakness. This afternoon, a beautiful day, he was with Louisa in her garden
very good & well amused, Spring in the country is quite

a novelty to him & his observation is quite awake—he was so surprised at the quantity of daffodils everywhere, but the subject of the greatest surprise to him was the *very* cruel behaviour of Louisa's cock which got down the poor hens & pecked them so. He took upon himself to be the hen's champion tho' Louisa told him the cock had a right to correct his wives if they did not behave well.

The Episcopals came last night—Uncle looked worn with his Chester business—3 days not going out of the house must have been trying as well as looking over, & settling about all the *goods*, several of which were labelled for more than one person.

How is Alice's health? Johnny told us that when she did not go out as much as Blanche some people said she had the scarlet fever, & others a disappointment.

You will be a lucky mother if you do keep clear from all shoals—the mischief is indeed soon done & it is so difficult to push off from the breakers in time, but the greatest difficulty is for the eyes of parents to be sufficiently open. *I* have always a fear of a certain Johnny C. nothing would make me if, I was you, comfortable but knowing he had some engagement or love. To a romantick girl such as Blanche he must be a dangerous acquaintance & there is a certain song book, prepared for illustration, which haunts my recollection.

I hope Henry will walk safely thro' Sardinia but is it not rather a lawless country? Affecly yours   M. J. S.

(288)   ALDERLEY *March* 21/49.
DEAR HEN,

I have sent Henry's letter to Ally—it is a very good account of the society he is in. You see I was not mistaken in thinking there were banditti—to be sure it was rather a queer idea wishing to pay them a visit.

Have you seen anything of Montemolin—I have not patience with his amusing himself playing about in London while his friends & adherents are fighting for him in Spain—he would do better to tell them to give up his cause at once as a hopeless one for he has neither money arms nor spirit to help them with.

I wonder you are ever guided by the Examiner's criticisms—they are very one sided, that is, governed by their friendships or *bribed* by some fair lady to give favourable opinions.

Yours affecly   M. J. S.

(289)   ALDERLEY *March 25th.*

You are so gloomy in your political views of European affairs one would think you had been reading Dr. Cumming's last series [1] about the pouring out of the 7th vial—he is a most eloquent & powerful writer & good on all subjects *except* the main spring of his writings— I like him so much whenever I can separate him from the Apocalypse. " 1848 or Prophecy Fulfilled " is admirable, but for my part I think it is presumptuous to fix the epochs that are to come.   The safety of England is to depend mainly, upon whether the Irish Catholick Church is to be endowed or not, if it *is* the Vial will be poured out on us without any doubt.   As I think I have heard Ld. John has attended the lectures, I hope he will pay proper attention to this circumstance.

Mr. White wishes to bring the hounds in Passion

---

1 " Apocalyptic Sketches," by John Cumming (1807–1881), bee-keeper and divine.

Week which makes one very cross, not for the impiety of the deed, but because the fences are made up everywhere & the fields sown.

My Lord keeps well though the East Wind penetrates to his fire side.

(290)   ALDERLEY *March 29th/49.*

I shall be very glad when you hear again from Henry as he talked of Genoa & one does not know whether he might not think it a pleasant excitement to join *one* of the armies. He would not be on the Italian side but he had rather a partiality I think for the Sardinian troops.

I wish poor Lady Vernon [1] may consent to separation but women are such fools & with some *no* ill treatment or neglect can wean them entirely from the attachment they blindly feel thro' everything. I know the Ellisons wish it.

Very interesting acc. of the Claremont [2] family—have you seen a little brochure called Une Visite à M. le Duc. de Bordeaux par Charles Didier a curious acc. of the life of those people & curious as being written & the visit made by a fierce republican.

Albert [Way] brought one over for the Queen, sent by Mr. Reeves with whom he was mostly living at Paris.

Mrs. Fleetwood is in labour & has been so all yesterday & all night I wish it was well over for her—her 11th— but it suits Johnny as I suppose Fleetwood does not like to be far off yet does not wish to be always in the house so he offered his services.

                              Yrs. affec.   M. J. S.

---

[1] Isabella Ellison married Lord Vernon, 1824.
[2] The French Royal Family.

(291)   ALDERLEY *April 1st.*

Poor Mrs. Fleetwood had a dead child yesterday after a great deal of suffering, & tho' Night: had been there several times he was not there at last—came *running* in such a *perspiration* but not in time—however the neighbouring gossips helped pretty well & she is doing well.

I suppose you are to be one of Lady Syke's guests—I do not know whether I despise most the lady who purchases such a lift into society by such means, or the lady who undertakes to introduce her.

You may not have heard of the Bishop intending to give 500 to the Parrys, Bella having been Mrs. Gibson's godchild as well as Mary to whom she left that sum. It is very liberal & will be very acceptable just as Sir E. has lost 3000 thro' the Australian Bank—& as Edward [1] is entering the University. The Bishop has been equally liberal in many things—I believe he can well afford it but it is not everybody who does the right thing if they can afford it ever so well. Adieu Yrs. affecly M. J. S.

(292)   ALDERLEY *April 3rd.*

. . . Algernon is very truthful—Rose [Rosalind] not so much so but you may always depend upon Algy—he is *very* sensitive & very observing—in short he is very near a paragon at present, & they do play & *sing* so prettily together. I hope they will not have time before we come to make up a shy face to receive us. It is such a beautiful day & such weather makes one very unwilling to move.

I was very glad to see a letter from Henry but I am not quite easy about the Curé & his books. In his

---

[1] Edward Parry became Suffragan Bishop of Dover.

present state of mind a clever votary of the church might do a great deal of harm & the conversion of an English aristocrat might gain him great praise & honour. The step from infidelity to blind belief is a short one— I should like to know the turn of his thoughts in his solitary rambles. Self examination may be of great use— but there must be some good foundation to start from which I am afraid he has not. I wish he was more particular in saying who he lives with, if any body. It must be a beautiful country. What great importance to him would be a sensible well principled companion to whom he could impart his thoughts.

[Lord and Lady Stanley and their household now removed to London for the summer, so no more letters passed until they returned to Alderley in July.]

(293)   A L D E R L E Y *July 8th*/49.

As we reached the door here at 8 o'clock on Friday My Lord had been in his carriage since 10 A.M. He *might* have been almost dead but tho' he complained of stiffness getting out & of palpitations from the exertion, in half an hour he walked from his own room to tea in the dining room. He is now gone out on the lawn. I should mention that on Friday night I watched the full moon from the arbour on the hill till after 10.

I would not exchange with anybody in London now I have smelt & looked at the country.

(294)   A L D E R L E Y *July 22nd*/49.

The little girls came quite well—but such objects ! with their long straight locks ! I cannot imagine they can ever be made to look presentable especially Kate who has not the same beauty as Rose to carry off any hideous appendage.

If you are not in bed[1] pray do not relax in your endeavours for emigration there is a very bad report of Jem—idle & impudent—& so filthy in his habits that, he chusing to lock his door (they had got him in the house) Walton was determined to get in at the window & found the room in such a nasty condition they soon helped him out of the house again. This comes of being romantick about interesting little outcasts, disappointment generally.

(295)   ALDERLEY *July 25th.*

Mr. Birkmore wrote to say the boys would be here (D.V. !) tomorrow at I. II. How absurd all the Parsons are that they will not take for granted such must be the case without the professing cant of expressing it.

LADY STANLEY TO BLANCHE STANLEY

(296)   ALDERLEY *July 26th/49.*

MY DEAR BLANCHE,

I think it would be quite wrong if Mama was able to receive a letter herself & as I *owe* you a letter I shall tell *you* that the boys are arrived looking well & in high spirits.

Mr. Bahin wears spectacles—looks a quiet sensible middle aged man, neither shy nor the reverse—I am happy to learn his name is pronounced Bin, for there

---

[1] Lady Eddisbury was expecting her twelfth child.

was such a baa-ing in the family *guessing* how it should be called that I was in a fright lest the boys should catch a wrong sound & make fun of it which might have been difficult to check.

Mama asks for new books, I think I ought to apply to her for information on that head. I can only recommend her as *new*, I say no more, Miss Martineau's History of the 30 year's Peace as large a volume as the thickest Elegant Extracts or Peerage & Baronetage & also the Lives of the Lindsays in 3 large octavo vols: in which there is a deal of family egotism & admiration of themselves. Goodbye with many loves but there is nobody in the house to send them so I suppose they are sent.   Yrs. affec   M. J. S.

LADY STANLEY TO LORD EDDISBURY

(297)   ALDERLEY *July* 27/49.

MY DEAR EDWARD,

Much congratulation on the birth of another Miss, & Henrietta's well doing—I hope all will go on as well as it has begun & the recovery be as expeditious as the delivery.

Nothing can begin better than boys & tutor—he seems to have the reins in hand. The schoolroom, being your room, commands an excellent & most desirable view of the dog kennel, which Fleetwood has tabooed. The young gentlemen made an escape into the yard before breakfast & Mr. Bahin was seen to follow them & request the pleasure of their company in the schoolroom. . . .

Loves from *all*   Yours affec.   M. J. S.

LADY STANLEY TO LADY EDDISBURY

(298)   ALDERLEY *Aug* 1/49.

I am sorry you cannot manage [to nurse the baby] as it would be both a pleasure & convenience. Do nothing rash to delay your recovery, & I hope you will be here before E. takes flight—but I can *imagine* he does not feel great interest in a Christening as he has had so many, & that the grouse would carry the day—tho' it would be but *pretty* of him to wait for you.

Instead of being a *lively* playfellow as I thought at first, poor Mr. Bahin looks most melancholy mild & gentle, but I do not doubt his firmness with the boys & he is very attentive to them.

MRS. HARE (LUCY) TO LADY EDDISBURY

(299)   *Undated.*

I cannot fancy you with a new baby of yr. own when one is beginning to think of you in the character of a grand-mother but I daresay you will be quite soft over it. I think Aunts Rianette & Louisa had better adopt Alger-non & Rosalind it would be everything to them if they had a child or two to take an interest in—I had a letter from Louisa lately so sad & melancholy about Penrhos, there is nothing to stand in the place of past happiness, & then it leads to such morbid feelings. *Unless* that *new* life has been given which changes the whole aspect of things, *all* things are over. We are so much too apt to think & talk as if *this* were our home, if we could more truly realise that it is the journey to our home, trials & vexations & partings would be met, as they are by travellers who cheer each friend they part with, with the hope of meeting at the end.

I daresay you are glad of this quiet month, to be taken away from things temporal, & able, while you watch your sleeping darling, to look back & to look forwards. If we do not write you know that you have always warm sympathy in all that concerns you & yours.

Yr. affec. sister LUCY.

LADY STANLEY TO LADY EDDISBURY

(300)   ALDERLEY *Aug. 5th.*

DEAR HEN,

I am glad you have a prospect of shipping off Jem & I hope he will not take to *crook*-ed ways on the road. I shall be ready to help you but you must pay something for your experiment. It *is* a difficulty *how* to send him, that is which way, there must be somebody at Plymouth to whom he would be consigned. Bob thought Jem did not *quite* like the thoughts of the voyage & destination & Maud tryed to point out the advantages. The boy was made too much of at first & taught to think himself an object of interest.

I have been obliged to give the boys each a room as Johnny broke a jug on Lyulph's head in a passion, which might have been very serious but only made a great bump. They are certainly not better friends than they were—never together by choice. I think Johnny was very much ashamed, he was not punished more than by hearing everybody's opinion on the matter, & knowing I should tell you, & I think that is more punishment than any deprivation we could have thought of. Poor Mr. Bahin is very dull—but he is very attentive to his charge.

I conclude the chloroform experiment was done by medical permission—I should be fearful of it, for you especially unless quite sure the headaches are simply nervous or else smothering the effect without removing the cause may be dangerous.   Yrs. affec.   M. J. S.

(301)   A L D E R L E Y *Aug.* 7/49

I hope Edward & you will not grudge Maude her peep at the country world, it is not like London & I do not think she is at all disposed to put herself forward. She went to practise shooting with Mr. Granville yesterday—I thought it would add very much to her pleasure if she took part in the amusement of the day, as an Archery Meeting is very dull to a mere looker on. Grandpapa has taken an interest in her practising promising her 1/- for every time she hits the target.

The boys have been in disgrace this morning, much to the advantage of the holiday task, in consequence of a great row last night. Mr. Bahin luckily heard the uproar & was on the spot—I am sure, poor man, it is a great exertion for him to punish them, he could not eat a bit of dinner today.

I shall be glad to hear the Queen met with no affront in Dublin—I cannot think it was a wise thing to go to Ireland & she does not manage her progresses wisely, taking the people by surprise as she has done at Cork.

(302)   T A T T O N *Aug.* 10*th.*

We had an awful storm yesterday [1] but the Egertons did the right thing handsomely & most good naturedly

---

[1] For the archery meeting.

opened the house to all. Of *grandees* there were Ly.
Delamere & daughter, Ld. & Ly. de Tabley, Leycesters
of Toft, the Astle party, Warburtons etc. lots of parsons
& very vulgar looking females. Chris: Sykes is here
who seems to have been Henry's companion at Peile's,
Alford's & Trinity, a very shy but not silly youth. He
is a son of Sir Tatton's & of Ly. Charlotte's protegée.
Mr. Wynne a son of Charles Wynne's is the only other
gentlemen at present, a lawyer without practise.

I don't agree with you that people's manners are
formed upon those they frequent, because the different
members of a family so often have different manners—
& I think both Alice's & Maud's are much better than
Blanche's. Figure however has a great deal to do with
what I mean by manners.

LADY EDDISBURY TO LORD EDDISBURY
(AT ALDERLEY)

(303)   GROV: CRES: *Sunday night.*
MY DEAREST LOVE,

I am so fretted about dear baby I must write to you.
Yesterday afternoon the little thing was uncomfortable
& when the nurse came she could not suck from wind.
She has continued poorly all night & today I was quite
shocked when I came upstairs at the change which had
taken place in the baby, so thin & its little hands cold &
shrivelled. Dr. Locock ordered her castor oil & sal
volatile which Williams had given. I had a very bad
night, never closed my eyes, first from pain & then from
the laudanum.

11 *o'clock.* I have just sent for Dr. Locock I am so
    uneasy about dear Baby.

7 o'clock Monday morg. Baby no better, pinched & blue Locock ordered brandy in her milk it is the nurses milk put down her throat in spoonfuls

6 o'clock. I think Baby is better, I have more hope.

12 o'clock. I am more & more anxious. Poor dear little lamb it looks so worn & piteous. When Locock comes again he is to decide about her being baptized. I shall be so wretched to lose her she is such a darling & I feel it quite a punishment for having said I did not wish for a child. I did not know how fast love grows for babies but as I sit by its cradle & hear its faint moans it goes thro' my heart. I feel very poorly quite knocked up. I am sure you will feel for the little soft thing you have watched the last fortnight as well as for me. She sleeps continuously & when she is roused to take food her eyes look quite dead.

2 o'clock. It has been a cholera attack without pain, & now she is exhausted. She has no disease. I cannot now say what day I can go I feel I shall not have my little darling to bring.

LADY STANLEY TO LADY EDDISBURY

(304)   ALDERLEY *Aug.* 14*th.*

DEAREST HEN,

While there is life there is so much ground for hope, with young children, that I look forward trustfully to a better account tomorrow, & if so much is gained then all will go well—we shall soon see you. I am longing for you & Alice to be with us.

One hears of cholera from many quarters—Emmy writes word their agents wife died of it in a very short time. . . .

LADY EDDISBURY TO LORD EDDISBURY

(305)   *Monday night.*

MY DEAREST LOVE,

I closed my letter before with a gleam of hope, Dr. Locock came just as I had sealed it he said Baby was less *prostrate* than in the morning but he would not say she was at all out of danger—she was not safe. Within half an hour of his going the blue look came on again. I then decided upon having her baptized at once & a curate came & the dear little lamb was baptized Mary Ethelflida, I did not care what name for I fear she will not bear it long here, but you had said you liked that & I thought it would be best. Since 9 o'clock she has been more natural in colour but the two last meals have been forced down her throat with holding her nose. I need not say how worn I am. It is difficult to say why Baby refuses all food she certainly has no organic disease, the bowels have acted twice this evg. We are sadly plagued with the wet nurse who just now wants to go home but Williams will send for her child tomorrow—we must do anything rather than lose the nurse, the only chance our darling has is having a good nurse.

I cannot sleep, I try to think of you as caring for me & not insouçiant as you sometimes appear. I am so unhappy I cannot write more. Yr. affec. wife

H. M. E.

LADY STANLEY TO LADY EDDISBURY

(306)   ALDERLEY *Augt.* 15*th.*

DEAREST HEN,

The message reached us at 2 o'clock, I did not think a
hope remained of recovery & I could only be glad you
was spared a prolonged anxiety & rejoiced to think
Edward would be with you so soon. How welcome he
must have been & he would not have been happy staying
here. Three weeks is quite long enough to have gained
your affections & the last few days nursing must have
added much to its hold upon you. I am glad you will
have a fortnight with us & all your children (poor Henry
excepted) before you go to Rhyl—many dear loves from
all—you *know* their hearts are with you.

Very affecly yrs.   M. J. STANLEY.

LADY EDDISBURY TO LORD EDDISBURY

(307)   ALDERLEY *Aug.* 22*nd.*

Poor Clarke has been very bad [with cholera] ever since
you went & two of the Somervilles are ill. It is very
fearful the suddenness of the complaint & dreadful to be
separated at such a time. It makes me feel all I suffered
with dear Baby. None of the people here are the least
contagionists, so we have not that folly to contend with.
I hope I shall hear, from Perth, Friday, & pray tell me if
you have the least indication of illness.

Ever yr. affec. wife   H. M. E.

(308)   ALDERLEY *Aug.* 23*rd.*

After the most dreadful anxiety Clarke has rallied &
Nightingale who was here till 1 O'clock this mg., went

251

away not expecting to find him alive, but says today if he has no relapse he will recover. Nightingale says it is the first case of real Asiatic cholera he has seen—all the symptoms, cramps, no pulse, cold sweats & rice water evacuations were there—cramps I am told frightful. Clarke thinks he will recover.

I am only very weak & that makes me low & nervous. How I wish all this horrid autumn & winter was passed I know we shall have more misfortunes.

(309) ALDERLEY *Aug.* 25/49.

My dear little one would have been a month old today—you can have no idea how present she is to my mind, I am surprised at it myself, still I do feel most thankful that up to this time we have been spared other losses by this dreadful disease. Clarke is better this morning having slept. I feel now he will recover.

I think your Mother is a little frightened tho' she always eats the wrong things from bravado.

(310) ALDERLEY *Aug.* 26/49.

Since this morg: a great change has come over poor Clarke. He is now insensible & I should greatly fear before this letter is closed all will be over. Nightingale has put mustard to his feet but he has no hopes. His wife has been sent for. It is very sad indeed.

Will you tell me what I had better do about the horses—poor Clarke, he was so anxious about them on Friday, he will be a great loss to us. When I asked Nightingale what was the cause he gave the same reason they did in London with our baby " It has fallen on the nerves ".

I am just told that all is over—his poor eldest boy is quite an orphan & he has left a child by this wife.

Nightingale says he never saw so mysterious a disease —there is no fighting against it.

(311)   ALDERLEY *Aug.* 27*th.*

Poor Mrs. Clarke came here with her two children.   She is very much afflicted that the whole time of his illness should have passed without any religious conversation, but in this dreadful illness there is no time & no opportunity for thought, & those who have left all to that moment are indeed in an awful position.

Mrs. Clarke tells me he was very much afraid of cholera & the day he came home from our funeral he told his wife he was struck with the smell of the grave, & was sure he was ill.   That must be quite a fancy but it shows what fright can do.

Maude Adeane has gone home as [the cholera] is in her village where most of her children are.

Your party seems dull enough—I should not think, with the difficulty of getting people, that it would answer to have Lady Ashburton who cannot exist without amusement.

LADY STANLEY TO LADY EDDISBURY

(312)   PENRHOS *Aug.* 30*th.*

We arrived quite safe at 6 o'clock—having had the honour of travelling in the same train with the D. of Cambridge & family from Chester to Bangor.   They were going to Plas Newydd[1]—when they got out at the

---

[1] Seat of the Marquis of Anglesey.

station I wondered what ill looking German had Pss. Mary on his arm & found it was P. George.[1] There was an attempt to raise a cheer by the loyal Taffys. The poor Duke looked very bothered I thought.

When I was in Chester I went to Browns to buy a gown & was tempted by " the next article ", a love of a cloak, like Blanche's in some respects but black instead of brown & longer, & two such delightful pockets in front. I shall wonder how I ever did without it, in cold weather. I am rather tired so adieu, with many loves

Yrs. ever M. J. S.

LADY EDDISBURY TO LORD EDDISBURY

(313)   ALDERLEY *Aug. 29th.*

MY DEAREST LOVE,

If you knew what a blank a day without a letter from you becomes & how low I feel I think you would spare me the 5 minutes it takes, even from Lady Ashburton's fascinating conversation.

I have settled poor Clarke's books & paid 2.10. for the funeral expences. It seemed to be expected & with such an old & valued servant I thought you would approve. Poor woman she has no savings at all & when she has collected his debts will not have above £40.

Johnny is so naughty & disagreeable he quite wears me out I shall not go out today—I suppose it is not cold but really the prospect of spending so much of my life without you is enough to make me wretched. It is useless to say anything as you only enjoy yourself you

[2] Princess Mary and Prince George were the daughter and son of the Duke of Cambridge.

say when you have your holiday as you call it from me.

I feel too wretched to write more.   Yrs. affecly

                                                    H. M. E.

(314)   ALDERLEY *Aug 30th.*

MY DEAREST DARLING,

I can not at all express what I feel for all your love & anxiety for me & the children.   I am truly grateful for it, & if what I have suffered in loss & anxiety brings out your affection I shall be well repaid.   Perhaps all this anxiety is sent to show us all how much we are dependant on each other, & if it only makes you care more for your home, & less for the allurements of the society you have lately been so devoted to, the gain to me will be too great to make me repine at any sacrifice.

Remember, love from you makes up to me for all troubles & that now my anxiety is to hear of you being well.   My beloved take care of yourself.

RHYL, [where Lady Eddisbury had taken a furnished house]

(315)   *Sept.* 3/49.

Do not take too much credit for writing every day—for you cannot believe how very much astonished every one expresses themselves that you should have left us all with the cholera in the family.   I only just say that, that you may see that there is even a higher standard of affection than that of writing to one when overwhelmed with anxiety.

I have heard from Aunt Kitty, the Bishop is better but has had a complication of nerves, bile, & determination of blood to the head, he is to return by steamer [from Scotland]

My head aches so much & I feel so low that I cannot collect my ideas to write more & I feel life a burden.

(316)   BODDLEWYDAN.[1]   *Friday.*

DEAREST LOVE,

I have had an accident—I was sitting on a bench reading the paper, I got up when, without any reason that we can find out I reeled round & fell on my back in such excruciating pain I could not move. Lady Sarah [Williams] thought my leg must be broke but it is only the ankle which is enormously swelled. I was got into the house & have got bran & vinegar they want me to stay but I would rather get back to Williams.

Rhyl. I came here without its hurting me much in Sir John's barouche. The staircase here was too narrow for me to be carried up so I had to drag myself one step at a time, Blanche carrying my leg. Henry came just as I was in the confusion of being settled. He looks so ill. I told you I should have misfortunes, this is nothing to what we shall have.

Dr. Roberts has just been & he says there is nothing broke or displaced in my foot, only a violent sprain & he thinks it was a spasm that sprained my ankle.

Yrs. affec.   H. M. E.

[1] Seat of Sir John Williams, brother of Ellin Stanley.

(317)   RHYL *Sept. 9th.*

MY DEAREST LOVE,

You will ere this have heard of the death of your Uncle [1] a kinder or better man never lived, & now death will have obliterated his small peculiarities people will do justice to his enlarged philanthropy & universal charity. I am much grieved at his loss for since I have been your wife I have had nothing but the greatest kindness from him & his family.

I received a long letter from Kate this morg., she said that Aunt Kitty was going to write to you to go to Norwich they wished particularely, as you saw the place when they first went, that you should see how they leave it.

I shall not be sorry that the boys go tomorrow, they have worn me out in my present nervous state they are selfish & quarrelsome.

I am very sad & feel as if every day brought a fresh sorrow.

Yrs. affec.   H. M. E.

LADY STANLEY TO LADY EDDISBURY

(318)   PENRHOS *Sept. 9th.*

Is it possible that being, so full of life & vivacity & warm feelings—is gone—I cannot realize it, yet. There is hardly an individual in the family I could not have sooner feared would be taken away. I will copy Mary's letter Sept. 7th.

" His redeemed Spirit was released at $\frac{1}{2}$ past 11 last night. All day we sat listening to the laboured breathing, praying that the Soul might be set free. At 11 we saw

1 The Bishop of Norwich, aged 70.

a change—we were all round his bed—we scarcely dared to break the silence by breathing ourselves— gradually the breathing became feebler & less frequent & then came one & no more. That moment it seemed as if the very life was drawn from one, no one moved for some time—then Arthur knelt down & prayed. Mama was quite calm & she has slept well—this morning she feels much exhausted but that is all. The remains will be brought by sea & laid in his own Cathedral. It was his wish expressed not long ago. Dearest Aunt you know what we have lost & what today is to us. Arthur will write to Edward, Mama wishes him to attend the funeral & dear William too. . . ."

I am *very* sorry *either* shd. be asked—Edward just beginning to recover his spirits & health I hoped, Wm. certainly very far from well. I could wish Ed. would not get the letter till too late as perhaps they wd. not know where to direct.

Rianette gives a very good acc. of the father—who has now seen all his sisters & brother go before him.

I fear [the Bishop] was not himself the last two days enough to have been able to speak to them clearly, a few last words are so valuable to think upon. Poor Owen & Charles, & to think of the unconscious letters that will come from them for months, & how Owen may hear it all of a sudden from a newspaper on his return to Sydney before he may receive a letter.

LADY EDDISBURY TO LORD EDDISBURY

(319) RHYL *Sept.* 10*th.*
The poor boys are just gone, Johnny crying & Lyulph making a noise saying he found *that* the best plan as stimulants kept up their spirits.

I have just had your letter—I am sorry, very sorry I made you unhappy about me, you say truly I am in the habit of making the best of what comes in my way, & shall still, but I have had a weight on my spirits partly from bodily weakness & partly from the repeated shocks I have had lately.

Is not Julia Hobhouse's[1] death most sad.   Only 19 & her father's idol.

Henry says he must go to town on Wednesday so you must write to him there—he does not do much here but reads Macaulay that is something.

I am very sorry you should make yourself unhappy at anything I say you know I shall not till my dying day like you to be with people who wean you from me. These people you become intimate with in the country then in London they ask you to dine without me, you go to the Opera to Richmond etc. with them, & get more intimate, & are more asked again & so on.   I am deprived of you more than half our married life, & I am not of your way of thinking that if I die it does not matter for I believe I could hardly forgive the world then for all it has robbed me of.   They say no couple love equally I wish it had fallen to my lot to have loved the least, those always manage to get on best where the husband loves the most—but now it is too late to alter. Be assured of my love now & ever   Yr. affec.   H. M. E.

LADY STANLEY TO LADY EDDISBURY

(320)   PENRHOS *Sept.* 18*th*.

I was not at all uneasy at being two days letterless, thought there was some delay, but never guessed such

---

[1] One of the two daughters of Sir John Hobhouse.

atrocity as one being left in a blotting book. I didn't suppose you quite well, though you are of Mother Hubbard's dog's breed, but I was glad you was able to move for it must be such a pleasure to be in E's company for the few days he is at Aldy.

I am wishing very much to hear more from Norwich—it seems so painful delaying the funeral so long & I cannot imagine why it should be so. We went to Church on Sunday—but I suppose it was not *right*—& taken as a hint we should see company—as two visitors came next day but really we thought it absurd to keep away as the funeral was so long delayed—we should not have visited anywhere.

I think you must have made a mistake in saying the Macclesfield acc. is *bombastic*—I think you mean the Carnavon paper the leading article of which is very absurd. I had rather the Times let him alone for I think it never *favoured* him.

(321)   PENRHOS *Sept. 23rd.*

I am afraid poor Cruttenden is getting very buzzardly. It is not the first time he has forgot what was told him & made great blunders, anyhow I think it was very inattentive not to ascertain when the funeral was to be.

I am very much hurried having taken the whole morning with copying for Emmy.

If the *evidence* of deep feelings which I know well always exist, could give me the hope that they would not re-enter the recesses of the heart but would now & then appear on slighter occasions, what heartfelt pleasure & satisfaction I should feel from K's account of dear

Edward's warm & affectionate sympathy shewn in this
hour of need to them, & which they so fully appreciate.
Kitty's concluding sentence: " It has put us all quite on
a different footing with him which with God's help, we
will not lose ".   She says they have pressed Henry to
stay till Monday, may those hours be blessed to him &
may Arthur's words sink into his heart & reach his head,
for I have no doubt he will make some attempt to converse
with him.

(322)   PENRHOS *Sept. 29th.*

What do you say about Arthur's refusal [1]—all I can say
is that I wish he had taken a different line in his profession
at first & that his ideas of *usefulness* had not taken such
an ambitious range.   But take him *as* he is I think he has
judged well, he could not have been happy, I believe, out
of Oxford.   Nothing can be more gratifying to the
family than the offer & the manner & words in which
it is conveyed.

I have a better acc. of William today—blisters behind
the ears & leeches at the bottom of the back have relieved
him very much & he is a great deal better.

The cholera is creeping on here, 8 cases since Sunday ;
most of them may be accounted for as predisposed from
drunkenness, unhealthy dwellings or previous weakness.

Shall we fight the Turks side by side with the French ?
I really think such a war would be quite popular—no
doubt My Lord is very warlike & ready for a 10 pr. ct.
income tax to carry it on.

Yrs. affecly   M. J. S.

[1] Of the Deanery of Carlisle.

LADY EDDISBURY TO LORD EDDISBURY
(AT ALDERLEY)

(323)   WINNINGTON *Oct.* 14*th.*

Maud heard from Mme. de Trey that Henry was paying little Wm. Clarke's schooling.   I often hear of his doing kind things.

As I am going to Alderley alone it will be to see you only, so I hope you will give me much of your company.

LADY STANLEY TO LADY EDDISBURY

(324)   ALDERLEY *Oct.* 18*th.*

As Edward's cold is heavy I should like to have you as soon as we can so I send the brougham for you this afternoon—but *please* not to be under any alarm it is quite a common cold.   *Fishing* is the bane of this family I am sure he caught it that way which reminds me I have not heard of Henry this age.

Mrs. Leycester has produced a son under chloroform—mother & child doing well.   Emma Mainwaring was with her all the time.   The last hour was an anxious one & would have been a very bad time in a common way—but there was little suffering.

Yrs. affecly   M. J. S.

(325)   ALDERLEY *Nov.* 16*th*

My Lord is rather taken with Shirley, thinks the author or authoress (he says the latter) is a person of no ordinary mind, & like you, cares more for the observations than the story.   I think I do not like it as well as you seem to do. Tho' there is nothing improper in one sense of the word I cannot think it is just the book to put into the hands of young ladies.

LADY EDDISBURY TO LORD EDDISBURY

(326)   WINNINGTON *Nov. 15th.*[1]

I am just returned from Church—I at first felt very sorrowful, for the memory of that wee thing is still very present to my heart, but I can feel truly thankful that all the other dear ones have been spared & you my chiefest & greatest blessing. The churches were very well attended & the day observed everywhere. I believe this is the only country in which there has been a national acknowledgement of God's directing Providence in the cholera, & I believe it is not a mere outward form but that more & more are becoming every day religious. At such a time one's heart is very full & many thoughts crowd that cannot be expressed. I hope I may show the fruits of religion more than hitherto. To attain this I feel I must mainly keep my temper under & I wish much to avoid those irritating topics which wound me deeply. My entire & absorbing love for you will I trust never change but when it does it will not be a question of degree but a total dispersion of illusion which I fear more than death to me.

My growing fat is not a façon de parler—it is really fat like a fatted oxen & very disagreeable.

Blanche & I have been asked by Mrs. Heber Percy to go to Hodnet. She is a very nice person but I suppose you wd. not think it worth while.

[1] A general day of thanksgiving for the cessation of the cholera epidemic.

LADY STANLEY TO LADY EDDISBURY

(327)   ALDERLEY *Nov. 20th.*

I doubt if a school to be called " ragged " [1] will answer
well in a small town, I think it may make an uncomfortable feeling between the National School & them, &
possibly the National scholars will despise the others &
taunt them with the name. However I shall not be
unwilling to help if necessary tho' I should *prefer* giving
farther help to the established schools at Northwich &
Baintree than see a new one attempted without a great
certainty of success. I do not suppose any child is
refused admission to those schools because he is poorly
clad now. I never liked the name *ragged* school—a sort
of opprobrium.

I sent Lyulph's Testament yesterday with a letter, a
hare, pheasant & 2 rabbits.

LADY EDDISBURY TO LORD EDDISBURY

(328)   WINNINGTON *Nov. 20th.*

I received the half notes, *all* are paid away—pray send
me some money. I really wish you would increase my
allowance I am so dunned for my debts. I have not been
extravagant, you know, but 100 a year for everything is
too little for living in London & going out as I am obliged
to do—you have now 3800 a year, more than either of
your married sisters & both Ally & Emmy have a great
deal more than I have. I find I have, with the utmost
economy, spent 140 a year & it is now 8 years since you
have reduced me to the bare 100 so I have above 300 of

---

[1] The " Ragged Schools " were started by Lord Shaftesbury.

debt, on most of my bills interest is charged so I am getting more & more involved. I never indulge in a fancy—I never bought a pretty thing in my life. Pray take this into your most serious consideration & send me £50 to appease Allenby who will persecute me once a week. I really can assure you that every woman I know in the same position has much more than I have, it is very disagreeable to have to beg what most people have naturally, & you may remember, when in office before you gave me 180 a year.

LADY STANLEY TO LADY EDDISBURY

(329)   ALDERLEY *Nov.* 27/49.

I am not sure if I said Sir Brooke [Boothby] has engaged himself to a poor cousin, to be married *when* he gets a living which he *now* feels he has a call for.

Strange changes come over the spirit of Maude [Adeane's] dream, she now wishes Robt. & Harry to come together, I thought her wish was to separate them, so I suppose some *miraculous* improvement has taken place in one or both—I hope we shall find it so. I do not think Henry is any loss to a young party, rather the reverse, so I do not care for his coming. Perhaps we may have a shooting day in the wood, as Fleetwood says there are too many cocks.

I suppose the *hitch* in Edward's advancement now is the place he was obliged to take on the return of the present Govt: to office. The foolish peerage was certainly his own cooking. His entire silence in the H. of Lords is also unfortunate, not having brought his abilities into play.

LADY EDDISBURY TO LORD EDDISBURY

(330)   WINNINGTON *Nov. 30th.*

MY DEAREST LOVE,

I can think of nothing but the change you mention
in the Cabt: & if *you* are not advanced I shall get a fever
from vexation—I wish I was near you to spur you up,
you are so supine, so engrossed with your frivolous companions. Now that poor Charles Buller is gone you have
never cared what became of your political career. I do
hope you will not allow yourself to be passed over any
longer—that tomfoolery of a peerage ought to have some
compensation.

Margaret [Hamilton] was confined a fortnight before
she expected.

As to my prospects, I feel well, not at all sick. Williams says she is sure I am not with child & that all will
come right. I really would not swear either way.

                        Yrs. affec.   H. M. E.

(331)   WINNINGTON *Dec. 2nd.*

MY DEAREST LOVE,

I received your letter from the Grange this morning
but none this afternoon, you have got your smart lot. I
hate them all so much.

You write most wisely about the Government & I will
try & feel the same but I cannot help being deeply morti-
fied for you & not less so for feeling that there is a great
deal in it that is your own fault—all the faults you used
to lament in Charles Buller you have taken up & exag-

gerated & you do not redeem them by brilliant speeches
but let the opportunies pass by. The society you have
lately chosen has been & will be the bane of your career
& you *ought* to be discontented at finding yourself after
15 years of office life, at the same point from which you
started. I began, intending to agree but when I go on
my blood boils & I feel indignant at your supineness.
Everyone is not like you & it *will* be taken for granted
you are satisfied & you will be left behind for ever. I
am too angry at it.   Yr. indignant   H. M. E.

(332)   WINNINGTON *Dec. 5th.*

I have to give you the most pleasing intelligence, that my
apprehensions are dispersed. It is a most singular circumstance, I have done nothing one way or another. I
certainly do wish some time or other to have another
baby but not next June as I would rather see after the
girls.

If *you* grumble I am satisfied, I was only afraid you
were supine & wanted stirring up—I know as well as
you can tell all the grievous disadvantages of having been
out of Parliament, & all the other mistakes, still in this
world we must take care of ourselves, & if I have roused
you to do that I am satisfied.

I have just had my bill again from Allenby, 332–12.
I am sorry to say the interest is 13–12 a year & I have no
means of reducing it. Economical & saving as I am I
cannot dress upon 100 a year.

You certainly have a much gayer life than your poor
girls who are moped to death here—I hope we shall not
have a party of bores & relations at the Grange but I
rather expect it.

LADY STANLEY TO LADY EDDISBURY

(333) ALDERLEY *Dec.* 6/49.

You will indeed be shocked to hear what I have to tell you. Charles Stanley [1] died at Hobart Town a fortnight before his father. Sir Edward [Parry] sent me the news from his nephew, & how & when Kitty will have heard it is my distress at this moment. The girls & Emmy will probably have had it broken to them before leaving Babraham; one cannot help wondering & wishing to know so much how K. will hear it first. I trust to her wonderful calmness of mind, but it is quite a new trial, so prosperous as her sons have been & she has never had any experience of the loss of a child. He died of gastro enteritis (a new disease to me) on the 13th Aug:—his poor widow in a most disconsolate state. Only in the last letter of hers which Kitty sent me she wrote so devotedly about him & of his birthday which she had been obliged to pass *alone* which she felt very much, (he was absent on business) & now for ever she will be alone.

Shall I send the brougham or the barouche? Yrs. affecly M. J. STANLEY.

LADY EDDISBURY TO LORD EDDISBURY

(334) WINNINGTON *Dec.* 7th.

MY DEAREST LOVE,

Have you heard the sad news that Charles Stanley died at Hobbart town. . . .

If in town pray call at Brook Street it may be fanciful but it will be taken kindly & surely in this world it is good to visit the house of mourning that we may be prepared

---

[1] He was secretary to the Governor of Van Dieman's Land, Sir W. Denison.

against the evil to come. I am very very sorry for this
additional grief to those poor people. Poor Katharine
will feel the loss of her nearest brother.

I have just had a most touching letter from Aunt Kitty
they are quite overwhelmed with this calamity.

Ever yrs. affec. H. M. E.

(335)   ALDERLEY *Dec.* 11*th*.

Poor Aunt she will feel it badly but to Kate it is the most
grievous & I long to hear that her health has not suffered.
I hear they all look very ill. I believe your mother has
been much grieved but nothing will soften them here, it
is a constant jar which is most painful, & the manner
they bully your Father is quite distressing, he might be
an idiot they coerce him so. Poor Moomie has had a bad
fall, the poor old soul complains she is badly served from
the kitchen but she does not dare speak—altogether I
think 4 weeks here will be quite long enough.

Nightingale came this morning—he thought Alice
only weak, no disease, but here they think her going in
a decline.

I am making out a list for the Tree. Maud wants a
locked morroco book with " Maud " on it.

Yrs. affecly   H. M. E.

(336)   ALDERLEY *Dec.* 14*th*.

Mrs. Davenport's party answered very well. Blanche &
I had our heads felt by Mr. Bally, a Swiss settled in Manchester & we got our characters for 5/–. I do not think
mine is a pleasant one tho' it may be true—but it is
represented as a strong character very practical & not

much benevolence or veneration. Both of us were deficient in hope.

Johnny wants a tolerable good paper knife with J. C. Stanley engraved on it will you order a 2/6 one.

(337)   ALDERLEY *Dec. 20th.*

I daresay I shall not get a letter or present from you tomorrow for my birthday—I did not remind you to see if you wd. remember it.

Lady Delamere has as usual asked us to go to her two evgs. for private theatricals which I have as usual declined.

Alice would like a fan, an old one, she does not like the gaudy new ones, Blanche a tortoiseshell comb & Lyulph any of Marryatt's novels—Midshipman Easy, Peter Simple, I send the list, any you like.

Blanche has got into disgrace by saying something against boys, but your mother is always snubbing the poor child. She is looking *very* handsome, quite a soft dreamy look.

The Globe says you have left London to visit your family I hope you have not another as you are not here.

If you cannot get Alice a fan any pretty thing would do, a statuette particularely. Algernon only wants a common whip.

Ever yr. affec. wife   H. M. E.

1850

(338)   ALDERLEY *Jan.* 10*th*/50.

Mary & Arthur arrived safe at ½ past 4 & it was with great difficulty I could get rid of the Crawfords in time to receive them alone.   Mary cryed very much at first but she was soon composed, & talks over every particular calmly & easily.   She thought her Mother was better the last 2 days.

There was a fat letter, besides those sent, which was so clearly a printed one that I ventured to open it & it proved to be a pamphlet about marrying a wife's sister— which I thought would not be worth the postage on.

(339)   ALDERLEY PARK *Jan.* 16*th*/50.

DEAREST HEN,

Your letter was the greatest possible comfort—I got precious Maude [Adeane's] letter early with the fullest details of everything from the beginning.   There never was such a human creature as she is—so much firmness of mind & determination to do what is right without a shadow of selfishness.   I am sure *seeing* her must be almost too much, so heavenly—what a blessing she will

271

have *you* in town, she could not have a more useful &
valuable friend, & it is good for her to have someone to
whom she can speak on the subject.

Rianette will go willingly if after a little while, when
recovering, you was less able to give her your time, &
she felt she wished for another companion—but I hardly
think she will.   The first horrible idea was cancer, but
is it only what you call it, a tumour, from some hurt
perhaps or the consequence of a very bad breast in one
of her early confinements.   I think Ally would be less
anxious knowing the whole truth, than in ignorance,
forming all sorts of fears in her mind when she knows
Maude is coming to town to be under medical treatment
but I will certainly say nothing on the subject without
Maude's wish & I shall equally keep silence with Lucy
& Emmy.

Lady O Montagu is to be married in a grey dress &
bonnet, but the worst exaction of Mr. T's is that she
must take an old lady's maid of his first wife's who had
married the butler.   I do not think this can answer.

Yrs. affecly   M. J. S.

(340)   ALDERLEY *Jan.* 20*th*.

I hope Maude will make no delay in coming up.   You
confirm my apprehension that the extension to the
neighbouring glands is a bad feature.   Our family, on
both sides, is so free from any glandular ailments, that it
must be quite spontaneous in her constitution & therefore, I hope, more curable.   Poor Maude knows the
complaint so well—she did so much to alleviate Miss
Lander's sufferings, how little thinking she should have
personal experience of what she saw was so dreadful.

If Aunt Kitty can be kept in ignorance I daresay it will be best, she is not a good keeper of a secret & it is sure to go to Lou Clinton at all events, & defend me, & Maude too, from her oppressive sympathy.

(341)   ALDERLEY *Jan.* 25*th.*

I am quite uncomfortable, writing to my absentees & not to name Maude even, which I think the safest plan, but it seems so odd to have a secret, & *such* a secret, from Ally & Emmy. But I would not do anything contrary to Maude's wishes.

I was thinking a large pélerine, to throw over My Lord's shoulders would be better than anything—& he always calls for a shawl over his knees, as much to keep them from his burning furnace of a fire, as for warmth. He is very well.

I hope you will not encourage Mary & Aunt about the inscriptions—that for Charley especially which is so very objectionable throughout—ill constructed, untimely & sudden, not appropriate. *Most* loved & *most* loving will certainly bear two interpretations, but the obvious one is that he was *most* loved of his family.

(342)   ALDERLEY *Jan.* 27*th.*

Emmy seems to be going on extremely well, says she has never had a pain anywhere & is following Locock's directions under the man at Reigate. It is an advantage, he has attended her in one of her mishaps & therefore must have got an insight into her constitution. She means to go through all with him should she be so fortunate as to go on to the end. I hope you will be able

to do something about Lucy Parry joining Albert without
the dear fussy old man being perplexed ; when the distant ones find Maude does not write to them it must
appear she is very unwell.

(343)   ALDERLEY *Jan.* 30*th.*
DEAREST HEN,

I did not expect to be so soon out of suspense & to
hear [the operation] was over. The next 2 or 3 days
must be very anxious ones. The fear is upon me that the
disease has gone deeper than was expected—I did not
know so much loss of blood was to be expected & her
great weakness alarms me for her. I hope you have told
Lucy, I cannot bear her being ignorant of anything, &
should anything go unfavourably Lucy would be so
vexed not to have known all. How much we owe you
for your truly sisterly kindness & devotion to her &
what would she have done without such a friend, there
is no one who could have supplied your place & been
what you are to her. All well here tho' most anxious.

Yrs. affecly   M. J. S.

(344)   ALDERLEY *Feb.* 3/50.
DEAR HENRIETTA,

I was indeed astonished by your letter of yesterday
but Lucy always did, & always will, act upon the impulse
of the moment, to her dying day. It would not have
been like her to wait another day for further accounts.
I wonder what you could have said to alarm her so much.

I *think* from a letter of Emmy's *she* does not take in the
whole truth, & as long as it can be avoided is it not better

to shirk the terrible *word* & keep to tumour, which will
satisfy almost anybody without they are very curious.
My Lord knows *nothing* & seems to have forgotten. I
told him Maude was gone to London. May he not as
well be spared—if it once got a hold on his mind I think
it would haunt him. Adieu—

Ever yrs. affecly   M. J. S.

(345)   A L D E R L E Y $\frac{1}{2}$ *past* 5 *8th Feb.*
We can decide nothing but to wait for tomorrow's letter
—we cannot leave the father quite alone, Louisa cannot
be here until tomorrow but if we heard tomorrow there
was a chance of another day perhaps we might *indulge
ourselves*, tho' I believe the best would be to wait till we
knew if we could be of any use. I had just finished
several letters full of hope. Ever yrs.   M. J. S.

(346)   A L D E R L E Y *Feb.* 10/50.
The letter of yesterday morning prepared us for hope—
I thought the preceeding night was a *crisis* & so it has
proved. The quantity of nourishment she has taken
seems quite wonderful & proves what unceasing attention she required, nothing less than such care could have
saved her. How well I understand you was her *tormentor*.
I remember so well when Rianette restored me to life
by her hourly feeding & how I disliked it. I have written
to Lucy.

(347)   A L D E R L E Y *Feb* 14*th*.
There are above 20 bottles of the best brandy in the
cellar, I wonder they did not catch your eye. To think

275

of you making such an expedition at such an hour. Dear Lucy is of no use on such occasions but to caress & soothe the invalid, & repeat Hymns & Texts, but she has no head for general overlooking, or bodily strength for night work. I am late & can write no more. Adieu & God bless you

Ever affecly yours   M. J. S.

(348)   A L D E R L E Y *Feb. 24th.*

Hopes & fears must still be balanced & I try to keep mine as evenly balanced as possible, as long as the doctors say *they* have hopes.

The length of time they say it may last is indeed very serious for all & I suppose you may be obliged to think of a regular nurse. It is too much for the [Adeane] girls & for you, tho' you have borne so much & so well, yet I cannot help feeling you *ought* not to persevere too long, however much they may wish for you. As Rianette is there with not much to do but write, do not think I shall expect regular details now.

I had a letter from Albert this morning—not very comfortable—it is a case in which I cannot pretend to have a wish except that if it is to end, as I fully expect it will, in disappointment, the sooner it is over the better.

Affecly yrs.   M. J. S.

(349)   A L D E R L E Y *Feb 27th.*

Letters indeed begin to be much more agreeable than they have been for a *month*—for it is so long that you have had the charge of this poor suffering creature, & when

you see her on the sopha you will feel rewarded for all
you have done.

We are surprised & much pleased at hearing we shall
see Henry today. He will find his poor friend Tom Trap
laid up in a rheumatick fever—he is so subject to these
attacks.

I saw an extract from something Carlyle has lately
published—such horrid nonsense, I never should wish
to see more of it, if it is what you mean.

I am sure I never thought of appropriating Mr.
Stanley to you. What a goose Ellin must be to repeat
what I said either to *Alice* or you—I certainly should not
mind saying the same to you, not to Alice. I have had a
good deal of experience in young ladies, & observation
of them, & the supposition is not very absurd tho' it may
be unfounded & whether it is so or not you certainly will
not avow it. All I can say is that after four years cam-
pagning she must be very heartless or very unpopular if
nothing of the sort has come across her path ; & I could
make out a very pretty romance how some thing may have
crossed it if I would.

I feel quite sure I shall not like Dr. Vaughan [1] *at first*.
What a curious contrast he must be to Cat: probably just
the man to correct her faults & bring out all her good
points—as the faults are chiefly those of manner, &
exaggeration, which I think would not suit him in a wife
even if he admires it as a lover.

(350)   ALDERLEY *Feb* 28*th*.

Henry certainly looks very far from well—Mr. Dean
felt his pulse & said it was not that of a young man, very

---
[1] Engaged to Catherine Stanley.

weak.   He recommends quinine but Hy. sets his face against it for many *bad* reasons, amongst the rest that he has taken so much it has lost all effect upon him.

As to his African mania I think he is most gratified by seeing how many & sensible people are interested in the same subject.   He cannot give up his present situation with common sense but I own, if he were to lose it, by any change, I should wish to see him indulged to the utmost *short* of going *alone* to lay his bones in a desert.

The father is going on well, gout looking *healthy* if one may use the expression, & he is in good spirits with the blue book before him.

(351)   A L D E R L E Y *March 3rd.*

I think we may begin to look up cheerily, but I am not expecting rapid progress.   The approximation to solid food in toast & rusks is something gained.

Henry is gone to Capesthorne between churches—not that he went to either.   He is certainly very languid & gives me the idea he has been paying the penalty of his sins, as most young men do.   When I said, (on purpose to see what he would say) I did not think he would make a very good M.P. he answered he thought as good or better than many who are in the house.   He is still very much at sea on many important points.   I should not wish to see him too intimate with a very clever Jesuit however, he would be a fish worth catching, & might be induced to bite if the angler was skilful.   Believing too little often ends in believing too much.

I have always forgot to ask about a surtout for My Lord.   It must not be lined with silk—the dear old man is so dirty, it should be something that could brush.   6 gns.

is a great sum but not to be thought about if he wd. like it.

What business had Ed. to be dining with the Ashburtons en garçon—I hope he does not do these things often.

I am afraid the rabbits are hardly worth sending & hares seem *very mad* Goodbye Yrs. affecly M . J.

(352)   ALDERLEY *March* 13*th.*

As the bright account [of Maude] was written after you had seen the doctors I hope your fear of the interminable duration of her illness got a comfortable check & that the prospect is really becoming much clearer. The mere *talk* of a drive exhilarates.

I never knew before what value oysters were & Moomie has so enjoyed half a dozen this morning it was a pleasure to see her gobble them up. She is much better.

How will you ever get out of this Greek scrape[1] & is it really according to the Law of Nations that you may take justice into your own hands ? It really looks very awkward, altogether.

Very glad to hear you *are* going to have a dinner, I have a nice hen turkey ready for you. You ought to have 5 or 6 people once a week & that number, which would make very good society would not be expensive—do tell Edward it is quite indispensible he should do something of the kind. I refrain from observations I could make, on another thing about dining, I wish I could make any that would do good.

---

[1] The Greeks having beaten up a Portuguese Jew of British nationality, Lord Palmerston sent the British Navy to demonstrate in the Piræus.

How can you tolerate Thackery for shewing you all up in the manner he does—mothers & daughters, & to call one of the latter Blanche ! Really he should be banished from the society he has so wonderfully found his way into only to hold it up to ridicule.

Yrs. affec. M. J. S.

LADY EDDISBURY TO LADY STANLEY

(353)   GROV: CRES: *March 23rd.*

MY DEAR LADY STANLEY,

I will begin my letter & dispatch the dinner as the least agreeable subject—I never had so much trouble & such a failure ! At 5 Macaulay sent word he was too ill to come, Ed. could get no remplaçant & so at ¼ to 8, our dinner having dwindled, we sent for Mama who good naturedly came, but altogether it was not at all like our dinners. Some of the people we had asked came in the evg., Rawlinson, Carlyle, Ellice & we all sat up till near 1 o'clock but I saw Ed: did not like it & I felt dispirited. Your turkey came in good time, many thanks for all.

Now to Lyulph. I think it was most fortunate I should have taken him to Eton as it may be the means of furthering his good. . . . We found Mr. Johnson, a young, *very* short sighted, man, he at once set to work with Greek exercise examining in many ways in Greek for half an hour. Lyulph had the most perfect self possession. When this was finished Mr. J. took me into another room & said that Lyulph was very superior to anything he had had brought to him and that he thought Coleridge's house the best for him. I was rather startled at so unexpected an observation but said I would

refer all he said to Ld. E.   I have now written to Mr. J.
to say we shall try to get him in there—he seemed to
think we could easily as Mr. Coleridge likes clever boys.
I was not able to visit Dr. Hawtrey [1] as I was to dine in
London.   Just now Lyulph is my brightest prospect I
am so pleased with all about him.

LADY STANLEY TO LADY EDDISBURY

(354)   ALDERLEY *March 27th.*

I think we may *almost* consider dear Maude *not* worth
writing about.   Have you tried to coax Edward to take
you to Paris ?   Do you *think* if the additional expence was
made easy he would consent ?   If you did I would write
to him & try—I should be so glad you had this little
amusement.

I am grieved by your account of Henry, he used to be
so glad to go to Thorpe I wonder why he is so unwilling.
There must be something very wrong about his state of
health—has he consulted any doctor lately or have you
or his *father* for possibly *you* might not be told exactly
what has been, if not *now*, the matter.   Do you suspect
anything of that kind ?

I shall be quite sorry to lose Harry [Adeane], Robert
may have a better temper but he is a wearisome companion in the long run.

(355)   ALDERLEY *April 10th 5 o'clock.*

Maud [Stanley] & I are just returned from the Edge &
found Edward in the wood busy planting yews & hollies

[1] Headmaster of Eton.

by the log house. I am always happy when he finds a little job to do & can be on the spot to see it is done as he likes. I am so anxious to have done what I think he will like, but it is generally odds whether what I have done is right or wrong. He seems to me as if he was not quite well, what do *you* think of him ?

The two younger generations are really less satisfactory in health than the Methuselah *old roots*.

Yrs. affecly   M. J. S.

LORD EDDISBURY TO LADY EDDISBURY

(356)   ALDERLEY *Ap.* 10/50.

MY DEAREST LOVE,

The weather is beautiful & I should enjoy myself very much if there was not so much questioning & molestation as to what I shld. do & when I stop. In fact I do not think it will be good for my health to stay beyond Friday on which day I propose returning to town.

My Father they say is much better than he was—I do not perceive much difference. Moomie is looking very ill indeed & I shld. think she could not last long.

Yrs. aff.   E.

LADY EDDISBURY TO LADY STANLEY

(357)   GROV: CREST: *April* 13*th.*

MY DEAR LADY STANLEY,

I must begin by expressing my great thanks for the *lovely flowers* they have embellished my room to a great degree. Nothing could give me more pleasure.

Edward says he is very well but he is wonderfully silent & not in good spirits.

I saw Mr. Coleridge yesterday, he called, & I was quite enchanted with his manners & conversation, he looks so firm & yet so kind. He has such a very good set of boys in his house. He says he thinks there is no place any where like Eton for the advantage of public & private education, but there are fearful stories of drunkenness & people do not scruple to name two of the masters as not being free from that vice.

Yr. affec. dau.   H. M. E.

LADY STANLEY TO LADY EDDISBURY

(358)   ALDERLEY *April 22nd.*

We shall lose a day of Albert, I am afraid, from a baddish acc. of Emmy, but as it seems to have been only a bilious attack which passed off without bad consequences in other ways I trust we may see only good in it, as proving she is strong in her vocation. The tremendous storm of Saturday tried her head & roused her bile.

I have said nothing to My Lord of moving but I think there is no doubt he would negative any proposal for *his* leaving Alderley, as there is so little to interest him elsewhere, & his *motions* are certainly weaker than they were last year. He is very willing to go out when it is fair. I took him a round he had probably not been for many years, & shewed him farm houses & new buildings that he had only heard of. From Soss Moss he went past Soss Moss Hall & Yarwood's & he was quite enlivened by it.

The beautiful scarlet rhodendrum Maud saw is quite over & I do not think common ones would look well in the hair, very heavy, & the colour not good for candlelight.

With Loves   Yrs. affecly   M. J. S.

(359)   ALDERLEY *May 2nd.*

I am just returned from Macclesd. where the bells were ringing very merrily for the addition to the country's family.[1]

Poor Blanche, the life you lead is murder—I am so tired of seeing your name in the newspaper lists, knowing how many hot crowded rooms you haunt. It is well *you* hold out so stoutly as you do. I do wish Alice had a good husband of some kind or other—she would be *so* well with a child every year I have no doubt.

Moomie goes on, I think, getting weaker, & that *animal* Nightingale told her yesterday she might slip off suddenly if anything hurried her, intending, I believe, only to induce her to be calm. There might have been some use in telling *us* so, & wishing that people should be very gentle with her.

We had frost last night alas ! for our cherry blossom.

Yrs. affecly   M. J. S.

(360)   ALDERLEY *May 7th.*

What a strange lottery marriage is—it is not every one would have chosen such a little stumpy dwarf—but I daresay she will make an excellent settler's wife. Williams will never come back—the Land of Liberty will just suit her democratic notions, yet I think she may look back sometimes with regret to her English home & nurse-

---

[1] H.R.H. the Duke of Connaught.

"MOOMIE"

NURSE TO MARIA JOSEPHA'S CHILDREN

lings.[1] One must *hope*, more than ever, that you have completed your number tho' one may not *expect* it—but it will be very hard to begin the world again if you should be put to the trial. And without *that* you will miss her very often.

I don't think Carlyle worth arguing with & I would as soon be called a fool by him as not—is there one *sentence* of sense in his last two numbers ?

(361)   A L D E R L E Y *May* 16*th*.

I think poor Moomie's end is now really near & if she remains to the last as she is now it will be comfortable. She is quiet & sensible. Louisa was sitting by her bed, when Moomie opened her eyes & said, low but very distinctly " Farewell farewell dear Miss Louisa—now leave me " Louisa asked if she would not like her to stay in the room—she said no, leave me to myself. If there is no change this is most comfortable & the last impression will be just what one would wish, & they will be so much more willing to part with her after this last fortnight's preparation, always having feared her end might be sudden. Louisa is very composed.

Nightingale has just been here—he says the congestion of the brain is caused by water on the heart & is of an intermittent nature.

(362)   A L D E R L E Y *May* 21*st*.

Not half an hour after I sent my letter she breathed her last. She must have been strangely altered for they would not let Rianette go up to see her, & altogether

---

[1] We find her with them again some twelve years later. Cf. " Amberley Papers."

there has been much painful in her end, but there were tranquil intervals & those were very valuable & she would repeat whole verses of hymns & other poetry.

(363)   ALDERLEY *May 22nd.*

Mrs. Davenport's fête & poor Moomie's funeral will be remembered for the most awful thunder storm I ever heard. The thunder & lightening have been incessant ever since 3 & it is now near 5. Rain & hail have fallen in torrents. The park has many ponds in it, & what is worse the water has found its way into the bow room over the drawing room & come down the walls of both those rooms. Pearce & almost all the maids & men gone, all the upper women to Moomie's house & the others to Capesthorne. Mr. Lloyd sent word during the worst of the storm that he would wait [for the funeral] till it was over, for fear they should set off at 4 o'clock. Rianette & Louisa sat on the hill listening to the musick of distant bands at C. mixed with the peals of thunder— no rain then.

Pray tell Aunt Kitty of the storm—you may tell her also that I have no doubt Lord P[almerston] will come off triumphantly [1] she must live with *very bad politicians* to doubt it, you ought to teach her better.

Yrs. affecly   M. J. S.

(364)   ALDERLEY *May 29th.*
I am sure you would cheer Emmy by telling her not to mind every little spasm she feels or fancy it a formidable symptom.

[1] He was in very hot water with the Queen and Prince Albert over the Greek question.

I hope there will be an opportunity [for Edward to speak] on the Greek business—only I am so vexed to hear he dines out so often I am hardly enough in charity with him to wish him any gratification. It is very *wrong* —but perhaps if I say so you will, wife like, make excuses for him—& after all he had better dine out than be grumpy & sleepy at home. It is a sad life you have been placed in, very inimical to domestick happiness. As it is I only wish you could have a little more society at home for the girls' sakes. But this is an episode I had not intended to introduce.

(365)   ALDERLEY *June 4th.*

I earnestly hope Maude will not hesitate—it is by far the best disposal that could be made of Edward [Adeane]. He is an active boy now in good health & the naval education is more likely to agree with him than any other school. When I saw the youngsters on board the Victory at their studies I thought any boy might envy them. Two of my naval grandchildren [1] are doing so well I should be very glad of another & in my own mind could wish Lyulph to be added to the list—if ever there should be war again perhaps he would get his peerage sooner than by the drudgery of the Bar. Surely Maude cannot be so unwise as to demur.

(366)   ALDERLEY *June 6th.*

Robert tells me Edward would like the sea very much & he (Robt.) hopes his Mama will let him go & so do I. He is just the boy for it, very active & *not very bright.*

---

[1] Parry and Hare.

287

Mrs. Whitby was my first cousin, Aunt to Albert—but she has lived so long out of the world that I never thought of your mourning for her, or doing so myself tho' I did seal with black to Emmy.

(367)   ALDERLEY *June 9th.*
I am very glad to hear from Maude it is decided as we wish. I think Mr. Andrew's letter very decisive of his opinion what would suit the boy best & I was much amused with his idea that the only éclat he could ever make must be by fighting in the field hereafter.

This is Maude's birthday, [44] how little you would have thought she could ever reach it, some weeks ago. It is fortunate Robert is as old as he is—he can be of great use to her.

(368)   ROCKEND *July 6th.*
I have so many correspondants with black edges that I opened yours quite unconsciously & read the first lines of your enclosure before your letter. I was truly thunderstruck & scarcely knew what I was about, only calling vehemently for Lucy & Louisa in such *distress* they felt *relieved* when they found the news was not from Alderley, or any other nearer & dearer than he who is taken from us.[1] But in the first moment, I could think of nothing that could be worse than what poor Kitty was suffering. Such repeated bereavements, this so unexpected & at a time when all thoughts were busied in his return. How she will cling to Arthur, & when I look at him I do feel such dread of farther & deeper trials.

I shall be very anxious until I know how Emmy hears,

[1] Captain Owen Stanley, R.N., son of Bishop Stanley, had died in New South Wales.

& bears this sad news—Sir Edward Parry says he wrote
to Albert immediately & you probably wrote also. It
would be impossible & foolish to try to keep it from her
—but how she will feel it.

Yrs. affec.   M. J. S.

(369)   ROCKEND *July 9th.*
The letters this morning have been great comforts. I
am especially relieved by a letter from Albert saying
Emmy had not suffered bodily, tho' she had learnt it in
the most sudden manner possible. It was very stupid in
him not to see the paragraph. I think upon consideration
you will excuse Albert & will have found he wrote as
soon as he could, he got your letter on Saturday & as no
letter he wrote could reach you before Monday I daresay
he sent his letter on Monday by the early post. I was
very glad to hear that tho' she had an indifferent night on
Sat. she had been in the drawing room on Sunday &
taken her usual walk.

I propose going to Babraham on Sat. if dear Maude
is well enough—what can this weakness end in? Or
rather what must it not end in? I should like to see her
again dear child.

[Two long letters from Lady Stanley, dated from
Babraham July 15th and 16th, make it evident that
Maude's recovery had been a temporary affair and that
she was very ill indeed.]

(370)   ALDERLEY *July 24th.*
DEAREST HENRIETTA,
What do we not owe you? But it was fitting you
should complete your work & be with her at the last as

in the beginning & I turn to every consolation I can think of. Had I indulged my wish to stay a few days longer, perhaps you would not have come, & I should not have carried away the image of her lovely, unsuffering, countenance as the last impression. So far for myself. For her, precious thing, how much better to be taken away now to perfect rest, & not to go on a few years longer, feeling how unequal she was to all she wanted to do.

I hope this will find you in London, for I think, while there is life & consciousness you will not leave her.

And now I shall be very anxious to hear of Emmy. I fear the effect of what may appear almost sudden to her will be very serious, yet if too late to see her alive she would be much better at home. There are indeed black clouds all around our prospect of the future—but I will not anticipate evil. Yrs. affecly M. J. S.

(371) ALDERLEY *July* 25/50.
DEAREST HENRIETTA,

It is for *you* I am now feeling the most—& tho' I said, & feel, *you* are the fitting one to be where you are, I also feel deeply that it is *my proper* post—mine ought to be the fatigue, the watchfulness & the anxiety, & nothing can reconcile me to what may appear almost a shrinking from duty, but the certainty that *I* should have been of little *real* use. To *us* it is such a comfort to have our last impression of her countenance with her lovely smile on it & not to *see* her in our memory, disfigured & a living corpse, as from your description she must have been. I say *must have been*, surely the struggle is over.

My Lord *says* little, only seems impatient for anxiety

to be ended. Extremes in age, are much alike, poor
little Fred & the Octogenarian willingly talk on *any*
other subject rather than that which fills our minds. And
now Adieu dearest Hen:

Yours affecly   M. J. STANLEY.

[There are some letters from Lady Eddisbury to her
husband written at this time with the most ghastly and
haunting accounts of Maude's last days.]

(372)   A L D E R L E Y *July* 29/50.

How you must feel deeply thankful you had not gone one
day sooner. If you had lost that last, most precious
revival, what grief & regret you would have felt. Such
a soothing end, to all who were there—but I can hardly
give you an idea what I have felt, in hearing she thought
I had come to take a last leave of her. I *can never forget*
it or think of it without the greatest pain. I have scarce
a tear for anything else. Could nobody remind her, I
had been with her so lately & only left her because I
thought it was right—for *her* sake. I have been spared
a most heart breaking scene, but should I have minded
anything, to have had a share in her last words ?

Lucy's day of sorrow is the 30th—how near the dates.

I was glad of a tolerable acc. of Emmy today—but this
great nervousness sickness & sleepless nights is a bad
preparation—I *hope* Ally will give up all thoughts of
leaving her.

[Lady Eddisbury now took Alice, Blanche, Maud,
Johnny and Lyulph for a tour on the Continent.]

LADY STANLEY TO LADY EDDISBURY

(373)   ALDERLEY *Aug.* 8/50.

Edward has sent me your letters from Ghent & Liège —very good of him. Do not grudge yourself anything reasonable you wish for—you shall have another 50 if you will not grudge yourselves doing things *genteely.*

Harry [Adeane] came yesterday—he loves to talk of *her* & looks dreadfully pale & thin—he told me, what I had not heard, the three letters she wrote on the Monday in the dreadful state she was then in. What amazing energy she had to the last.

Ally writes in great spirits about Emmy, the poor thing is suffering very much from uncomfortable nights, but her mind is in a most comfortable state & has been much relieved by talking of dear Maude to one who could give her such full answers to all she could ask. To poor, almost broken down old Albert, Ally is a great comfort.

(374)   ALDERLEY *August* 16/50.

All well here, but our fears & anxieties are very much excited not having one line from Ally for *three* days, & nothing she could have told us, if silent on acct. of protracted or dangerous labour, would go beyond the apprehensions one conjures up, in ignorance—ready as I am for almost anything, I have such fears of want of strength.

I wonder, as you seem to travel for *nothing,* almost, that you do not aim at a sight of Switzerland,—a peep at those mountains wd. be worth all the Churches & pictures in the world. You have too much society for 2 thirds of the year to want *that* abroad.

Harry has been very happy here & I am sure the more the brothers are separated the better for both. Robert

has offered himself on the 26th which of course I have
accepted, but he writes in such an unfeeling way of the
arrangements, from the *bustle* of which he is very glad to
get away, tho' he says everything is settled very satisfactorily—not a word of reference to their loss.   He will be
as jolly at Cambridge as ever.

(375)   ALDERLEY *Aug*: 19*th*.
You will have heard from Ally—but I must write to say
how happy I am tho' you can *guess* that without being
told.   I can hardly believe the full extent of what I have
heard—not very long suffering, a live, fat, blue eyed
beautiful girl, as Ally says, as if a new born baby was ever
beautiful ugly little red things, but I *can* imagine she as
well as Emmy would think it beautiful.   Ally called it
IT all through her letter—but luckily Albert said it was
a girl, not that I cared nor they either, I daresay, *which*
it was.   Poor Albert how very happy he must have been,
& it was so nice that he happened to be dining out, & so
escaped the 2 hours of real labour, returning only just
before the final, for Ally says it was not serious before 9
o'clock & born at ½ past 11.   If you have heard all this
& more you must excuse it, as it is so pleasant to relate
& dwell upon it.

Williams [who came to say goodbye] was quite satisfied with the children *except* that they did not testify any
great regret at parting with her.   The ship is expected to
sail on Tuesday she says it is a very large one—it is a
great undertaking, from her acct. the settlement seems so
new & very little money amongst them.   She *says* she
will only stay a year.

Edward looks very well but very fat.

                         Yrs. affecly   M. J. STANLEY.

BLANCHE STANLEY TO LORD EDDISBURY

(376)   SCHWALBACK. *Aug 20th.*

MY DEAR PAPA,

We find this place as quiet & more strengthening than the sea—Alice is getting robust. We have made the acquaintance of the Miss Leighs [1] there are 4 of them the eldest I should think is 30, they are very nice & one of them paints in oil. We get on very well with our German—the master teaches well, but seemed surprised to find we knew where Asia is, which does not say much for the education of the German young ladies. Mr. & Mrs. Selwyn are here, she looks so old, like his mother, but they seem to get on well together.

Yr affec. & dutiful daughter   BLANCHE STANLEY.

LADY EDDISBURY TO LORD EDDISBURY

(377)   SCHWALBACK. *25th August.*

MY DEAREST LOVE,

I have had a letter from Ally with the welcome news of Emmy's well-doing. I am very glad indeed for poor Emmy.

I must tell you about our clergymen. Last Sunday the service was very well performed by a clergyman travelling with Dr. Pusey's only son, a poor deformed, deaf, youth—the clergyman came over from Wiesbaden but declined doing so again, having scruples at officiating in a Lutheran Church. Everyone thought him prejudiced, & today we had a wild Irishman, quite the other way, who spent his time in finding fault with the Pusey-ite & making colloquial remarks to his congregation.

[1] Daughters of Lord Leigh of Stoneleigh.

Mrs. Selwyn is in an interesting situation & looks so old. I never saw anyone more in love than her boy husband is with her.

Yrs. affec.   H. M. E.

[William Stanley had an appalling carriage accident on the 24th Aug.—the horses he was driving bolted down a steep hill and he was pinned between the wheel and the wall of a cottage. At first they feared that he was dying, but he made a good recovery. Lady Stanley wrote " how short a time we have been out of trouble ".]

LADY STANLEY TO LADY EDDISBURY

(378)   ALDERLEY *Aug. 29th.*
[Much about William]   I only hope Emmy will not be too venturesome Lou Way tells me she tried to *read* & *write* on the 9th day, but found her eyes would not stand *that* effort, & Albert quickly removed the book & pen— but the mere wish shows how well she felt.

LADY EDDISBURY TO LORD EDDISBURY

(379)   WIESBADEN *Aug. 31st.*
A very uncomfortable account from Lady Stanley of poor William, & Sir B. Brodie speaking of creeping palsy is too frightful.

I heard from Aunt Kitty, she had arrived at Strasbourg an hour before Louis Napoléon & seen his arrival, which she described as spiritless & he looking jaded & tired, & just after his troop came a smart carriage driven by a woman in Alsatian peasant's dress & that woman, Mrs. Howard ! It caused great scandal.

(380)   ON BOARD THE STEAMER,

LAKE OF LUCERNE *4th. Sept.*

We had only time at Frankfort to walk about the Fair
& dine.   I met Sir John Warrender at Koch's the
bankers who told me there was no news.   At dinner
we met a number of English, Lady Ashbrook, Lady
Galloway, the Stuart Mackenzies—at 3 we left.   Lady
Pollington [1] was at the station, surrounded by German
officers & seeming much as of old, but coarse & plain.

Johnnie's boil has broken.   He wishes you to be told
he has seen two cretins.

(381)   UNDER THE JUNG FRAU *Sept. 7th.*

I hope you received the letter I wrote on the Lake of
Lucerne.   We are now still more romantically situated,
sitting under the shelter of a châlet expecting avalanches.

I never saw any people enjoy anything more than the
boys—all enchantment.

The guides here talk with horror of the chamois hunting, they say it becomes such a passion, people never
leave off until they get killed & that they become as wild
as the chamois.

Beautiful weather.   Yrs. affec.   H. M. E.

LADY STANLEY TO LADY EDDISBURY

(382)   ALDERLEY *Sept. 27th.*

You can hardly receive this I fear but I will try a last
letter to say all's well here.

Emmy talks of coming here in Nov:—she is going to
the sea, probably Dover, but not for another week as

---

[1] Sister to Lady Dolly Walpole.

Baby is to be vaccinated next Monday. It is very well
if Emmy survives tomorrow, [christening] with such a
large party. It *must* be a great excitement tho' one of
great happiness. Kitty & Arthur, perhaps Mary, Emma
Leycester & three of his sisters in the house, & the Scotts
for the day.

I had a letter from William today, of a sheet & a half,
proving his *head* is clear at all events.

Mr. Dean will be here on Saturday to pull out a few
of the Grandfather's stumps & he cannot do better than
to operate on the youngest [Rosalind] as well as the
oldest of the family, as she has a bad tooth, a very decayed
double one.

[In the next letters, the black edge, for Maude, now
becomes twice as thick, for late in October Lord Stanley
died, aged nearly 84. There are no letters giving details
of his death as presumably the family was gathered together for the occasion.]

HENRIETTA MARIA, LADY STANLEY OF
ALDERLEY, TO HER HUSBAND THE 2ND
LORD STANLEY OF ALDERLEY

(383)   WINNINGTON *Nov. 7th* 1850.

MY DEAREST LOVE,

This is the first letter I address you by your new name
& I must wish you all happiness & honour in bearing it.

Surely if it was not for the last time I see Wing: it
would be enough to give one the utmost melancholy. It
is in a more deplorable condition than ever. Alice is
looking wretchedly ill, she lies on a sofa without opening
her mouth.

The gentleman who wanted to hire Wing: turns out to be a " party " & I think a myth.

Bennet seems to think our white horse will do very well at Alderley with Old Ben, so we shall be able to go to Church on a wet day, the only use of a coach.

Yr. affec. wife   H. M. S. of A.

LORD STANLEY TO LADY STANLEY

(384)   F . O . *Nov. 8th/50.*

MY DEAREST LOVE,

You need not I think write your name with all its distinctions at the end of a letter & indeed I see my Mother is satisfied with signing her name as M. J. Stanley without the appendage.

I heard from her this morning—she has had a flattering account of St. Anne's Hill from Lord Holland's agent, the place, 250 clear of taxes & with 30 acres of meadow land. The last tenant had a family of 7. She likes the description of the place & looks for Ld. Holland's answer with impatience.

I am sorry to hear that you do not look upon Winnington with more complacency even though it is for so short a time, you must console yourself with the feeling that it is not for long.

Love to the children,   Yr. affec.   S.

MARIA JOSEPHA LADY STANLEY TO LADY
STANLEY

(385)   ALDERLEY *Nov. 7th.*

Sir Edward [Parry] has sent me such a flattering report of Charley from his Captain " I shall be wofully dis-

appointed if he does not make a first rate officer for I
believe him to be both clever & good "—what a delightful letter for a father to receive.

Mrs. Hibbert has just been here. With all her
oddities & crooks of character she is one of the very few
I shall be sorry to leave behind.

Mr. Cruttenden called yesterday & I spoke about the
Hatchment which he thought as objectionable as we did,
but he had not liked to say a word unless it was noticed
by the family. We settled it should be put in front of
the pew, where there are arms, & will not be in sight of
those in the pew. He said *he* thought there never were
supporters to Hatchments.

LADY STANLEY TO LORD STANLEY

(386)   WINNINGTON *Nov.* 11*th.*

MY DEAREST LOVE,

I only signed my name in full for the novelty of it, I
will not do it again as you do not like it tho' I know
your mother signs herself so in all letters not to her
intimes.

Why did you not observe upon that disagreeable
article in Sat: Chron: ? I only read it yesterday & was
most indignant, you see what comes of not exerting
yourself & not speaking oftener in the H. of Lords, you
are considered a nonentity ; it has made me very angry
—& your mother has written about it, also indignant.
Do you not begin to suspect that Lord John's letter of
condolence was a feeler as to whether you were giving
up your office, he may want the U.S. of F.A. for someone
else.   Yrs. affec.   H. M. S.

MARIA JOSEPHA LADY STANLEY TO LADY
STANLEY

(387)   ALDERLEY *Nov. 17th.*

Do not fancy I am hurrying myself *too much* on your
account—tho' I do wish for you to come as soon as you
can. You & E. are so very kind, so sincerely so I am
sure, that I do not for a moment think you are impatient,
& so all the more I wish to make all as easy & comfortable as possible for you. I have no arrears of accounts
to do. It is only looking over papers & all sorts of
things, & making preparation for packing.

I think Albert will not be sorry to leave, he gets
fidgetty about the small pox. The poor lad [Fleetwood's
eldest son] is *very* ill with it.

Nov. 18*th.* Poor James Fleetwood has died—his parents
in great affliction.

LADY STANLEY TO LORD STANLEY

(388)   WINNINGTON *Nov. 15th.*

I had a letter from Alethea Scott this mg. She says she
thinks your mother very far from well, she is very low &
subdued, & in her own room most of the day busy with
accounts.

Fancy Johnny going in a cab to Harrow, it must have
taken all his pocket money.

I hear a bad account of the Adeane girls, more thin &
low than ever. I enclose a note from Kate [Vaughan]
if you can do the kindness she wants I hope you will. I
send her private note you may as well know Johnny's
faults & it is one that distressed Wee very much.

M J Stanley of Alderley
1859

MARIA JOSEPHA
LADY STANLEY OF ALDERLEY

CATHARINE VAUGHAN TO LADY STANLEY

(389)   HARROW *Nov.* 16*th*.

MY DEAR HENRIETTA,

I cannot bear asking favours but I cannot refuse to do so in this case as it is on behalf of the greatest friend my dearest Charley ever had [she asks if Edward will speak to Lord Grey with a view to getting a Mr. Simpkinson made Port of Harbour Master at Hobart Town]. I am too shy to write to Edward.

Johnny is going on very well.

Yrs. very affec.   C. Vaughan.

enclosed note. As my letter is intended for Edward I will add what I have to say separately. The only real fault found with Johnny is that he *swears* so much. He is a dear child & I love him & I am sure he *wishes* to keep out of evil, though he is easily led away at the moment. My heart yearns over him, you don't know what it is to see his dear little face here, the only thing wh. reminds me of days & years that are past. He so little associates me with Dr. Vaughan that one day when I sent him a note he thought it was from Dr. Vaughan & wondered it should be so familiar.

MARIA JOSEPHA LADY STANLEY TO LADY STANLEY

(390)   ALDERLEY *Nov.* 23*rd*.

I shall be very glad to give you Lucy—she has not the same employment we all have to turn her thoughts from what is melancholy & Louisa does not help people on in such a case, tho' I believe she tries to do her best—but

301

as in all cases, that concern her, she thinks *she* has a heavier load to bear than anybody else.

I should like to know if you have a coffee pot, & how many salt cellars—I must & will think of you & it will not distress *me* to do so, so it need not, *you.*

LADY STANLEY TO LORD STANLEY

(391)   WINNINGTON *Nov.* 24*th.*

MY DEAREST LOVE,

I do not know what is going on at Alderley. Yesterday I had a letter in very low spirits from Lucy & today she offers to come here—by her mother's desire. I believe the poor sisters are so miserable they cannot bear to see anyone & your mother will like to be quite alone.

I wish I could have some books—I want Ruskin's Modern Painters & Olive. Are all the books here to go to Alderley? I particularly wish to know about Mitford's Hist: of Greece. The other books are chiefly mine.

Lady Stanley has written to me about the forks etc.— she is dreadfully afraid of distressing us. She wishes to enquire if we have coffee pot & salt cellars & will let you have the coach for what it is worth, viz *nothing.*

She says Louisa is very low, poor thing one ought to pity her more but she does not deserve as much as those who behave better.

The Adeanes have had such a kind loving letter from Robert [who, up to this, has been much criticized for his heartless behaviour] expressing an earnest wish that they should not leave Babraham for many years to come, that it sends them on their hard task with a more lively heart.

Yrs. affecly   H. M. S.

(392)   WINNINGTON *Nov. 25th.*

Lucy is come & brings but a poor account of Alderley,
poor Fleetwood is very ill with small pox, & several other
cases.   I think your mother must be very unwell, so low
about herself, she makes all arrangements as if it were not
for long.[1]   She has been sadly vexed about Penrhos.[2]   I
do not know exactly what, but Rianette says that there is
such a contrast between our letters & theirs & it has
quite upset Lady Stanley.

I believe Louisa has been very miserable taking leave
& your mother makes her worse by calling her precious
relics rubbish, & sometimes referring to their having
had too much left them.   They do not take the piano-
forte, nor indeed hardly anything, & your mother continually repeats, all she takes shall be returned at her
death.   She means to give the £100 left in the will to
the poor, now, that we may not be obliged to give it.   It
it quite impossible for any person to have acted more
kindly & generously than she has done, & her only
feeling seems to be anxiety for you.

Fleetwood much better, & not the small pox.

LORD STANLEY TO LADY STANLEY

(393)   FOREIGN OFFICE *Nov. 27th/50.*

I think Dr. Vaughan seems to give the boys too long
impositions to write out, as it occupies their time &
takes them from their usual studies.   After all, the good
old whipping is perhaps as good or better than anything
for young boys.

[1] She lived another thirteen years, however.
[2] The property of William Stanley since his father's death.

I heard from my Mother today again, nothing can be clearer than her letters on business & nothing kinder than all she says & does towards us. She wishes to leave her diamonds & her best jewels to you & to the family. They were her mother's.

LADY STANLEY TO LORD STANLEY

(394)   WINNINGTON *Saturday.*
Mme. de Flahault's cook might do if she has been in the country—we give 30 gns. *no perquisites* & I pay my own bills.

The dining-room I should like a pale yellow. I taboo green, it is so unbecoming to Blanche. It is very difficult to judge of colours in little bits & I do not profess to be skilful in choosing decorations.

You had not told me about Ed. Mildmay,[1] I am sorry for him for there is good in him, wretched man.

(395)   ALDERLEY *Dec. 9th.*
MY OWN DEAREST LOVE,

Here I am in our future home—but it is very sad to come to an empty house, full of old voices. I found it very melancholy & when I was in that room, with the cold reminding me of Winnington & not an old association with it, I felt so wretched I quickly came back to my old room where I shall stay for the present.

Downs sent to know if the tenants dinner was to be as usual on the 18th.

I have had the keys given me but could not go into

---

[1] Married an adventuress.

your mother's room it was too cold—tomorrow I hope
to go about the house.

Maud is rather cross because she is not to have a new
bed—poor child she is like her neighbour, we each wish
for our toy.

I found very kind letters from them here.

      Goodbye dearest,

             Yr. affec. wife   H. M. S.

INDEX

INDEX

Way, Albert, 89–95, 102, 103, 233, 240, 274, 276, 283, 289, 292, 293, 295

Mrs. Albert (Emmeline Stanley), xvii, 3, 4, 5, 6, 21, 23, 57, 59, 62, 66, 70, 75, 79, 88, her engagement and marriage 89–95, 103, 120, 130, 139, 168, 171, 179, 189, 208, 209, 210, 211, 213, 233, 273, 283, 286, 288, 290, 291, 292, her daughter is born 293, 294, 295, 296, 297

Wellington, Duke of, 43

Wharncliffe, Earl and Countess of, 141

White, Miss, 93–5, 100, 134, 135

Mr., M.F.H., 60, 239

Wilberforce, Bishop, 188

Williams, Sir John, 39, 256

Lady Sarah, 39, 256

Williams, "Wee," 12, 38, 42, 119, 130–1, 133, 143, 169, 225, 229, 234, 248, 256, 284, 293, 300

Woburn, 115, 116, 141

Wodehouse, Lord, 75

Wortley, Lady Georgina, 12

Winnington, 24–5, *passim.*

Winterhalter, 61

Wynne, Mr., 248

Did you enjoy reading this book?

If you did we believe that you would be equally pleased with other titles on our list.

May we keep you advised of our latest publications? We shall be happy to do so, if you will kindly send a postcard, giving your name and address, to :—

CHAPMAN & HALL LTD.

II HENRIETTA STREET

LONDON, W.C. 2